ARTIFICIAL INTELLIGENCE TECHNIQUES IN BREAST CANCER DIAGNOSIS AND PROGNOSIS

SERIES IN MACHINE PERCEPTION AND ARTIFICIAL INTELLIGENCE*

Editors: **H. Bunke** (Univ. Bern, Switzerland)
P. S. P. Wang (Northeastern Univ., USA)

*For the complete list of titles in this series, please write to the Publisher.

Series in Machine Perception and Artificial Intelligence – Vol. 39

ARTIFICIAL INTELLIGENCE TECHNIQUES IN BREAST CANCER DIAGNOSIS AND PROGNOSIS

Editors

Ashlesha Jain

Ajita Jain

Sandhya Jain

Lakhmi Jain

World Scientific

Singapore • New Jersey • London • Hong Kong

Published by

World Scientific Publishing Co. Pte. Ltd.

P O Box 128, Farrer Road, Singapore 912805

USA office: Suite 1B, 1060 Main Street, River Edge, NJ 07661

UK office: 57 Shelton Street, Covent Garden, London WC2H 9HE

British Library Cataloguing-in-Publication Data
A catalogue record for this book is available from the British Library.

ARTIFICIAL INTELLIGENCE TECHNIQUES IN BREAST CANCER
DIAGNOSIS AND PROGNOSIS
Series in Machine Perception and Artificial Intelligence — Vol. 39

For photocopying of material in this volume, please pay a copying fee through the Copyright Clearance Center, Inc., 222 Rosewood Drive, Danvers, MA 01923, USA. In this case permission to photocopy is not required from the publisher.

ISBN 981-02-4374-X

This book is printed on acid-free paper.

Printed in Singapore by World Scientific Printers

This book is dedicated to
the victims of cancer

The proceeds of royalty will be donated to the Anti-Cancer Foundation

Contributors

Chapter 1

R. Kates, **N. Harbeck**, and **M. Schmitt**
Technische Universität München
Munich
Germany

A. Jain
Private Practitioner
Adelaide
Australia

A. Jain
University of Adelaide
Adelaide
Australia

Chapter 2

M. Bottema, **G.N. Lee**, and **S. Lu**
Flinders University of South Australia
Adelaide
Australia

Chapter 3

R. Kates, **N. Harbeck**, **K. Ulm**, **H. Graeff**, and **M. Schmitt**
Technische Universität München
Munich
Germany

F. Jaenicke
Universitätsfrauenklinik Eppendorf
Hamburg
Germany

Chapter 4

L.M. Roberts
University of Wisconsin-Milwaukee
Milwaukee, WI
U.S.A.

Chapter 5

M.G. Daidone and **D. Coradini**
Istituto Nazionale per lo Studio e la Cura dei Tumori
Milan
Italy

Chapter 6

H.-P. Chan, **N. Petrick**, and **B. Sahiner**
University of Michigan
Ann Arbor, MI
U.S.A.

Chapter 7

S.S. Cross, J. Downs, P. Drezet, Z. Ma, and **R.F. Harrison**
University of Sheffield
Sheffield
U.K.

Chapter 8

W.N. Street
University of Iowa
Iowa City, IA
U.S.A.

PREFACE

The main aim of this book is to present a sample of recent research in the application of novel artificial intelligence paradigms to the diagnosis and prognosis of breast cancer. These paradigms include neural networks, fuzzy logic and evolutionary computing. Artificial intelligence techniques offer advantages, such as adaptation, fault tolerance, learning and human like behavior, over conventional computing techniques.

The idea is to combine the pathological, intelligent and statistical approaches to enable simple and accurate diagnosis and prediction of prognosis.

This book contains 8 chapters. Chapter 1 provides a brief background on breast cancer including epidemiology, diagnosis, prognosis and management of the disease. It also highlights the benefits of artificial intelligence paradigms.

Bottema, Lee, and Lu present the techniques for automatic image feature extraction for diagnosis and prognosis of breast cancer in Chapter 2. Artificial intelligence methods process information in order to arrive at decisions. Image analysis methods are described in the context of extracting information from images relevant to the detection, classification, and prognosis of breast cancer.

Chapter 3, by Kates, Harbeck, Ulm, Jaenicke, Graeff, and Schmitt, discusses the clinical requirements for decision support strategies in breast cancer. It is demonstrated that a statistical mode of neural network operation emphasizing the avoidance of unnecessary complexity can recognize and represent the complicated dependence of the disease on factors, and distinguish this dependence from the noise.

Roberts presents MammoNet, a Bayesian network aiming to perform accurate, reliable and consistent diagnosis of breast cancer in Chapter 4. The network creates a differential diagnosis by specifying the observed symptoms and computing the posterior probability of the various diagnoses using standard probability formulas.

Daidone and Coradini focus on predicting prognosis and treatment response in breast cancer patients in Chapter 5. Integration of patho-biological, clinical and statistical approaches is shown to contribute significantly to the prediction of prognosis.

Chapter 6 by Chan, Petrick, and Sahiner is on computer-aided breast cancer diagnosis. It discusses computer vision techniques for detection and characterization of masses and microcalcifications on mammo-grams as well as the effects of computer-aided diagnosis algorithms on radiologists' diagnostic accuracy.

Cross, Downs, Drezet, Ma, and Harrison examine in Chapter 7 four different decision support technologies: logistic regression, data-derived decision trees, multilayer perceptrons, and adaptive resonance theory mapping neural networks.

The final chapter, by Street, discusses Xcyt, a system for remote cytological diagnosis and prognosis of breast cancer. Xcyt is a software system for providing expert diagnosis and prognosis of breast cancer based on fine needle aspirates. This chapter addresses important topics in imaging, diagnosis and prognosis. The Xcyt system is being made available via the World Wide Web.

It is our objective to develop an intelligent, cost-effective, reliable and easily accessible system for the diagnosis and prognosis of breast cancer. It is our belief that this book will stimulate the imagination of researchers in the application of artificial intelligence paradigms in this important area of medicine.

This book will be useful to researchers, physicians, and students who are interested in the application of artificial intelligence paradigms in breast cancer diagnosis and prognosis.

We are grateful to the authors for their contributions and to all the reviewers for their expertise in the various fields. We acknowledge the assistance of Berend Jan and Irene van der Zwaag and Shaheed Mehta in the preparation of the manuscript. We thank Professor H. Bunke for the opportunity to publish this book, and the World Scientific Publishing Company for their excellent editorial assistance.

CONTENTS

Chapter 3.

Decision Support in Breast Cancer: Recent Advances in
Prognostic and Predictive Techniques 55
R. Kates, N. Harbeck, K. Ulm, F. Jaenicke, H. Graeff, and M. Schmitt

Chapter 4.

***MammoNet*: A Bayesian Network Diagnosing Breast Cancer** **101**

L.M. Roberts

Chapter 5.
**Predicting Prognosis and Treatment Response in
Breast Cancer Patients** **149**
M.G. Daidone and D. Coradini

Chapter 6.
Computer-Aided Breast Cancer Diagnosis 179
H.-P. Chan, N. Petrick, and B. Sahiner

Chapter 7.
Which Decision Support Technologies are Appropriate

Chapter 8.

Xcyt: A System for Remote Cytological Diagnosis and
Prognosis of Breast Cancer **297**

W.N. Street

Chapter 1

An Introduction to
Breast Cancer Diagnosis, Prognosis,
and Artificial Intelligence

N. Harbeck, R.E. Kates, M. Schmitt, A. Jain, and **A. Jain**

This introductory chapter gives a synopsis of breast cancer including epidemiology, diagnosis, prognosis and management of the disease. Taking into account the particular features of breast cancer, this chapter will point out where modern modeling approaches can bring us closer to achieving key medical objectives. Of particular interest in this book are artificial intelligence approaches, which include knowledge representations such as artificial neural networks and expert systems, and techniques such as evolutionary computing, fuzzy logic and their fusion.

Knowledge-based systems employ a number of novel techniques, many of which are inspired by the performance of biological systems. *Artificial neural networks* are designed to mimic the biological information processing mechanism, at least in a limited sense; *evolutionary computing* algorithms are used for optimization applications; *fuzzy logic* provides a basis for representing uncertain and imprecise knowledge. The trend is to fuse these novel paradigms so that the demerits of one technique may be offset by the merits of another. These fundamental paradigms form the basis of the novel design and application related projects presented in the following chapters.

1   Breast Cancer Characteristics

1.1   Epidemiology

Breast cancer is the most common malignancy in women in the western world after lung cancer. Roughly ten percent of all western women will develop breast cancer during their lifetime, and more than half of these women will eventually die of the disease.

In Australia, for example, breast cancer is the most common cause of death by cancer in females [19]. In 1994, breast cancer accounted for 29.5% of all new cancers in females and 18.6% of all cancer deaths in females [22]. In 1996 there were 2,623 breast cancer deaths among females, resulting in approximately 31,000 potential years of life lost before the age of 74 years.

The Australian breast cancer mortality rate has remained unchanged over the past 20 years [19]. However, the incidence has increased by 1.5% annually over the period 1982-1992, resulting in significant morbidity from the disease. Internationally, the incidence and mortality rates of breast cancer are greater in North America, New Zealand and some parts of Western Europe, as compared to Australia. In some parts of the world, such as Eastern Europe, Asia and China, the incidence and mortality rates are lower than in Australia.

The statistics presented above illustrate the significant impact of breast cancer in terms of both mortality and morbidity.

The causes of breast cancer are still uncertain. A number of causal factors are thought to contribute to its development. Epidemiological studies have led to the identification of several measurable risk factors [22]:

- Increasing age: breast cancer mostly affects females after the age of 40 years. Females over 50 years old account for over 74% of all new cases.
- Breast tissue alterations: biopsy confirming benign disease with atypical cells.

- Family history: risk depends on number of relatives affected, age of relatives at diagnosis, and type of breast cancer [24].
- Hereditary gene mutations: A family history of breast cancer has been linked to specific gene mutations in approximately 5% of breast cancers. If such a gene mutation is present, the lifetime risk of developing breast cancer is 85%-90%.
- Cancer history: history of primary cancer of the ovary or endometrium.
- Previous breast cancer - there is increased risk of developing a new cancer in the previously unaffected breast.
- Exposure of breast tissue to ionising radiation (especially before 20 years of age).
- Suspected behavioural and lifestyle factors:
  - never having children (nulliparity) or having the first full-term pregnancy after the age of 30.
  - diet high in animal fat, low in fibre and fresh fruit and vegetables.
  - obesity in post-menopausal females.
  - menarche (first period) at an early age and menopause (last period) at a late age.
  - high alcohol intake.
  - long-term smoking.
  - inactive lifestyle.
  - long-term use of exogenous oestrogens in hormone replacement therapy.

1.2 Biology

Breast cancer occurs when cells in the breast tissue begin to behave in an abnormal way and grow into a mass of tissue (*tumour*). However, tumours may be benign or malignant, and benign tumours do not spread. Malignant tumours, on the other hand, can invade neighbouring tissue, and may then spread to other parts of the body resulting in secondary deposits of tumour cells (*metastases*). Hence, diagnostic accuracy is of fundamental importance in classifying tumours as malignant or benign. Techniques that cause the least possible harm to the patient are preferred.

The three main modes of spread of breast cancer are by *local invasion*, *lymphatic spread*, and *vascular spread*. Breast cancer can spread locally and invade neighboring organs such as the overlying skin or the chest wall. The lymphatic system is composed of glands known as lymph nodes that are connected by a system of channels. The major lymphatic drainage of the breast is via lymph nodes located in the armpits (*axilla*). Hence, lymphatic spread of breast cancer cells can occur via local lymphatics within the breast itself, leading to the axillary lymph nodes and other sites. Nowadays, microscopically detectable tumor spread to the axillary lymph nodes will have occurred in about 50% of patients at the time of primary therapy. The chances of long-term survival decrease with the number of involved axillary lymph nodes [1].

Cancer cells may also invade the blood vessels within the breast leading to dissemination of tumour cells to distant sites in the body (metastatic sites) even without axillary lymph node involvement. The most frequent site of distant metastasis in breast cancer is the bone, followed by the lungs, the liver and the ovaries [24]. Recurrence and metastatic spread can occur even after primary surgical and systemic treatment. If the disease spreads to distant loci, breast cancer is no longer considered to be curable by present techniques. About 30% of all node-negative patients and 75% of all node-positive patients will eventually experience a relapse and subsequently die of breast cancer. For all patients, the 5-year survival rate is approximately 75% [22].

2   Breast Cancer Diagnosis and Management

2.1   Diagnosis

The *diagnosis* of breast cancer is performed by a combination of clinical, imaging, and histology findings.

As a non-invasive technique, *mammography* is the most useful imaging tool in the detection and further investigation of suspected breast cancer. It is useful for defining the extent of a lesion, demonstrating other abnormalities, and obtaining a baseline image before biopsy

distorts the normal architecture of the breast. Mammographic abnormalities suggestive of tumour include irregular densities, microcalcification and architectural distortion. Mammograms can detect cancer earlier than any other method. Frequently they can detect breast cancers even before they can be felt by clinical examination. Mammograms decrease premature death from breast cancer by over 30%. They are of greatest benefit to females aged 50 to 69 years.

However, mammograms are not 100% foolproof. Firstly, they are not specific to cancer, i.e., they also detect many breast changes that may not be cancerous. Secondly, their sensitivity is not perfect, i.e., occasionally a lump may be felt that is not seen on a mammogram. They are less sensitive for younger females (as younger females have greater breast tissue density, and therefore very small changes cannot be detected as readily). Additional imaging information can be gained in such cases by ultrasound and MRI (magnetic resonance imaging). These techniques may also add diagnostic security to a mammographic finding.

2.2   Disease Management

Once a suspicious breast lesion has been identified, a histopathological diagnosis must be performed. For this purpose, tissue cells may be obtained by fine-needle aspiration, core-cutting needle biopsy, or lump incision or excision biopsy.

In addition to the histopathological diagnosis, further histomorphological factors are determined at time of primary therapy in order to define the individual tumor characteristics for further treatment decisions. These so-called *established prognostic factors* include tumor size (in centimeters), numbers of involved axillary lymph nodes, tumor (malignancy) grade, and steroid hormone receptors. The presence of these oestrogen and progesterone receptors indicates whether the cancer is likely to respond to hormone treatment.

Treatment options for primary breast cancer include locoregional surgery and radiotherapy, as well as systemic chemotherapy and hormone therapy. Systemic treatment may be administered before surgery ("neoadjuvant," i.e., preoperative chemotherapy) or, as is usually the case, afterwards ("adjuvant" chemo- or hormone therapy).

Factors determining which treatment modalities are used include the type and size of the tumour, presence or absence of distant metastasis or axillary lymph node metastases, and patient factors such as general health.

In the past, breast cancer treatment comprised radical surgical procedures. Current treatment involves the use of more breast-sparing forms of surgery with the addition of radiotherapy [5].

Mastectomy is the removal of all breast tissue including skin and nipple, but without removal of the chest muscles. Mastectomy decreases the risk of *lymphoedema* (arm swelling) and allows for easier breast reconstruction than the previously used "radical mastectomy" in which the chest muscles were also removed. *Subcutaneous mastectomy* is removal of just the breast tissue whilst leaving the skin intact (allowing for later insertion of an implant to restore breast contour).

An alternative to mastectomy is the so-called *breast conserving* approach which includes removal of the tumor lesion and subsequent irradiation of the breast. Large studies have shown that local recurrence rates, distant disease-free organs and overall survival of breast conserving treatment are comparable to that of mastectomy [4]. *Lumpectomy* is the removal of the tumor lesion together with a small margin of normal tissue. In the case of larger tumors, a *quadrantectomy* or partial mastectomy may be required which involves removal of a larger part of the breast. *Radiotherapy* is then used after surgery to decrease the risk of local recurrence of the tumour.

Although other options are being actively investigated, removal of all axillary lymph nodes remains an essential element of every surgical approach to primary breast cancer. These lymph nodes are examined microscopically by a pathologist for evidence of tumor spread. In addition to removal of potential tumor burden, lymph node metastasis is the strongest established single prognostic factor in breast cancer and provides an important input to determination of adjuvant therapy strategies.

After primary surgery, *adjuvant systemic therapy* (chemo- or hormone therapy) is often used to decrease the risk of breast cancer recurrence.

Chemotherapy is the administration of cytotoxic agents, with the aim of eliminating undetected tumour cells that have already spread to other parts of the body, thus decreasing the risk of breast cancer recurrence. The main disadvantage of this modality is the (mostly reversible) side effects of the agents used, such as nausea, leukopenia, diarrhea, and hair loss. Some of these side effects may however be controlled by efficient medications.

Tumours which are positive for steroid hormone receptors may be treated primarily by hormone therapy, which inhibits hormone action within the body and changes body oestrogen and progesterone levels, or by administration of these hormones in high doses.

At present, breast cancer cannot be prevented. Therefore, in countries where breast cancer is a significant health issue, such as Australia or other Western countries, strategies to decrease the impact of breast cancer mortality have been implemented. These comprise *early detection*, *prompt diagnosis*, and *effective treatment* based on the best available evidence [22]. Of these, it is generally accepted that increasingly early detection of breast cancer (ie. detection in the early stages of the disease - while the disease is localised) will give the greatest possible reduction of mortality of all of these strategies [5].

3   Breast Cancer Prognosis and Risk Assessment

In contrast to other malignancies, breast cancer is a potentially curable disease due to favorable tumor-biological criteria of some breast lesions as well as very effective drug regimens. However, as mentioned above, once the patient has developed overt distant metastases, the disease is no longer curable by presently available therapies. Hence, the major challenge for the physician is to accurately assess each patient's risk situation at the onset (*prognosis*) and individualise loco-regional and systemic treatment modalities accordingly (*prediction* of therapy response).

At primary surgery, breast cancer is considered a potentially systemic disease even if no clinical signs of metastases can be detected. Large meta-analyses have demonstrated that adjuvant systemic hormone or cytotoxic therapy in addition to loco-regional therapy (surgery, radiation) is able to reduce the overall odds of recurrence by about 25% [3]. Thus, the higher the risk of recurrence for any given group of patients, the greater the expected potential absolute risk reduction by this treatment regimen [20]. However, there may be risk groups with a lower or higher than expected response to therapy due to specific tumor biology.

In the context of treatment strategy, the concepts of *therapeutic efficiency* and *therapeutic security* are often discussed:

- High therapeutic efficiency: exclude patients from therapy unless the risk is sufficiently high to justify adjuvant therapy.
- High therapeutic security: administer adjuvant therapy unless the risk can be proved to be very low.

The first of these concepts is related to the *specificity* of prognosis, while the second is related to the *sensitivity*. Ideally, both of these goals should be achieved. As mentioned above, at present axillary lymph node status is considered the strongest established prognostic marker: "Node-negative" breast cancer patients have a lower risk of suffering disease recurrences than "node-positive" breast cancer patients, whose lymph nodes show tumor cell involvement at time of primary therapy. About 70% of node-negative patients will be cured by surgery alone. Nevertheless, even within this low-risk breast cancer group, up to 30% of the patients may relapse within 10 years after surgery and eventually die of metastasis [2]. In other words, achieving both high therapeutic efficiency and security is impossible based only on nodal status, as too many "low-risk" patients would still relapse if the node-negative group were not treated. Hence, the side effects and other risks of therapy still represent the lesser of two evils even for this group.

In view of known drug side effects and long-term toxicity, the currently prevalent practice in the USA of treating nearly all patients for whom treatment is an option is not necessarily the strategy of greatest benefit to patients. Hence, *accurate risk group selection* for adjuvant systemic therapy could help to avoid over-treatment of patients who would have been cured by loco-regional treatment alone. Unfortunately, even augmenting nodal status with other established histopathological prognostic factors such as tumor size, grading, and steroid hormone receptor status is still not sufficient for such risk group assessment [1].

Advanced statistical modeling approaches may enhance the clinical impact and usefulness of the established biological markers. On the other hand, new tumor-biological factors have been evaluated for their ability to allow improved prognostic estimates at the time of primary therapy. Chapter 3 of this book discusses the use of both new tumor-biological factors and advanced statistical modeling techniques including neural networks to achieve improved decision support in breast cancer management.

4   Artificial Intelligence

It is obvious from the previous sections that in breast cancer, a large number of factors need to be considered for accurate classification (in the diagnostic context) or forecasting (in the prognostic/predictive context). This property of breast cancer, coupled with the existence of complex and only partially understood processes linking the factors, strongly suggests the application of artificial intelligence to these problems.

As is typical of an emerging field of scientific research, there is no precise definition of artificial intelligence (AI). Generally speaking, however, so called intelligent techniques are inspired by an understanding of information processing in biological systems. In some cases an attempt is made to mimic some aspects of biological systems. When this is the case, the process will include an element of adaptive or evolutionary behavior similar to biological systems, and like the biological model there will often be a very high level of connectionism between distributed processing elements [6]-[11]. Data and information processing paradigms that exhibit these attributes can be referred to as members of the family of techniques that make up the knowledge-based engineering area. Researchers are trying to develop AI systems that are capable of performing, in a limited sense, "like a human being." [12]-[13].

The main artificial intelligence paradigms include artificial neural networks, evolutionary computing and fuzzy logic. Artificial neural networks (ANNs) [14] [15] mimic biological information processing mechanisms. They are typically designed to perform a non-linear mapping from a set of inputs to a set of outputs. ANNs are developed to try to achieve biological system type performance using a dense interconnection of simple processing elements analogous to biological neurons. ANNs learn from experience and generalise from previous examples. They modify their behaviour in response to the environment, and are ideal in cases where the required mapping algorithm is not known and tolerance to faulty input information is required [21]. Artificial neural networks have been used in the area of breast cancer diagnosis and prognosis [25]-[26]. They have been used to predict the clinical course of breast cancer patients. They can be used for the analysis of complex data for predicting outcomes in medicine. ANNs can be used successfully when the relationship between variables is governed by a complex nonlinear function.

Evolutionary computation is the name given to a collection of algorithms based on the evolution of a population towards the solution of a certain problem. [16], [17], [28], [29]. These algorithms can be used successfully in many applications requiring the optimisation of a certain function on a multidimensional space. The population of possible solutions evolves from one generation to the next, ultimately arriving at a satisfactory solution to the problem. These algorithms differ in the way a new population is generated from the present one, and in the way the members are represented within the algorithm. Three types of evolutionary computing techniques have been widely reported recently. These are Genetic Algorithms (GAs), Genetic Programming (GP), and Evolutionary Algorithms (EAs). The EAs can be divided into Evolutionary Strategies (ES), and Evolutionary Programming (EP).

Evolutionary programming is currently experiencing a dramatic increase in popularity. This technique manipulates entire computer programs, and hence can potentially produce effective solutions to very large scale problems. Several examples have been successfully completed that indicate the tremendous potential of EP. Koza and his students [18] have used EP to solve problems in various domains including process control, data analysis, and computer modelling. Currently, however, the complexity of the problems being solved with EP lags behind the complexity of applications of various other evolutionary computing algorithms. These computing techniques can be used successfully in the selection of effective features for the classification of mammographic microcalcifications for diagnosing breast cancer.

Fuzzy logic was first developed in the mid 1960s for representing uncertain and imprecise knowledge [23]. It uses continuous set membership from 0 to 1 instead of the traditional Boolean values of 0 (for false) and 1 (for true). Thus, fuzzy logic allows elements of a set to have degrees of set membership. In this way, a set of rules can be built up to translate human knowledge, which is usually in a natural language. Example of a typical rule:

IF	Lump in the breast	**OR**	Changes in the colour of the skin
THEN	Consult your health nurse		

Fuzzy logic techniques have been successfully applied in a number of applications [27] such as computer vision, decision making, and system design including ANN training. It has been successfully used in microcalcification detection.

Neural networks, fuzzy logic and evolutionary computing have shown capability on many problems, but have not yet been able to solve the complex problems that their biological counterparts can (e.g., vision). It is useful to fuse neural networks, fuzzy systems and evolutionary computing techniques, thereby offsetting the demerits of one technique by the merits of the other techniques. Some of these techniques have been fused as follows:

- Neural networks for designing fuzzy systems.
- Fuzzy systems for designing neural networks.
- Evolutionary computing for the design of fuzzy systems.
- Evolutionary computing in automatically training and generating neural network architectures.

5   Summary

The preceding discussion highlights the potential benefits of knowledge-based systems in the diagnosis, prognosis and management of breast cancer because the impact of each available data source can be enhanced.

Improved *diagnostic accuracy*, i.e., increased specificity and sensitivity, avoids unnecessary invasive diagnostic procedures and reduces the potentially harmful time delay between initial examination and final diagnosis.

Improved assessment of *patient prognosis,* i.e., risk-group assignment, as well as improved *prediction of therapy response* allows individualized therapy decisions that could potentially meet the goals of high therapeutic security and efficiency. In particular, side effects of aggressive therapies for selected risk groups would be justified by high response rates.

We have seen that artificial intelligence methods are typically used to solve difficult modeling problems that are of very high priority. Considering that proper management of breast cancer is a life and death matter for countless women, the problems discussed above are of phenomenal importance to society. In view of this importance and the complexity of the biological processes involved, intelligent approaches are clearly warranted. As will be seen in the following chapters, application of soft computing techniques, especially artificial intelligence systems has the potential to enable *effective use of resources* and *patient-oriented management of breast cancer.*

References

[1] Clark, G. (1996), "Prognostic and predictive factors," in Harris, J.R., Lippmann, M.E., Morrow, M., Hellmann, S. (Eds.), *Diseases of the Breast*, Lippincott-Raven Publishers, Philadelphia, pp 461-485.

[2] Clark, G.M. and McGuire, W. (1988*)*, "Steroid receptors and other prognostic factors in primary breast cancer," *Semin Oncol* 15: 20-25.

[3] Early breast cancer trialists' collaborative group (1992), "Systemic treatment of early breast cancer by hormonal, cytotoxic, or immune therapy," *Lancet* 339, pp. 1-15 and 71-85.

[4] Harris, J. and Morrow, M. (1996), "Local management of invasive breast cancer," in Harris, J.R., Lippmann, M.E., Morrow, M., Hellmann, S. (Eds.), *Diseases of the Breast*, Lippincott-Raven Publishers, Philadelphia, pp 487-547.

[5] Henderson, I.C. (1994), "Ch. 319: Breast Cancer," in Isselbacher, K.J., Braunwald, E., Wilson, J.D., Martin, J.B., Fauci, A.S., and Kasper, D.L. (Eds.), *Harrison's Principles of Internal Medicine*, 13th edition, McGraw-Hill, Inc., vol. 2, pp. 1840-1850.

[6] Jain, L.C. and de Silva, C.W. (Eds.) (1999), *Intelligent Adaptive Control: Industrial Applications*, CRC Press, U.S.A.

[7] Jain, L.C., Johnson, R.P., Takefuji, Y., and Zadeh, L.A. (Eds.) (1998), *Computational Intelligence Techniques in Industry*, CRC Press, U.S.A.

[8] Jain, L.C. and Vemuri, R. (Eds.) (1998), *Industrial Applications of Neural Networks*, CRC Press, U.S.A.

[9] Jain, L.C. (Ed.) (2000), *Innovative Teaching and Learning: Knowledge-Based Paradigms*, Springer-Verlag, Germany.

[10] Jain, L.C (Ed.) (2000), *Evolution of Engineering and Information Systems and their Applications*, CRC Press, U.S.A.

[11] Jain, L.C. and Lazzerini, B. (Eds.) (1999), *Knowledge-Based Intelligent Techniques in Character Recognition*, CRC Press, U.S.A.

[12] Jain, L.C. and Martin, N.M. (Eds.) (1999), *Fusion of Neural Networks, Fuzzy Systems and Evolutionary Computing Techniques: Industrial Applications*, CRC Press , U.S.A.

[13] Jain, L.C., Halici, U., Hayashi, I., Lee, S.B., and Tsutsui, S. (Eds.) (1999), *Intelligent Biometric techniques in Fingerprint and Face Recognition*, CRC Press, U.S.A.

[14] Jain, L.C. (Ed.) (1997), *Soft Computing Techniques in Knowledge-Based Intelligent Engineering Systems*, Springer-Verlag, Germany.

[15] Jain, L.C. and Jain, R.K. (Eds.) (1997), *Hybrid Intelligent Engineering Systems*, World Scientific Publishing Company, Singapore.

[16] Karr, C.L. and Freeman, L.M. (Eds.) (1998), *Industrial Applications of Genetic Algorithms*, CRC Press, U.S.A.

[17] Karr, C.L. (Ed.) (1999), *Practical Applications of Computational Intelligence for Adaptive Control*, CRC Press, U.S.A.

[18] Koza, J.R. (1997), "Introduction to Evolutionary Computation," in Jain, L.C. (Ed.), *Soft Computing Techniques in Knowledge-Based Intelligent Engineering Systems*, Springer-Verlag, Germany, pp.71-111.

[19] Kricker, A. and Jelfs, P. (1996), *Breast Cancer in Australian Women 1921-1994*, Canberra: Australian Institute of Health and Welfare, Cancer Series No.6., NHMRC National Breast Cancer Centre.

[20] McGuire, W. and Clark, G.M. (1992), "Prognostic factors and treatment decisions in axillary node-negative breast cancer," *N Engl J Med* 326: 1756-1761.

[21] Medsker, L. and Jain, L.C. (Eds.) (2000), *Recurrent Neural Networks: Design and Applications*, CRC Press, U.S.A.

[22] Commonwealth Department of Health and Family Services, *National Health Priority Areas. Cancer Control.*

[23] Sato, M., Sato, Y., and Jain, L.C. (1997), *Fuzzy Clustering Models and Applications*, Springer-Verlag, Germany.

[24] Stevens, A. and Lowe, J. (1995), *Pathology*, Times Mirror International Publishers Limited, London.

[25] Teodorescu, H.N., Kandel, A., and Jain, L.C. (Eds.) (1999), *Fuzzy and Neuro-Fuzzy Systems in Medicine*, CRC Press, U.S.A.

[26] Teodorescu, H.N., Kandel, A., and Jain, L.C. (Eds.) (1999), *Soft Computing in Human-Related Sciences*, CRC Press, U.S.A.

[27] Teodorescu, H.N. and Jain, L.C. (Eds.) (2000), *Intelligent Systems and Techniques in Rehabilitation Engineering*, CRC Press, U.S.A.

[28] Vonk, E., Jain, L.C., and Johnson, R.P. (1997), *Automatic Generation of Neural Networks Architecture Using Evolutionary Computing*, World Scientific Publishing Company, Singapore.

[29] Van Rooij, A., Jain, L.C., and Johnson, R.P. (1996), *Neural Network Training Using Genetic Algorithms*, World Scientific, Singapore.

Chapter 2

Automatic Image Feature Extraction for Diagnosis and Prognosis of Breast Cancer

M.J. Bottema, **G.N. Lee**, and **S. Lu**

Image analysis methods are described in the context of extracting information from images relevant to the detection, classification, and prognosis of breast cancer. The discussion includes the roles of techniques across various modalities of image data as well as the techniques themselves.

1   Introduction

Artificial intelligence (AI) systems process information in order to arrive at decisions. In the case of systems that make decisions regarding the diagnosis or prognosis of breast cancer, the information supplied to the system, the input, can take the form of clinical data, non-clinical data such as statistics regarding family history, and image data such as mammograms, ultrasound images, and fine needle aspiration (FNA) slides. The performance of the system in terms of the proportion of correct and incorrect decisions clearly depends on the design of the system but also depends on how information is made available to the system. This is particularly important for image data because, in the information theoretic sense, the amount of information of diagnostic or prognostic value in an image is generally small compared to the great volume of information represented by the entire image. For example, a single screening mammographic image typically consists of more than 10^7 picture elements (pixels) while the evidence of cancer may be confined to fewer than 100 pixels which together represent a cluster of microcalcifications. In principle, an AI system could learn to distinguish between normal images and ones showing evidence of cancer by using raw images as input. In practice, it is necessary to reduce the information in the image to a manageable set of parameters which serves as input to the AI system. The process of reducing an image to a small set of parameters is called feature extraction and the parameters are called features. This chapter provides an overview of automatic image feature extraction for detection, diagnosis, and prognosis of breast cancer.

The literature on automatic image feature extraction related to breast cancer has focused on three types of images: mammographic images, ultrasound images, and images of FNA slides. The next section provides a brief description of these modalities in the context of image feature extraction and reviews several methods reported in the literature. Although the images in these three categories vary greatly both in terms of acquisition and utilization, the image features which must be extracted overlap significantly. Section 3 describes some of the methods which pervade the modalities.

2   Image Modalities

2.1   Mammography

2.1.1   Screening Mammography

The objective of screening mammography is not to diagnose cancer but to ascertain if there is enough evidence of cancer to warrant calling the subject back for more tests. Numerous computer algorithms have been designed to detect major signs of cancer in mammograms such as masses, stellate lesions, and clustered microcalcifications. The prime requirement of a screening program is high sensitivity and hence algorithms for detection must be tuned to yield very high detection rates. It has been found that in order to detect essentially all cancers, the false positive rate is prohibitively high for fully automated screening.

Some elaboration on this point is worthwhile. Current AI systems for screening mammography generally aim to provide assistance to radiologists in reading screening mammograms. They are designed to work with the radiologist by highlighting suspicious regions in the mammogram or to work as a second (or third) reader. They are not designed to replace the radiologist altogether. Accordingly, the specificity and sensitivity of the algorithm alone must be distinguished from the specificity and sensitivity of the human-computer system. The contribution of the algorithm is to detect cancers that are missed by the radiologist. If several false detections are found by the algorithm along the way, they can be dismissed by the radiologist so that the human-computer system operates at a sensible level of specificity. The limiting factor for the algorithm is the tolerance of the radiologist. If the algorithm reports false detections too often, the radiologist will soon ignore the reports and the AI system provides no benefit. The level of tolerance of radiologists is not known and surely varies between individuals, but as an indication of possible bounds, a false detection rate on the part of the algorithm of one per mammogram is definitely too high but a rate of one per ten mammograms might be reasonable.

In order to design algorithms that perform near these specifications, some attempt must be made to classify the detected anomalies even for screening applications. For example, if all microcalcifications are reported by the algorithm, a very large fraction of all screening mammograms will be marked by the algorithm. At the very least, isolated calcifications and "obviously benign" clusters such as vascular calcification must not be reported.

2.1.2   Clinical Mammography

Clinical mammography is one of several methods used to analyze suspicious regions initially identified at screening or through the presence of a lump or other symptoms. One or more high resolution images of the region of interest (ROI) are obtained. The aims of AI systems in this setting include classifying masses as malignant or benign or classifying types of microcalcifications. Usually it is known that a particular anomaly is present and it may be quite obvious visually, but in order to extract features such as size, shape, or texture automatically, the exact location of the anomaly within the image must still be determined. This means that many of the detection methods used for analyzing screening mammograms also apply here.

Thus, detection and classification play roles in both screening and clinical mammography and, from the point of view of automatic image analysis, there are no outstanding differences between them.

2.1.3   Detection and Classification of Masses

Masses appear as bright regions in the mammogram which must be distinguished from other bright regions such as the nipple, the pectoral muscle, and normal dense tissue. Although masses vary in form, especially malignant ones, their overall shape and density distribution does set masses apart fairly well as a general class of objects in mammograms. Geometric properties are therefore natural candidates for features. Petrick *et al.* used zero crossings of the Laplacian of Gaussian filter to detect closed boundaries in the image. Five geometric features were measured on the objects defined by these boundaries: the number of boundary pixels, area, circularity, rectangularity, and contrast with background [40]. In this paper circularity was computed using formula (2) in Section 3.1.3. Qian *et al.* used wavelets (Section 3.5) for preprocessing and computed circularity by formula (1) in Section 3.1.3, measured the standard deviation of the boundary viewed as a radial function (Section 3.1.4), the variation of the intensity surfaces, contrast, and the mean gradient on the boundary [44]. A simpler approach to preprocessing was taken by Zheng *et al.* who used difference of Gaussians to suppress noise and enhance suspected masses. Candidate masses were identified by thresholding and three level sets were formed from each candidate mass by thresholding at different values. A collection of geometric and texture features were computed for each level set as well as some parameters relating properties of adjacent layers [67]. An altogether different approach was taken by Li *et al.* who used a multi-resolution Markov random field model for detection [34].

Malignant masses are characterized by rough boundaries, possibly with spicules radiating from the center, irregular shape, and non-uniform surfaces. Automatic classification of masses has concentrated on measuring geometric features similar to those used for initial detection of masses, texture features of the image intensity surface and surrounding area, and the irregularity of the boundary [9], [22], [29], [34], [41], [42], [45]. Pohlman *et al.* computed several properties of the boundary viewed as a radial function (Section 3.1.4) including the fractal dimension (Section 3.2.5) [41]. Huo *et al.* computed the maximum gradient at points in the mass and recorded the orientation of this gradient with respect to the ray from the center of the mass to the point in question (not with respect to a fixed direction). The gradient magnitudes for each direction were summed over local neighborhoods to form a histogram of edge gradients [22]. Kobatake *et al.* used a filter called the iris filter on the gradient field of the image for initial detection and used snakes (Section 3.4) as part of a boundary detection scheme. Features for classification included measurements of a co-occurrence matrix (Section 3.2.2) defined on an array of values representing the probability of a mass boundary being present at a particular point in the image [29]. A method for focusing attention to the boundary was introduced by Sahiner *et al.* who excised a band of fixed width along the boundary, straightened this band into a rectangle and measured many features from co-occurrence matrices (Section 3.2.2) derived from the rectangle [9], [46]. Instead of characterizing spiculation at the boundary, Rangayyan *et al.* measured the sharpness of the boundary [45]. The boundaries of malignant masses tend to be diffuse while boundaries of benign masses tend to be well defined.

When examining screening mammograms, radiologists compare current and previous mammograms and look for asymmetry between images of the left and right breasts. Attempts to gain information from such comparisons in automatic systems has proven to be a formidable task. Inconsistent tissue deformation during image acquisition, and natural changes in breast tissue over time pose serious difficulties in image registration. Several studies have been reported which may point the way to overcoming these problems [19], [30], [47], [54], [62], [66].

2.1.4 Detection of Stellate Lesions

Stellate lesions are identified by linear structures radiating from a common central region. In many mammograms, linear structures in normal tissue tend to orient toward the nipple. This means that a histogram of edge orientations measured over a small region of normal tissue typically contains a single peak corresponding to the direction of the nipple.

If the region includes a stellate lesion, there are edges in all directions and the histogram is more uniform. Kegelmeyer *et al.* measured edge orientations using a Sobel gradient filter and analyzed histograms of orientations to detect stellate lesions [27]. An edge does not necessarily indicate a linear structure, so another approach is to detect lines directly. One method is to apply a set of oriented line filters at every pixel. This approach is computationally expensive especially if the width of the lines is not known and the process must be repeated for several line models. Karssemeijer and te Brake used just three filters based on second order derivatives of a Gaussian kernel to compute a line orientation value at each pixel. This was followed by a statistical analysis of orientation values in various sectors about the center [25].

2.1.5   Detection and Classification of Microcalcifications

Microcalcifications are an important sign of cancer in mammography. As many as 95 percent of cases of ductal carcinoma in situ (DCIS) are detected because microcalcifications are discovered in mammograms [20]. Many microcalcifications are also fairly easy to detect. They appear on the mammogram as bright spots above background. As a result, automatic detection of microcalcifications was one of the first aspects of computer-assisted mammography to receive serious attention. In 1987, Chan *et al.* designed a filter similar to a matched filter for detecting round microcalcifications [8].

However, linear filters alone just do not suffice for detecting microcalcifications. In the first place, variation among the appearance of microcalcifications (Figure 1) coupled with even greater variation in background tissue prevents the construction of sufficiently reliable models on which to base optimal linear filter design. In the second place, a very large fraction of normal images also contain calcification which is not associated with cancer. Thus an algorithm which detects all calcification without error, reports too many cases of obviously benign examples to be of clinical value. The correct goal for designing an algorithm for detection of microcalcifications is to target only calcification associated with cancer. This means that classification of calcification type must be included to some extent.

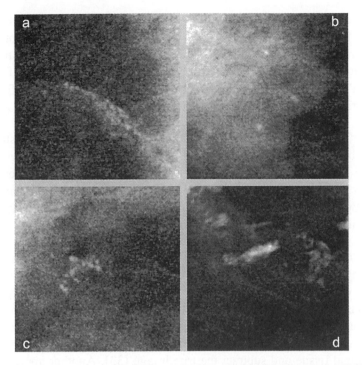

Figure 1. Four types of calcification: (a) vascular, (b) lobular, (c) DCIS cribriform, and (d) DCIS comedo. Vascular and lobular do not indicate cancer. All four images show a 1 cm × 1 cm region in a mammogram. For display purposes, the intensity values in each image have been scaled to fill the available range of gray levels so intensities between images cannot be compared.

Another difficulty in designing algorithms for detection of microcalcifications is that it is not possible to train methods on data sets in which the location of all microcalcifications are known absolutely. Through biopsy it is possible to learn the disease state associated with a particular cluster of microcalcifications, but is not possible to map the location of individual microcalcification found in tissue back to the location on the mammogram. Most microcalcifications can be identified in the mammogram by a radiologist but this identification cannot be expected to be free of error, especially in the case of subtle microcalcifications.

Initial detection often involves some form of background subtraction followed by a method for identifying clusters. Combinations of simple linear filters and non-linear filters have been used by many authors for background subtraction [8], [37], [65]. Filters organized into a multi-resolution filter bank or wavelet analysis for initial segmentation of clusters of microcalcifications are a natural extension and provide a framework for controlling parameters [31], [43], [52], [55], [63].

Linear filters generally distort objects of interest more than is desirable for subsequent feature extraction. In order to assign a local background which is largely independent of the object of interest, splines offer better performance than linear filters without excessive extra computational cost. Schmidt *et al.* used polynomials of degree three to approximate and then subtract the background for initial detection [48].

Background subtraction may be avoided altogether if detection relies on morphological or texture features instead of geometric ones. Detection based on statistical texture features (Section 3.2) measured on the regions immediately surrounding candidate calcifications was reported by Kim and Park [28]. Texture in images can also be quantified by fractal dimension (Section 3.2.5). One method is to construct a fractal model of normal tissue and subtract the true image [33]. Another approach is to measure the degree to which local tissue displays self-similar patterns by seeing how well the log-log plot of size vs. scale fits a straight line [32]. A straight line indicates a normal self-similar pattern, while a broken line indicates a disruption of the self-similar pattern, possibly due to the presence of calcification. Detection based on mathematical morphology (Section 3.3) was reported by Betal *et al.* The top-hat algorithm was used for initial detection and the watershed algorithm was used to segment individual microcalcifications [3].

A separate step is often needed to eliminate localized bright regions not associated with calcification such as film flaws, linear features in normal tissue, and scar tissue from previous surgery [15], [65].

Interpretations of mammograms involving microcalcifications are based on clusters rather than individual microcalcifications. The true disease state associated with clusters can be verified by biopsy and so proper training of algorithms is possible. Features for classification include distributions of properties of microcalcifications within the cluster such as averages, maxima, or standard deviations of densities, sizes, and shapes as well as size and shape properties of the cluster itself [3], [10], [14], [24], [39].

Texture measures of clusters such as features computed from co-occurrence matrices (Section 3.2.2) [10] and texture measures of the region surrounding calcifications [53] have also been reported.

2.2   Ultrasound

Ultrasound imaging is widely used to distinguish cysts from solid mass tissue in lesions detected through mammography. Improved technology has recently lead to the use of ultrasound for classifying lesions into subtypes for the purpose of deciding if fine needle aspiration (FNA) is necessary or to guide such a procedure if required [50]. With increased image quality and higher expectations of ultrasound, work has started on automating image interpretation. Differences between various lesions appear in the sonogram on the side of the lesion away from the transducers.

Zheng *et al.* measured texture features on several portions of the ROI relative to the location of the linear transducer array [68]. The texture features consisted of seven run-length features computed from a run matrix (Section 3.2.1), twenty-one Markov texture features (Section 3.2.3), and three novel features, relative through transmission, transmission rate, and anterior-posterior to transverse ratio, designed specifically to measure properties of sonograms reported by radiologists to be of diagnostic significance.

A variation of ultrasound, called color doppler ultrasound, produces images in which color is a measure of blood flow velocity. The distribution and level of blood flow is used to distinguish benign and malignant lesions. Image analysis can be used to replace subjective evaluation of color images by quantitative measurements. Huber *et al.* calculated average color values and color pixel densities and deduced flow rates to classify benign and malignant lesions [13], [21].

2.3 Fine Needle Aspiration Slides

FNA is used to determine if a breast mass is malignant or benign and to provide information for prognosis. A small amount of material is aspirated from breast masses, fixed onto a microscope slide and stained. Diagnostic and prognostic information is derived by analyzing cell nuclei. Computer algorithms for automatic feature extraction measure geometric properties and texture properties of the cell nucleus [18], [35], [56], [57], [58], [59], [60], [64] and the relative location and arrangement of nuclei from local cell groups [17], [38].

To identify the nucleus of a cell, Wolberg *et al.* required that the user determines the approximate boundary of the nucleus manually. The nuclear boundary was then identified more accurately using a snake (Section 3.4). The features measured were radius, perimeter, area, perimeter^2/area (Section 3.1), the second derivative of the boundary viewed as radial function (which the authors call smoothness), two measures of concavity, a measure of symmetry, the fractal dimension of the boundary of the nucleus (Section 3.2.5), and the variance of image intensity values within the nucleus [60].

Weyn *et al.* used wavelets (Section 3.5) to obtain multi-resolution texture measures. Eight features were measured on co-occurrence matrices at three distances (Section 3.2.2). In addition, the total optical density, mean optical density, standard deviation of the optical density and several geometric features similar to those described in the previous paragraph were computed [56].

3 Image Features and Analysis

A description of image features cannot be extricated from a description of feature extraction techniques. In many cases there is a loose consensus as to the definition of a particular image feature stemming from a suggestive name. For example, the feature "average radius of a region" is self explanatory, at least at the coarsest level of agreement. However, to actually compute this feature requires many choices. One must define the boundary of the region, decide if the average should be taken over all boundary pixels or over all directions, and in the case of the latter, how to manage the unequal sampling of directions. The exact definition of any feature is only given by the algorithm used at implementation. It is not unreasonable to view the terms "feature" and "feature extraction" as being synonymous.

This section comprises an introduction to image feature extraction biased toward the features encountered in the previous section. The criterion for inclusion represents a compromise between ubiquity in the literature, and personal taste. The choices are not meant to imply that those included are necessarily superior to others.

An analysis of the relative merits of features would be of great benefit, but is not realistic for two reasons. Firstly, the quality of a feature is measured by its contribution to detection, classification, or prognosis of cancer. This measure also depends on the other features extracted, the preprocessing steps, and classification methods. By fixing all other aspects of an algorithm, it is possible to ascertain the contribution of a single feature within a particular study. Unfortunately, the validity of such results seldom extend to other studies where the same feature is emersed in an altogether different scheme. Secondly, the performance of various methods reported in the literature, in most cases, have been measured on different data sets. The choice of data set can influence the performance significantly [6]. (It should be noted that choosing a "good" data set is in itself a difficult task. For example, randomly selecting screening mammograms which show masses for the purpose of testing a detection algorithm, probably biases the set toward cases which are not likely to be missed by radiologists.) A comprehensive study testing a wide range of algorithms implemented faithfully on a single data set has not been reported.

3.1   Geometric Features

Geometric features are used to measure various notions of size and shape of objects in images. There are nearly as many geometric features as there are papers on image analysis. The emphasis in this section is on general techniques and a few pitfalls.

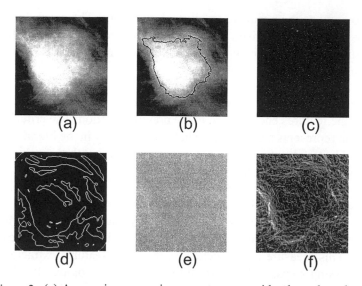

Figure 2. (a) A mass in a screening mammogram with a boundary that is obvious to the human eye in some places but fuzzy in other places. (b) The boundary of the set found by simple thresholding and identifying the largest connected component in the resulting binary image. The boundary is superimposed on the original. (c) The image obtained by applying a Gaussian filter of width $\sigma = 3$ to the image in (a) followed by the Laplacian. The displayed pixels are those for which at least one 4-connected neighbor had value above zero and one 4-connected neighbor had value below zero in the resulting image. (d) The same process as in (c) was applied after subsampling the image in (a) by a factor of 5 (5×5 patch $\rightarrow$ 1×1) and applying a 41×41 2-dimensional median filter. (e) The image of $\|\nabla f\|$ computed directly on (a). (f) The image of $\|\nabla f\|$ computed on (a) after subsampling by a factor of 5.

3.1.1   The Boundary

The boundary of an object in an image is the starting point for extracting geometric features and is often of interest in itself. Though the notion of boundary is intuitive, defining or extracting the boundary of an object is fraught with difficulties. The different methods listed below lead to different boundaries. Evaluating the merits of these boundaries should be based on their contribution to the extraction of features and eventual analysis of the image. As this depends on the particular application, none of the methods can be said to be inherently better than the others.

Too much emphasis is sometimes placed on constructing a method that automatically finds the boundary assigned by a human. Human interpretation of the boundary often depends critically on the contrast curve used for display and should not be regarded as categorically correct.

Binary sets

Images relevant to breast cancer are nearly always gray scale images and objects of interest are nearly always represented by pixels with a variety of intensity values. Segmentation algorithms for identifying objects usually result in a binary image where "on-pixels" represent the location of the object of interest. The segmentation may comprise simple thresholding of the image itself (Figure 2(b)) or thresholding of a function computed on neighborhoods of pixels, such as texture features (Section 3.2). Typically, thresholding does not result in a clean definition of the object. Additional processing, especially morphological processing (Section 3.3), can result in a binary image where the on-pixels accurately represent the object (Figure 6).

Once a set of pixels has been identified as representing the object, the boundary can be defined in several ways. Some authors use the vertical and horizontal line segments which separate the on-pixels from the off-pixels as the boundary. A variation of this approach is to allow diagonal line segments where pixels belonging to the set form corners. Another possibility is to view the boundary as a set of boundary pixels. The set of on-pixels for which at least one of its immediate eight neighbors is an off-pixel is called the 4-connected boundary. The set of on-pixels for which at least one of its four neighbors with which it shares an edge is an off-pixel is called the 8-connected boundary. The convention is that only pixels inside the set can be part of the boundary, but this is somewhat of an arbitrary choice. Either of these sets of boundary pixels or a subsampled version of one of them can be used to generate a smooth boundary using snakes (Section 3.4) or control points (Section 3.1.4).

Edge detection

The boundaries of many objects in images are defined by "edges" which are locations of transition from high to low or low to high intensity values. For an image given by intensity function $f(x, y)$, the magnitude of the gradient and the Laplacian are given by

$$\|\nabla f\| = \sqrt{\left(\frac{\partial f}{\partial x}\right)^2 + \left(\frac{\partial f}{\partial y}\right)^2} \quad \text{and} \quad \nabla^2 f = \frac{\partial^2 f}{\partial x^2} + \frac{\partial^2 f}{\partial y^2},$$

respectively. Edges can be characterized as places where $\|\nabla f\|$ is large or, alternatively, as places where $\nabla^2 f = 0$. These methods for detecting edges, as well as the Canny algorithm [7], are popular in the general literature, but are not always useful in delineating the boundaries of objects of interest in images relevant to breast cancer. In the first place, the presence of noise, particularly in ultrasound and x-ray images, requires that substantial smoothing be done before applying the methods (Figure 2(c)-(f)). In the second place, the structure of normal tissue near the object contributes additional edges which are confused with the target boundary. At best, the result is an edge image in which prominent features are not clearly connected to form an identifiable boundary (Figure 2(f)). However, edge images can be used as a basis for defining connected boundaries using the methods of the next section.

Global boundaries

Forming a connected boundary from an edge image is sometimes accomplished by searching a large collection of possible boundaries and scoring the candidate paths according to total edge intensity and other traits such as smoothness or deviation from an *a priori* model. This approach is often referred to as edge linking [23]. Other methods for identifying a global boundary from local edge data include using Fourier descriptors and control points (Section 3.1.4) and snakes (Section 3.4).

Examples: Mammography [22], [40], [41], [45], [46], [67], FNA [17], [60].

3.1.2   Area, Volume, Radius, Height, Contrast

Once a boundary is assigned, features such as area, volume, height, contrast with background, can be computed without difficulty. Counting the pixels inside the boundary approximates the area and the sum of the pixel values approximates the volume. Although these two methods represent the crudest form of numerical integration, increased precision obtained by more sophisticated integration schemes are seldom justified by the limits of accuracy incurred by discretization and assigning the boundary.

Often the average radius is computed, but this number is simply $r_{ave} = \sqrt{\text{area}/\pi}$ and so supplies no new information. However, it may happen that either area or r_{ave} provides better classification when combined with other features.

In some situations it is possible to determine geometric parameters without explicitly assigning a boundary. For example, a plausible model of a microcalcification in a mammogram consists of five parameters: gradient of the background, intensity of the background, and the radius and density of the microcalcification. These parameters can be found by minimizing the error between the model and the image over the set of parameters [5].

Examples: Mammography [3], [10], [14], [24], [39], [40], [44], [67], FNA [18], [35], [56], [60], [64].

3.1.3   The Curse of Perimeter^2/4π Area

Many authors use a version of the quantity

$$\frac{\text{perimeter}^2}{4\pi \text{ area}} \tag{1}$$

as a feature. This is fine as long as it is understood that this formula is not minimized by a disk as is often claimed. The confusion stems from the fact that for a disk in the continuous plane $\mathbb{R}^2$, the formula in (1) has value one and the value is strictly greater than one for other shapes. This fact simply does not carry over to the discrete setting. The details depend on the method used for computing the perimeter. For example, if the perimeter is taken to be the number of pixels in the four-connected boundary of a set, the shape with the smallest value of (1) is achieved by a square, not a disk (Figure 3). If the perimeter is taken to be the number pixels in the eight-connected boundary of a set, the smallest value is achieved by an octagon. These phenomena are due to fundamental difficulties encountered in defining the length of a curve which is given by

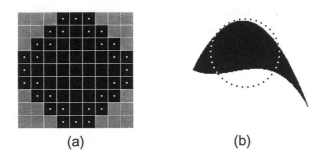

(a)   (b)

Figure 3. (a) The discrete disk (black) and the square both have a perimeter of 32 if measured as the number of 4-connected boundary pixels. The
4-connected boundary pixels of the disk are indicated by white dots. Using formula (1) the circularity of the disk is ≈ 1.430 and the circularity of
the square is ≈ 1.006. Hence the square is more circular than the disk. (b)
The black region is a set S and the dotted circle indicates the boundary of
the disk D having the same center and area as S. Using formula (2), the
circularity of of the disk in (a) is 1.0, the circularity of the square in (a) is
≈ 0.951, and the circularity of the set S in (b) is ≈ 0.771.

discrete data.

Fortunately, alternative measures of circularity exist which avoid the
problem of measuring the perimeter of the set. Consider a set S having area A. A reasonable measure of the circularity of S is given by the
formula

$$\frac{\text{Area}(S \cap D)}{\text{Area}(D)} \tag{2}$$

where D is the disk centered at the geometric center of S and having
radius $r = \sqrt{(A/\pi)}$ [16], [4]. The disk D can be viewed as the disk which
best approximates S. Formula (2) has value one for disks and has smaller
values for other sets (Figure 3). This definition of circularity depends
only on areas of sets, which, unlike the perimeter, is well defined for
discrete sets.

Examples: Mammography [34], [40], [44], FNA [18], [60].

3.1.4 Shape

No single description or parameterization of shape provides useful features in all situations. For example, the term "irregular boundary" in the case of mass boundaries in mammograms refers to local linear features radiating from the mass while the same term is used in the case of cell nuclei in FNA images to refer to large scale deviations from elliptic shape such as concavities [60]. Accordingly, a wide variety of methods have been used to describe shape.

Radial functions

A common device for capturing important aspects of shape is to measure properties of the radial function description of the boundary, $r(\theta)$. This function measures the distance from the geometric center of the object to the point on the boundary lying on the ray through the center which makes an angle θ with a fixed reference direction. The radial function is only defined for regions which are "star shaped" with respect to their centers. This means that there is exactly one boundary point for every angle θ. This is not the case for many boundaries, including the boundary of the mass shown in Figure 2(b).

A variation of the radial function is shown in Figure 4. Here the boundary points are indexed (parameterized) and the radius is recorded as a function of the index instead of the angle θ. Low frequency changes in this function measure global variation, high frequency changes measure local features.

Fourier Descriptors

Suppose N points with coordinates $(x(n), y(n))$, $n = 0, 1, \ldots, N - 1$ have been identified in an image as belonging to a boundary. A useful representation of the contour can be constructed by viewing the discrete functions $x(n)$ and $y(n)$ as the real and imaginary parts of a complex valued function f. That is,

$$f(n) = x(n) + i\,y(n).$$

The discrete Fourier transform coefficients of f are called the Fourier descriptors of the boundary. The letter a will be used to denote these

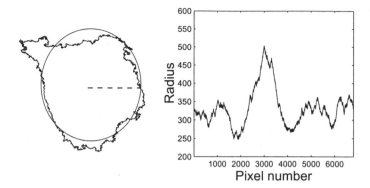

Figure 4. On the left is the boundary from Figure 2b and the concentric circle of the same average radius. The dashed line connects the geometric center of the region to the "first" point on the boundary. The other points on the boundary are indexed consecutively in a counter clockwise direction. On the right is the plot of the distance of each boundary point from the center. The horizontal axis is the index of each point.

descriptors, so

$$a(k) = \sum_{n=0}^{N-1} f(n)e^{-\frac{2\pi ikn}{N}}, \qquad 0 \le k \le N - 1.$$

The number $a(k)$ can be viewed as the shape at frequency k. A subcollection of these can be used as a list of shape features. Since the discrete Fourier transform is invertible, the complex numbers $a(k)$ provide a complete description boundary. The function f can be recovered by the Fourier inversion formula

$$f(n) = \frac{1}{N} \sum_{k=0}^{N-1} a(k)e^{\frac{2\pi ikn}{N}}, \qquad 0 \le n \le N - 1.$$

Fourier descriptors may also be used to measure the "distance" between two boundaries [23]. Suppose that $f(n)$ and $g(n)$ are two boundaries with Fourier descriptors $a(k)$ and $b(k)$. If both boundaries are laterally shifted so that their geometric centers are at the origin, then

$$\sum f(n) = a(0) = 0 \qquad \text{and} \qquad \sum g(n) = b(0) = 0$$

and the distance between the two curves is given by

$$d = \min_{\alpha,\theta,n_0} \left\{ \sum_{n=0}^{N-1} |f(n) - \alpha g(n + n_0)e^{i\theta}|^2 \right\}. \tag{3}$$

The expression inside the brackets is minimized when

$$\tan \theta = -\frac{\sum_k c(k) \, sin(\psi_k + k\phi(n_0))}{\sum_k c(k) \, cos(\psi_k + k\phi(n_0))}$$

$$\alpha = \frac{\sum_k c(k) \, cos(\psi_k + k\phi(n_0) + \theta)}{\sum_k |b(k)|^2}$$

where $c(k) = |a(k)b^*(k)|$, $a(k)b^*(k) = c(k)e^{i\psi_k}$, and the angle ϕ is $\phi(n_0) = -2\pi n_0/N$. With these values of θ and α, the distance between the curves becomes

$$d = \min_{n_0} \left\{ \sum_k |a(k) - \alpha b(k)e^{i(k\phi(n_0)+\theta)}|^2 \right\}. \tag{4}$$

Since the possible values of n_0 are $n_0 = 0, 1, \ldots, N-1$, finding d is not unreasonable computationally. Most importantly, the distance obtained is independent of the size, location, and orientation of the two boundaries. It only depends on the shapes.

One problem with this method is that the boundaries of the two shapes must be described using the same number of points. This problem can be alleviated by the use of control points [23]. A boundary described initially by N points $P_n = (x(n), y(n))$ is identified with the continuously defined curve $\gamma(t)$ by

$$\gamma(t) = \sum_{n=0}^{N-1} P_n B_{n,k}(t) \tag{5}$$

where $B_{n,k}(t)$ is the B-spline of degree k [23]. The curve $\gamma(t)$ may then be resampled to obtain a description of the original boundary in terms of fewer or more points.

The formula in (5) also provides a method for defining a global boundary based on a few, possibly sparse, boundary points detected locally by methods such as edge detection (Section 3.1.1).

Moments

The shape descriptors discussed above are useful for representing the outline of a region in an image. Moments provide a representation of the gray values within the region as well as the shape of the boundary. For a function $f : \mathbb{R}^2 \to \mathbb{R}$ with support in a bounded region $\Omega \subset \mathbb{R}^2$ and integers $p, q \in 0, 1, 2, \ldots$ the p, q-moment of f is defined to be

$$m_{p,q}(f) = m_{p,q} = \iint_{\mathbb{R}^2} f(x, y)\, x^p y^q dx dy = \iint_{\Omega} f(x, y)\, x^p y^q dx dy. \tag{6}$$

The gray scale values of the image in the region Ω, the function f in our case, can be recovered completely from all the moment values by the formula

$$f(x, y) = \int_{-\infty}^{\infty} \int_{-\infty}^{\infty} e^{-\pi i(x\xi_1 + y\xi_2)} \sum_{p=0}^{\infty} \sum_{q=0}^{\infty} \frac{(2\pi i)^{p+q} \xi_1^p \xi_2^q}{p! q!}\, m_{p,q}\, d\xi_1 d\xi_2. \tag{7}$$

Hence, in principle, no information is lost by representing a region by its moments. The formula in (7) is not very practical for computations mostly because the basis functions $x^p y^q$ do not form an orthogonal set. This shortcoming can be removed by using Legendre polynomials as basis functions instead. Translation and size invariant versions are obtained by considering normalized central moments. Formulas for combining moments to achieve rotation invariants are available [23] although the full story leads to the study of algebraic invariants.

Other shape features

The previous representations of regions are satisfying from a mathematical view in that they retain full information. Even though these representations are usually truncated in practice there is comfort in having control of fidelity by choosing the number of terms retained.

Many other shape features have appeared in the literature which do not obviously form part of a collection that fully represents regions. This means there is no guarantee that, given a set of such features, a better description of the region can be attained, even in principle, by including others.

However, this consideration does not preclude such features from contributing to classification. Understanding of the data often provides strong expectation that specific *ad hoc* features will provide crucial discriminatory power. This certainly is the case in the applications considered here since many features recommended by radiologists and pathologists to analyze images are manifestations of known biological processes.

- **Bounding boxes.** The smallest rectangular box which includes the region is called the bounding box. In some implementations only boxes with sides parallel to the natural axes are allowed, while in other cases all orientations are considered. Possible features are the dimensions of the bounding box, the ratio of the sides (eccentricity), and the orientation of the major axis.

- **Best fit ellipses.** An ellipse with the same second moments as the region is sometimes used to define the best fit ellipse. The lengths of the major and minor axes are possible features as are their orientations and their ratio (eccentricity).

- **Curvature.** If $\gamma(s) = (x(s), y(s))$ is a curve and the parameter s represents arc length, then the tangent angle is given by

$$\Phi(s) = \tan^{-1}\left(\frac{dy/ds}{dx/ds}\right)$$

and the curvature is given by

$$\kappa(s) = \frac{d\Phi}{ds}.$$

Discrete versions are

$$\Phi(s_j) = \tan^{-1}\left(\frac{y(s_j) - y(s_{j-1})}{x(s_j) - x(s_{j-1})}\right), \qquad \kappa(s_j) = \Phi(s_j) - \Phi(s_{j-1}).$$

Possible features include the number of corners, (taken to be the number of places where $|\kappa(s)|$ exceeds a given threshold) and the bending energy given by

$$E = \frac{1}{T}\int_0^T |\kappa(s)|^2 \, ds$$

where T the length of the curve. The bending energy can also be computed from the Fourier descriptors (Section 3.1.4) by the formula

$$E = \sum_k |a(k)|^2 \left(\frac{2\pi k}{T}\right)^4.$$

Examples: Mammography [28], [43], [44], [45], FNA [18], [60].

3.2   Texture Features

3.2.1   Run-Length Matrices

For a given direction θ, $w(m, n)$ is defined to be the number of runs in direction θ of m consecutive pixels having gray level n. The matrix $W_\theta = [w(m, n)]$ is the run-length matrix in direction θ (Section 3.2.4). The number of columns of W is determined by the number of gray levels in the image. In practice, it is often necessary to compress the gray scale in order to avoid excessively large and/or sparse arrays. Run length features refer to properties of the run-length matrix which summarize trends in pixel value distributions.

Examples: Mammography [46], Ultrasound [68], FNA [35].

3.2.2   Co-occurrence Matrices

A co-occurrence matrix, also known as a concurrence matrix, or a spatial gray level dependence (SGLD) matrix, is an array of joint probabilities for pairs of pixels separated by a given distance, d, at a given orientation θ. In other words, the co-occurrence matrix is $W_{\theta,d} = [w(m, n)]$, where $w(m, n)$ is the proportion of pixels p_1 and p_2 with intensity values $p_1 = m$ and $p_2 = n$ such that $\|p_1 - p_2\| = d$ and the ray $\vec{p_1 p_2}$ makes an angle θ with a fixed reference direction (Section 3.2.4). Examples of features derived from a co-occurrence matrix include

$$\text{energy} = \sum_{m,n} w(m, n)^2$$

$$\text{inertia} = \sum_{m,n} (m - n)^2 w(m, n)$$

$$\text{entropy} \; = \; -\sum_{m,n} w(m,n) \log(w(m,n))$$

$$\text{inverse difference moment} \; = \; \sum_{m,n} (1 + (m-n)^2)^{-1} w(m,n)$$

$$\text{difference entropy} \; = \; -\sum_{k} w_{m-n}(k) \log \, w_{m-n}(k)$$

where

$$w_{m-n}(k) = \sum_{|m-n|=k} w(m,n).$$

Examples: Mammography [10], [29], [46], FNA [35], [56], [64].

3.2.3 Markovian Statistics

Markovian statistics are very similar to co-occurrence features (Section 3.2.2). If $w(m,n)$ is the conditional probability that p_2 has value n given that p_1 has value m (rather than the joint probability), then the features measured on the matrix $W_{\theta,d} = [w(m,n)]$ are called Markovian statistics (Section 3.2.4).

Examples: Ultrasound [68].

3.2.4 Example of Texture Arrays

The three texture arrays introduced in Sections 3.2.1 - 3.2.3, are computed below for a 5×5 image consisting of 4 colors (gray scales). For each texture array, the direction is $\theta = 0$, meaning the direction of the positive x-axis, and the distance parameter needed in the co-occurrence and Markov statistic matrices is $d = 1$.

							n			
4	4	3	1	1			1	2	3	4
1	2	4	4	2		1	5	4	2	3
3	1	4	4	4	m	2	1	0	1	2
2	4	3	3	1		3	0	0	0	1
4	2	1	4	1						

Image array   run length

m	n 1	2	3	4		n 1	2	3	4
1	1/20	1/20	0	2/20	1	1/4	1/4	0	3/4
2	1/20	0	0	2/20	2	1/3	0	0	2/3
3	3/20	0	1/20	0	3	3/4	0	1/4	0
4	1/20	2/20	2/20	4/20	4	1/9	2/9	2/9	4/9

co-occurrence   Markov

3.2.5 Fractal Dimension

A set is said to be self-similar if general patterns are the same at many scales of resolution. For a scale factor, r, and a measure of the size of the set, $S(r)$, at scale r, the plot of $\log(S(r))$ vs $\log(r)$ is a straight line if the set is self similar. In this case, the fractal dimension of the set can be computed from the slope of this line (Figure 5). If the set in question is the boundary of a tumor, for example, then the measure of size, $S(r)$, is the length of the curve at scale r. If the set is the image intensity surface of a tumor, the size measure, $S(r)$, is the area of the surface at scale r [2], [36].

Examples: Mammography [32], [33], [41], [53], FNA [35], [60].

3.3 Morphology

Mathematical morphology refers to a collection of image processing methods based on Minkowsky set addition. For two sets A and B, the Minkowsky sum is

$$A \oplus B = \{a + b : a \in A, b \in B\}.$$

For applications to image analysis, the sets of interest are sets of pixels in the plane or sets of volume elements (voxels) in a 3-dimensional array. For example, if A and B are the sets of pixels

$$A = \{(0,0), (0,1), (1,1)\} \quad \text{and} \quad B = \{(0,0), (1,0)\},$$

then

$$A \oplus B = \{(0,0), (1,0), (0,1), (1,1), (0,2)\}.$$

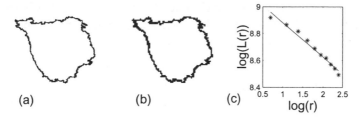

Figure 5. Box counting dimension. One method for computing the fractal dimension of a boundary is to cut the image into boxes of size $r \times r$ and count the number of boxes $N(r)$ containing at least one boundary point. The length of the boundary at scale r is then estimated to be $L(r) = rN(r)$. In this case the fractal dimension is defined as the number d such that $N(r) = \alpha r^{-d}$. Hence $d = 1 - m$, where m is the slope of graph of $\log(L(r))$ vs $\log(r)$. For the boundary of the mass in Figure 2(b), the boxes containing at least one boundary point for scales $r = 5$ and $r = 10$ are shown in (a) and (b) respectively. The graph in (c) shows plots of $\log(L(r))$ vs $\log(r)$ for $r = 2, 3, \ldots, 11$. A line of slope $m = -0.256$ gives the best fit so that the fractal dimension of this boundary is estimated to be $d = 1.256$.

There is also Minkowsky set subtraction defined, in general, by

$$A \ominus B = (A^c \oplus B)^c,$$

Where A^c, called the "complement" of A, is the set of all pixels that are not in A. For our example,

$$A \ominus B = \{(1,1)\}.$$

In most cases, there is a set X of pixels in an image from which features are to be extracted and a set B, called a "structure element", which is used to modify X by one or more of the following operations.

- **Dilation** of X by B: $X \oplus \bar{B}$
- **Erosion** of X by B: $X \ominus \bar{B}$
- **Opening** of X by B: $(X \ominus \bar{B}) \oplus B$
- **Closing** of X by B: $(X \oplus \bar{B}) \ominus B$

Here $\bar{B}$ denotes the reflection of the set B

$$\bar{B} = \{-b : b \in B\}.$$

Figure 6 illustrates the use of these operations in restoring an object in an image that has been corrupted by noise and in extracting the boundary. The structure elements used in this example are

$$
B_1 = \begin{matrix} & 0 & 1 & 1 & 1 & 0 \\ & 1 & 1 & 1 & 1 & 1 \\ & 1 & 1 & 1 & 1 & 1 \\ & 1 & 1 & 1 & 1 & 1 \\ & 0 & 1 & 1 & 1 & 0 \end{matrix} \quad
B_2 = \begin{matrix} 1 & 1 & 1 & 1 & 1 & 1 & 1 \\ 1 & 1 & 1 & 1 & 1 & 1 & 1 \\ 1 & 1 & 1 & 1 & 1 & 1 & 1 \\ 1 & 1 & 1 & 1 & 1 & 1 & 1 \\ 1 & 1 & 1 & 1 & 1 & 1 & 1 \\ 1 & 1 & 1 & 1 & 1 & 1 & 1 \\ 1 & 1 & 1 & 1 & 1 & 1 & 1 \end{matrix} \quad
B_3 = \begin{matrix} 0 & 1 & 0 \\ 1 & 1 & 1 \\ 0 & 1 & 0 \end{matrix}
$$

$$(8)$$

Morphologic operations can be applied to gray scale images as well as binary images. If the intensity surface of an image is given by $f(x, y)$, then the 3-dimensional set X is defined as

$$ X = \{(x, y, z) : z \leq f(x, y)\} $$

The structure element B must also be a 3-dimensional set, such as a ball. Combinations of erosions and dilations can be used to reduce noise in f with minimal blurring.

In addition to reducing noise and finding boundaries, morphological filters have been used to thin sets, to thicken sets, to find "skeletons" of sets, and to prune sets [23], [49].

3.4   Snakes

Boundaries such as the nuclear membrane in an FNA slide or the border of a tumor in a mammogram, are marked by a transition in pixel intensity values. Often, part of the boundary is not very clear or is obscured but the human eye infers a reasonable connection. Local methods for automatic detection of boundaries, such as gradients, often leave gaps. A snake is a model for a boundary which is assumed at all times to be continuous. The model is further endowed with physical properties which determine how much the contour can be stretched or bent and a potential energy which determines how well the snake fits boundaries in the image.

The original snake [26] is defined as the contour $v(s) = (x(s), y(s))$

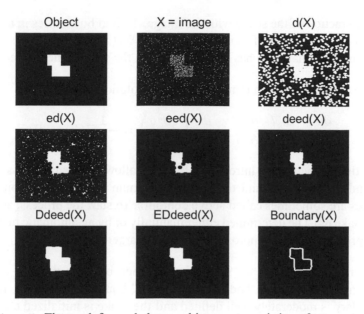

Figure 6. The top left panel shows a binary set consisting of two rectangles. The next panel to the right is an image of the set which has been corrupted by noise. The density of "on" pixels within the set is 50 percent and the density of "on" pixels outside is 3 percent. The sequence of panels left to right and top to bottom show the effects of consecutive morphological filters. The letters "d" and "e" denote dilation and erosion by the structure element B_1 in (8) and the letters "D" and "E" denote dilation and erosion by the structure element B_2 in (8). The boundary in the lower right panel was obtained by eroding the image EDdeed(X) by the structure element B_3 in (8) and retaining only the pixels in EDdeed(X) that did not appear in the eroded version. This process always results in a minimally thin 8-connected boundary which is often a very convenient form. In this case, the boundary was thickened via dilation by the structure element B_3 in order to make it visible in the figure.

which minimizes the energy functional

$$E(v) = \alpha(s)\left|\frac{\partial v}{\partial s}\right|^2 + \beta(s)\left|\frac{\partial^2 v}{\partial s^2}\right|^2 + G(v(s)). \qquad (9)$$

The first term of the energy functional models the snake's internal tension, the second term models the flexibility and the third term specifies the interaction of the snake with the image. To find boundaries in an image, a common form of G is $G(x, y) = -\|\nabla I(x, y)\|$, where $I(x, y)$ is the image, so that $E(v)$ has low values when the snake is near an edge.

The contour $v(s)$ which minimizes (9) is a solution to

$$\gamma \frac{\partial v}{\partial t} - \frac{\partial}{\partial s}\left(\alpha \frac{\partial v}{\partial s}\right) + \frac{\partial^2}{\partial s^2}\left(\beta \frac{\partial^2 v}{\partial s^2}\right) = -\frac{1}{2}\nabla G(v(s, t)). \qquad (10)$$

The time dependence introduced by (10) allows the snake to slither around the image to find the energy minimum and is the reason that snakes are sometimes called active contours. To start the process, an initial snake must be determined either manually or by an automatic method that produces a crude approximation of the target boundary.

The energy functional in (9) is often plagued by local minima which prevent the snake from finding the "correct" boundary. However, if the boundary is moderately well defined and the snake is initialized close to the desired boundary, impressive results can be obtained [61].

Examples: Mammography [29], FNA [60]

3.5   Wavelets

Wavelet theory provides a method for choosing a pair of linear filters, one lowpass filter and one highpass filter, which individually and as a pair, possess many useful properties for analyzing signals and images. Methods for constructing such filters, their properties, the relationship between them, the role and definition of wavelets themselves, and methods for implementing these filters appear elsewhere [1], [11], [12], [51].

The simplest way to apply wavelet analysis to images is to apply the 1-dimensional highpass and lowpass filters to the columns and rows of the image separately. This results in four new versions of the image: V_1, the image of vertical details obtained by applying the lowpass filter to rows and the highpass filter to columns; H_1, the image of horizontal details obtained by applying the highpass filter to rows and the lowpass filter to columns; D_1, the image obtained by applying the highpass filter in both directions; and A_1, the approximation of the original image obtained by

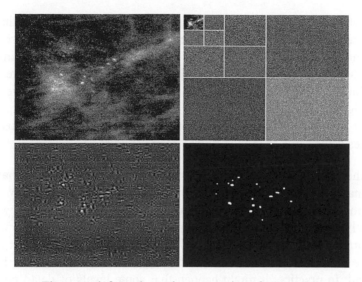

Figure 7. The upper left quadrant shows a portion of a screening mammogram with a cluster of DCIS microcalcifications. The upper right quadrant shows the ten images which make up the 3 level wavelet decomposition. Within this group of ten images, the upper left image is A_3, the level 3 approximation, the three images surrounding it are the level 3 details, the three images surrounding these are the level 2 details, and the outer shell of three images are the level 1 details. The lower left quadrant shows the reconstruction of the original image with the level 3 approximation set to zeros and retaining only the pixels in each detail image with absolute value greater than 90 percent of all pixel values in that detail image. The lower right quadrant was obtained by thresholding the image in the lower left quadrant.

applying the lowpass filter in both directions. The images V_1, H_1, and D_1 together form the level 1 details of the image and A_1 is the level 1 approximation of the original image. The same combinations of the lowpass and highpass filters can now be applied to A_1 to obtain V_2, H_2, and D_2 which form the level 2 details of the image, and A_2, the level 2 approximation of the original image. In principle, this pattern can continue many times, but in practice, the number of useful levels of decomposition is usually no more than about six. An N level wavelet decomposition of an image consists of the N level approximation, A_N, and $3(N-1)$ detail images, V_i, H_i, and D_i for $i = 1, 2, ..., N-1$.

One of useful property of the lowpass and highpass filter pair is that no information is lost if at each level every second row and every second column are removed from the detail images and the approximate image. This is called subsampling. The result is that V_1, H_1, D_1, and A_1 are each one fourth of the size of the original image, V_2, H_2, D_2, and A_2 are each one eighth of the size of the original image, and so on. One consequence is that the total number of pixels in the aggregate of the decomposition images is the same as in the original image (Figure 7).

Another nice property of the lowpass and highpass filter pair is that the original image can be recovered without error by combining the N level decomposition images correctly using upsampling and the same lowpass and highpass filters used for decomposition! If such a reconstruction is performed with the N level approximation set to zero, the result is an image containing just the details of the original image without the background. In practice, it might happen that some levels of detail contain mostly noise but that other levels of detail contain objects of diagnostic interest. Hence, by adjusting the weights of various detail images (or applying other processing steps), details in the original image of particular scales can be enhanced or suppressed (Figure 7).

Wavelet analysis can be used for background subtraction, detection (Figure 7), and preparing images for analysis, especially texture analysis, at several resolutions. Many authors prefer to skip the subsampling step when computing wavelet decompositions so that the detail images at every level can be easily compared with the original image. This convenience is at the expense of having to process unnecessarily large images.

Examples: Mammography [31], [43], [44], [52], [55], [63], FNA [56].

4   Summary

The performance of an AI system is limited by the quality of the information with which it is provided. Information from images is supplied in the form of features computed from the intensity function representing the image. Features are defined by the algorithms used to extract them. These algorithms are often integrated with the methods used for preprocessing and image segmentation. While this complicates the task of discussing details of image features in isolation, the ubiquity of general methods across a variety of images related to detection and prognosis of breast cancer motivates a discussion of general methods. At present, it is not possible to ascertain the relative merits of various algorithms. Comprehensive studies to remedy this situation would be valuable in advancing the role of AI in analyzing images related to breast cancer.

Acknowledgments

The authors would like to thank The Cooperative Research Centre for Sensor Signal and Information Processing (CSSIP) for support and BreastScreen SA for supplying mammographic images.

References

[1] Aldroubi, A. and Unser, M. (1996), *Wavelets in Medicine and Biology*, CRC Press, Boca Raton, FL.

[2] Barnsely, M. (1988), *Fractals Everywhere*, Academic Press, San Diego, CA.

[3] Betal, D., Roberts, N., and Whitehouse, G.H. (1997), "Segmentation and numerical analysis of microcalcifications on mammograms using mathematical morphology," *British Journal of Radiology*, 70(837):665–672.

[4] Bottema, M.J. (2000), "Circularity of objects in images," *ICASSP 2000*. To appear.

[5] Bottema, M.J. and Slavotinek, J.P. (1998), "Detection and classification of lobular and dcis (small cell) mircocalcifications in digital mammograms," in Ersbøll, B.K. and Johansen, P. (Eds.), *Proceedings of the 11th Scandinavian Conference on Image Analysis*, pp. 431–437.

[6] Brown, S., Li, R., Brandt, L., Wilson, L., Kossoff, G., and Kossoff, M. (1998), "Development of a multi-feature CAD system for mammography," in Karssemeijer, N., Thijssen, M., Hendricks, J., and van Erning, L. (Eds.), *Digital Mammography*, pp. 189–196.

[7] Canny, J. (1986), "A computational approach to edge detection," *IEEE Transactions on Pattern Analysis and Machine Intelligence*, PAMI-8(6):679–698.

[8] Chan, H.-P., Doi, K., et al. (1987), "Image feature analysis and computer-aided diagnosis in digital radiography. I. Automated detection of microcalcifications in mammography," *Medical Physics*, 14(4):538–548.

[9] Chan, H.-P., Sahiner, B., Helvie, M.A., Petrick, N., Roubidoux, M.A., Wilson, T.E., Adler, D.D., Paramagul, C., Newman, J.S., and Sanjay-Gopal, S. (1999) "Improvement of radiologists' characterization of mammographic masses by using computer-aided diagnosis: an ROC study," *Radiology*, 212(3):817–827.

[10] Chan, H.P., Sahiner, B., Lam, K.L., Petrick, N., Helvie, M.A., Goodsitt, M.M., and Adler, D.D. (1998), "Computerized analysis of mammographic microcalcifications in morphological texture feature spaces," *Medical Physics*, 25(10):2007–2019.

[11] Chui, C.K. (1997), *Wavelets: a Mathematical Tool for Signal Processing*, SIAM, Philadelphia, PA.

[12] Daubechies, I. (1992), *Ten Lectures on Wavelets*. SIAM, Philadelphia, PA.

[13] Delorme, S., Zuna, I., Huber, S., Albert, B., Bahner, M.L., Junkermann, H., and van Kaick, G. (1998), "Colour doppler sonography in breast tumour: an update," *European Radiology*, 8(2):189–193.

[14] Dhawan, A.P., Kaiser-Bonasso, C., et al. (1996), "Analysis of mammographic microcalcifications using gray-level image structure features," *IEEE Transactions on Medical Imaging*, 15(3):246–259.

[15] Ema, T., Doi, K., et al. (1995), "Image feature analysis and computer-aided diagnosis in mammography: reduction of false-positive clustered microcalcifications using local edge-gradient analysis," *Medical Physics*, 22(2):161–169.

[16] Giger, M., Doi, K., and MacMahon, H. (1988), "Image feature analysis and computer-aided diagnosis in digital radiography. 3: Automated detection of nodules in peripheral lung fields," *Medical Physics*, 15(2):158–166.

[17] Herrera-Espineira, C., Marcos-Munoz, C., and Esquivias, J. (1997), "Diagnosis of breast cancer by measuring nuclear disorder using planar graphs," *Analytical and Quantitative Cytology and Histology*, 19(6):519–523.

[18] Herrera-Espineira, C., Marcos-Munoz, C., and Esquivias, J. (1998), "Automated segmentation of cell nuclei in fine needle aspirates of the breast," *Analytical and Quantitative Cytology and Histology*, 20(1):29–35.

[19] Highnam, R., Kita, Y., Shepstone, B., and English, R. (1998), "Determining correspondence between views," in Karssemeijer, N., Thijssen, M., Hendricks, J., and van Erning, L. (Eds.), *Digital Mammography*, pages 111–118.

[20] Holland, R., Hendricks, J.H.C.L., et al. (1994), "Microcalcifications associated with ductal carcinoma in situ: mammographic-pathologic correlation," *Seminars in Diagnostic Pathology*, 11(3):181–192.

[21] Huber, S., Delorme, S., Knopp, M.V., Junermann, H., Zuna, I., von Founier, D., and van Kaick, G. (1994), "Breast tumors: computer-assisted quantitative assessment with color doppler US," *Radiology*, 192(3):797–801.

[22] Huo, Z., Giger, M.L., et al. (1995), "Analysis of spiculation in the computerized classification of mammographic masses," *Medical Physics*, 22(10):1569–1579.

[23] Jain, A.K. (1989), *Fundamentals of Digital Image Processing*, Prentice Hall, London.

[24] Jiang, Y., Nishikawa, R.M., et al. (1996), "Malignant and benign clustered microcalcifications: automated feature analysis and classification," *Radiology*, 198(3):671–678.

[25] Karssemeijer, N., te Brake, G.M., et al. (1996), "Detection of stellate distortions in mammograms," *IEEE Transactions on Medical Imaging*, 15(5):611–619.

[26] Kass, M., Witkin, A., and Terzopoulos, D. (1987), "Snakes: active contour models," *International Journal of Computer Vision*, 1(4):321–331.

[27] Kegelmeyer, W.P., Pruneda, J.M., et al. (1994), "Computer-aided mammographic screening for spiculated lesions," *Radiology*, 191(2):331–337.

[28] Kim, J.K. and Park, H.W. (1999), "Statistical textural features for detection of microcalcification in digitized mammograms," *IEEE Transactions on Medical Imaging*, 18(3):231–238.

[29] Kobatake, H., Murakami, M., Takeo, H., and Nawano, S. (1999), "Computerized detection of malignant tumors in digital mammograms," *IEEE Transactions on Medical Imaging*, 18(5):369–378.

[30] Kok-Wiles, S.-L., Brady, M., and Highnam, R. (1998), "Comparing mammogram pairs for the detection of lesions," in Karssemeijer, N., Thijssen, M., Hendricks, J., and van Erning, L. (Eds.), *Digital Mammography*, pages 103–110.

[31] Lado, M.J., Tahoces, P.G., Mendez, A.J., Souto, M., and Vidal, J.J. (1999), "A wavelet based algorithm for detecting clustered microcalcificaitons in digital mammograms," *Medical Physcis*, 26(7):1294–1305.

[32] Lefebvre, F. and Benali, H. (1995), "A fractal approach to the segmentation of microcalcifications in digital mammograms," *Medical Physics*, 22(4):381–390.

[33] Li, H., Liu, K.J.R., et al. (1997), "Fractal modeling and segmentation for the enhancement of microcalcifications in digital mammograms," *IEEE Transactions on Medical Imaging*, 16(6):785–798.

[34] Li, H.D., Kallergi, M., et al. (1995), "Markov random field for tumor detection in digital mammography," *IEEE Transactions on Medical Imaging*, 14(3):565–576.

[35] Markopoulos, C., Karakitsos, P., Botsoli-Stergiou, E., Pouliakis, A., Ioakim-Liossi, A., Kyrkou, K., and Gogas, J. (1997), "Application of the learning vector quantizer to the classification of breast lesions," *Analytical and Quantitative Cytology and Histology*, 19(5):453–460.

[36] Mendelbrot, B.B. (1977), *The Fractal Geometry of Nature*, W.H. Freeman, New York.

[37] Nishikawa, R.M., Giger, M.L., et al. (1993), "Computer-aided detection of clustered microcalcifications: an improved method for grouping detected signals," *Medical Physics*, 20(6):1661–1666.

[38] Ozaki, D. and Kondo, Y. (1995), "Comparitive morphometric studies of benign and malignant intraductal proliferative lesions of the breast by computerized image analysis," *Human Pathology*, 26(10):1109–1113.

[39] Parker, J., Dance, D.R., et al. (1995), "Classification of ductal carcinoma in situ by image analysis of calcifications from digital mammograms," *British Journal of Radiology*, 68(806):150–159.

[40] Petrick, N., Chan, H.-P., et al. (1996), "An adaptive density-weighted contrast enhancement filter for mammographic breast mass detection," *IEEE Transactions on Medical imaging*, 15(1):59–67.

[41] Pohlman, S., Powel, K.A., et al. (1996), "Quantitative classification of breast tumors in digital mammograms," *Medical Physics*, 23(8):1337–1345.

[42] Polakowski, W.E., Cournoyer, D.A., et al. (1997), "Computer-aided breast cancer detection and diagnosis of masses using difference of Gaussians and derivative-based feature saliency," *IEEE Transactions in Medical Imaging*, 16(6):811–819.

[43] Qian, W., Clarke, L.P., Song, D., and Clark, R.A. (1998), "Hybrid four-channel wavelet transform for microcalcification detection," *Academic Radiology*, 5(5):354–364.

[44] Qian, W., Li, L., and Clarke, L.P. (1999), "Image feature extraction for mass detection in digital mammography: influence of wavelet analysis," *Medical Physcis*, 26(3):402–408.

[45] Rangayyan, R.M., El-Raramawy, N.M., et al. (1997), "Measures of acutance and shape for classification of breast tumors," *IEEE Transactions on Medical Imaging*, 16(6):799–810.

[46] Sahiner, B., Chan, H.-P., et al. (1998), "Computerized characterization of masses on mammograms: the rubber band straightening transform and texture analysis," *Medical Physics*, 25(4):516–526.

[47] Sallam, M., Hubiak, G., et al. (1993), "Screening mammogram images for abnormalities developing over time," *1992 IEEE Nuclear Science Symposium and Medical Imaging Conference*, pp. 1270–1272.

[48] Schmidt, F., Sorantin, E., Szepesvàri, C., Graif, E., Becker, M., Mayer, H., and Hartwagner, K. (1999), "An automated method for the identification and interpretation of clustered microcalcifications in mammograms," *Physics in Medicine and Biology*, 44(5):1231–1243.

[49] Serra, J. (1982), *Image Analysis and Mathematical Morphology*, Academic Press, London.

[50] Staren, E.D. and O'Neill, T.P. (1998), "Breast ultrasound," *Surgical Clinics of North America*, 78(2):219–235.

[51] Strang, G. and Nguyen, T. (1996), *Wavelets and Filter Banks*, Wellesley-Cambridg Press, Wellesley, MA.

[52] Strickland, R.N., Hahn, H.I., et al. (1996), "Wavelet transforms for detecting microcalcifications in mammograms," *IEEE Transactions on Medical Imaging*, 15(2):218–229.

[53] Thiele, D.L., Kimme-Smith, C., et al. (1996), "Using tissue texture surrounding calcification clusters to predict benign vs malignant outcomes," *Medical Physics*, 23(4):549–555.

[54] Vujovic, N. and Brzakovic, D. (1997), "Establishing the correspondence between control points in pairs of mammographic images," *IEEE Transaction on Image Processing*, 6(10):1388, 1997,"

[55] Wang, T.C. and Karyiannis, N.B. (1998), "Detection of microcalcifications in digital mammograms using wavelets," *IEEE Transactions on Medical Imaging*, 17(4):498–509.

[56] Weyn, B., van de Wouwer, G., van Daele, A., Scheunders, P., van Dyck, D., van Marc, E., and Jacob, W. (1998), "Automated breast tumor diagnosis and grading based on wavelet chromatin texture description," *Cytometry*, 33(3):32–40.

[57] Wolberg, W.H., Street, W.N., Heisey, D.M., and Mangasarian, O.L. (1995), "Computer-derived nuclear "grade" and breast cancer prognosis," *Analytical and Quantitative Cytology and Histology*, 17(4):257–264.

[58] Wolberg, W.H., Street, W.N., and Mangasarian, O.L. (1993), "Breast cytology diagnosis with digital image analysis," *Analytical and Quantitative Cytology and Histology*, 15(6):396–404.

[59] Wolberg, W.H., Street, W.N., and Mangasarian, O.L. (1995), "Image analysis and machine learning applied to breast cancer diagnosis and prognosis," *Analytical and Quantitative Cytology and Histology*, 17(2):77–87.

[60] Wolberg, W.H., Street, W.N., and Mangasarian, O.L. (1997), "Computer-derived nuclear features compared with axillary lymph node status for breast cancer carcinoma prognosis," *Cancer Cytopathology*, 81(3):172–179.

[61] Yezzi, A., Kichenassamy, S., Kumar, A., Oliver, P., and Tannenbaum, A. (1997), "A geometric snake model for segmentation of medical imagery," *IEEE transactions on Medical Imaging*, 16(2):199–209.

[62] Yin, F.-F., Giger, M.L., Doi, K., Vyborny, C.J., and Schmidt, R.A. (1994), "Computerized detection of masses in digital mammograms: automated alignment of breast images and its effects on bilateral-subtraction technique," *Medical Physics*, 21(3):445–452.

[63] Yoshida, H., Doi, K., et al. (1996), "An improved computer-assisted diagnostic scheme using wavelet transform for detecting clustered microcalcifications in digital mammograms," *Academic Radiology*, 3(8):621–627.

[64] Yu, G.H., Sneige, N., Kidd, L.D., and Katz, R.L. (1995), "Image analysis-derived morphometric differences in fine needle aspirates of ductal and lobular breast carcinoma," *Analytical and Quantitative Cytology and Histology*, 17(2):88–92.

[65] Zheng, B., Chang, Y.-H., et al. (1995), "Computer-aided detection of clustered microcalcifications in digitized mammograms," *Academic Radiology*, 2(8):655–662.

[66] Zheng, B., Chang, Y.-H., et al. (1995), "Computerized detection of masses from digitized mammograms: comparison of single-image segmentation and bilateral-image subtraction," *Academic Radiology*, 2(12):1056–1061.

[67] Zheng, B., Chang, Y.-H., et al. (1995), "Computerized detection of masses in digitized mammograms using single-image segmentation and a multilayer topographic feature analysis," *Academic Radiology*, 2(11):959–966.

[68] Zheng, Y., Greenleaf, J.F., and Gisvold, J.J. (1997), "Reduction of breast biopsies with a modified self-organizing map," *IEEE Transactions on Neural Networks*, 8(6):1386–1396.

Chapter 3

Decision Support in Breast Cancer: Recent Advances in Prognostic and Predictive Techniques

R. Kates, N. Harbeck, K. Ulm,
F. Jaenicke, H. Graeff, and M. Schmitt

This chapter describes some recent advances in prognostic and predictive techniques for clinical decision support in breast cancer based on factors that can be measured at the time of primary therapy. In particular, tumor biological factors enhance predictability, especially in combination with advanced statistical methods and intelligent systems such as CART and neural networks, viewed as statistical models. A survival model using neural networks and application to simulated nonlinear diseases are described. These examples support the conclusion that the use of knowledge based systems offers potentially substantial benefits for application to decision support in breast cancer.

1 Clinical Requirements for Decision Support Strategies in Breast Cancer

1.1 Risk-Group Assessment

As stated in the introduction, breast cancer is a potentially curable disease. However, once the patient has developed overt distant metastases, the disease is no longer curable by presently available therapies. Hence, the major challenge for the clinician is to assess accurately each patient's risk situation right at the beginning and to individualize loco-regional and systemic treatment modalities accordingly.

Accurate risk group selection for adjuvant systemic therapy could help to avoid over-treatment of *low-risk* patients who would have been cured by loco-regional treatment alone. Unfortunately, established prognostic factors are not sufficient for accurate determination of this low-risk group [7]: A good example is node-negative breast cancer: In order to obtain an acceptably small number of relapses in the untreated group (high therapeutic security, i.e., <<10 % over ten years) on the basis of established prognostic factors such as tumor size, grading, and hormone receptor status, more than 75 % of all node-negative breast cancer patients would be placed in the high-risk group, even though only about 30 % of all node-negative patients will eventually develop systemic disease [6]. According to current guidelines, all of the node-positive patients will receive adjuvant systemic therapy.

A further application of accurate risk group selection concerns the *very-high-risk* patients who do not benefit sufficiently from conventional therapy approaches. One option for these patients could be the use of more aggressive therapies whose side effects are severe enough to preclude using them without a clear indication.

Moreover, in view of the broadening spectrum of new treatment options, including tumor-biological therapy approaches such as Herceptin™ [44], accurate *prediction of response to therapy* will be the prerequisite for clinical indications and could thus bring us closer to the goal of *optimal individualized breast cancer therapy*.

1.2 Tumor-Biological Factors: the Plasminogen Activation System

The tumor biology of breast cancer cells determines the occurrence and severity of processes such as proliferation, neo-vascularization, invasion and metastasis. In the last decade, the determination of factors characterizing some of these processes has become possible using new laboratory techniques. Indeed, these *tumor-biological* factors can be determined in the tumor tissue obtained in the course of primary surgery and thus provide important clues to the biological properties of the individual tumor.

For this reason, tumor-biological factors have become increasingly important for the development of treatment strategies for breast cancer patients: First of all, the obvious discrepancy between the true risk groups and the classification provided using established prognostic factors has stimulated the search for new prognostic factors [23]. In particular, tumor-biological factors have been proposed for more accurate prognostic estimates. Second, as mentioned above, tumor-biological factors that have proven to be strong prognostic markers may serve as future targets for tumor-biologically oriented therapy approaches.

Since at present breast cancer must be regarded as incurable once metastatic spread of tumor cells has occurred, the crucial determinants of long-term health of the patient are those that govern invasion and metastasis. Important prerequisites for tumor cell spread and formation of distant metastases are local proteolysis with subsequent invasion of extracellular matrix and basement membranes. The plasminogen activation system, including the serine protease uPA (urokinase-type plasminogen activator), its cell surface receptor uPA-R, and its inhibitor PAI-1 (plasminogen activator inhibitor type 1), play a key role in these proteolytic processes [41].

In the early 1990s, our group was the first to report on the prognostic strength of uPA and its inhibitor PAI-1 in node-positive [26] and node-negative [27] breast cancer patients: Patients with high antigen levels of either proteolytic factor in their tumors had a significantly worse survival than patients with low levels of uPA and PAI-1. The prognostic impact of both invasion markers uPA and PAI-1 on disease-free (DFS) and overall survival (OS) in breast cancer has since been confirmed by several investigators [3], [12], [15], [18], [19], [31], [32]. The clinical finding that an enzyme inhibitor (PAI-1) does not play a protective role, but itself is an indicator of bad prognosis, was initially somewhat surprising. However, sufficient explanatory data from basic research has emerged in the meantime [1]: Independent of its inhibitory effect on uPA, PAI-1 plays an important role in tumor cell migration by inhibiting cell adhesion to extracellular matrix components through interaction with vitronectin [33].

As we shall see in this chapter, it is the *combination* of the additional information provided by the new tumor-biological factors uPA and

PAI-1 with advanced statistical methods which are expected to lead to better risk group assessment and hence improved decision support in breast cancer.

1.3   The Role of Statistical Models in Clinical Decision Support for Breast Cancer

The clinical decision environment is complex and includes both subjective and objective influences on physician and patient. Often, subjective or intangible considerations having little to do with statistics are the most important ones from the patient's point of view. Physicians also take non-quantitative factors into account in their advice. In particular, much of the information available to physicians for decisions is not necessarily derived from empirical patient data such as that provided by clinical studies, but rather from considerations relating to general medical knowledge and fundamental understanding of a disease.

Nonetheless, no matter how strong the subjective and non-empirical basis for decisions, those components of the decision environment that *are* driven by empirical patient data should reflect the true risk structures underlying the data in question. This requirement defines the role of statistical modeling in a decision support environment. It does not imply that every clinical decision should be based solely on a rigid system of classification based purely on empirical results.

2   Intelligent Systems and Statistical Techniques for Prognosis and Prediction

2.1   Advanced Statistical Models as Intelligent Systems

As discussed in Chapter 1, a system is considered to be *intelligent* in the present context if it is able to improve its performance or maintain an acceptable level of performance in the presence of uncertainty. This definition can easily be interpreted as including *statistical inference*: For example, as we will see below, statistical "survival" models can be used to forecast the course of disease (e.g. risk of death or expected time to relapse) for a new patient on the basis of explanatory (measurable or controllable) factors and follow-up data compiled for a sample of patients with the same disease. Known explanatory factors in breast cancer include established histomorphological quantities and tumor-biological markers as discussed above, while controllable factors consist mainly of treatment options. The explanatory factors may represent uncertain knowledge in several respects: First, the measurement process may include uncertainties. Second, the available factors may contain only partial information about the determining disease processes. Third, there is usually uncertainty associated with follow-up due to censoring, i.e., clinical studies often end before the outcome of all patients is known.

Typical attributes of intelligence as mentioned in Chapter 1 include learning, adaptation, fault tolerance and self-organization. Generally speaking, these attributes can be characterized on a continuous scale. Hence, statistical techniques can be considered as intelligent systems to the extent that they possess these attributes. Learning and adaptation, and (perhaps to a lesser degree) self-organization, correspond essentially to the well established statistical concept of *estimation*. Statistical models can of course also be designed to be fault tolerant in several ways; for example, a measurement model may include a statistical error model as in Kalman filtering [4], or a repeated measurement model may include deviations from intended measurement intervals within the design matrix [48].

2.2 The Cox Proportional Hazards Model and Generalizations

The Cox proportional hazards model [8] is the most frequently used method for analyzing censored survival data. We give a non-rigorous discussion here (for a rigorous treatment see [29]) in order to illustrate the above points:

Assume that one is given a patient data set (collective) consisting of the following data for J patients:

1. Covariates (explanatory variables) labeled x_j (j) (in vector notation: $\mathbf{x}(j)$), which are measured at a reference time t=0 when no events

have yet occurred. In the case of breast cancer, for example, t=0 might correspond to the time of the primary operation. Here, the index j =1,J refers to the patient number in any order.

2. Endpoints t_j at which the outcome (say, relapse or censored) is recorded.

We now imagine that each patient represents a random sample drawn from a large pool of patients with identical covariates x. For this pool of patients, let $S(t|x)$ represent the percentage of surviving patients at time t (here „surviving" refers to the event under consideration, e.g., in the case of relapse it refers to relapse-free survival) with covariates x. This can be thought of as the conditional probability for surviving to time t given x. It is assumed that $S(\infty|x) = 0$ and $S(0|x) = 1$. According to the usual notation, one may define an event density $f(t|x)$ and a hazard function $\lambda(t|x)$ by

$$f(t \mid x) \equiv -\frac{dS}{dt} \tag{1}$$

$$\lambda(t \mid x) \equiv \frac{f}{S} \tag{2}$$

These definitions imply that

$$\lambda(t \mid x) = -\frac{d}{dt}\big[\log S(t \mid x)\big] \tag{3}$$

The proportional hazards assumption is

$$\lambda(t \mid x_i) = h_0(t)\exp(\sum_{i=1}^{p} \beta_i x_i) \tag{4}$$

Here, $h_0(t)$ is the baseline hazard. If this model were an accurate description of the true hazard, then the constant of proportionality of the hazards for any two patients with different covariates would be a constant in time, hence the name "proportional hazards." The term "Cox model" will be used interchangeably in what follows to refer to this particular formulation.

Estimation of the parameters β_i is performed by maximizing a so-called partial likelihood function that does not require estimating the function $h_0(t)$ and does not use the time intervals between events, only their order. The estimation procedure also produces confidence intervals for the parameters β_i.

As the model stands, the logarithm of the hazard log $\lambda(t|x)$ depends linearly on covariates. In many medical applications, continuous factors are converted to binary variables (1/0), often making use of cutoffs optimized by some preliminary procedure such as a log rank test. Corrections to confidence intervals (p-values) arising from the use of optimal cutoffs have been given by Hilsenbeck & Clark [25].

Whether or not binary covariates are introduced, covariate interactions are not explicitly included in the original Cox model. However, the covariates do not necessarily have to coincide with the original values of measured factors. Indeed, there are many generalizations [24] that essentially amount to allowing the list of covariates to include nonlinear functions of the measured quantities. In particular, statistical programs in common use include polynomial interaction terms. If a nonlinear interaction present in the underlying disease is not orthogonal to the polynomial terms included in the model, it can be detected and thus modeled to a certain level of accuracy as a nonzero β coefficient. However, finite polynomial expansions are not "universal approximators" in the well-known sense of neural networks, i.e., an arbitrary nonlinear interaction cannot be "discovered" by a polynomial model.

In breast cancer and other diseases, different internal processes may be associated with different time scales for failure ("Failure" here refers to the patient's point of view, e.g., failure to avoid neo-vascularization). However, failure of an individual internal process may or may not manifest itself immediately as an observed "event" (death or relapse). One can thus imagine that the long-term prognosis of a disease could depend on covariates in a different way than the short-term prognosis. Hence, it should not be surprising that diseases do not always obey the assumption of proportional hazards. In particular, if a factor is associated at early times with, say, an increased relative risk and at later times with a decreased relative risk, then its importance may be underestimated by the proportional hazards assumption.

Indeed, a generalization of the Cox model was introduced by Gray [17] and applied to demonstrate a time-varying impact of axillary lymph node and steroid hormone receptor status on prognosis in breast cancer patients. In this time-varying coefficient model, the coefficients $ß_i$ are considered to be functions of time $ß_i(t)$ in Eq. (4). The function $ß_i(t)$ is obtained by estimating it at numerous intervals in time and then smoothing over these pointwise estimates using spline functions. Alternative estimation procedures are available using fractional polynomials to approximate the time dependence. In either of these cases, the time dependence, if found, is associated with coefficients of individual covariates.

The estimation procedures for these survival models all have the property that they can maintain acceptable performance in the presence of uncertainties such as those due to measurement errors, missing information about disease processes, and censoring. However, a prerequisite for acceptable performance is that the assumptions underlying the statistical model used must be satisfied by the disease in question, which is not always the case.

2.3   Classification and Regression Trees

Recursive partitioning methods were introduced by Breiman *et al.* [5] and later applied to censored data [34]. Our theoretical discussion will follow that of Dannegger [9], [10], who gave a thorough treatment of classification and regression trees (CART), as the method is known in the medical literature and optimized the method for use with censored survival data.

Among currently available advanced statistical approaches, recursive partitioning methods offer some attractive advantages:

- They can handle covariates measured on a variety of scales naturally without requiring any arbitrary coding.
- Variable selection and interaction detection are highly automatic and data driven
- Trees handle missing values gracefully
- Tree-based classification has an intuitively clear interpretation
- They include nonlinear effects, though not always all

- They often provide very good performance, even in the presence of uncertainty

Limitations or difficulties (in a statistical context with sparse data resources) include the following

- As in most advanced statistical methods, stability of the explanatory structure (here, the tree) is a problem, because small random changes in the data sample can result in important qualitative changes in tree structure.
- As in neural networks, trees are subject to over-learning and "optimism."
- If the partitioning algorithm stops too soon, the algorithm may miss certain nonlinear effects, such as XOR (exclusive or) structures
- Splits often tend to involve highly disproportionate daughter nodes
- Existing programs are not yet designed to associate a time varying risk structure to a set of covariates

Using a learning sample, CART forms subgroups of elements with similar response expectation by recursively partitioning (splitting) the predictor space into disjoint subsets, called nodes. The resulting construction may be visualized as a tree. The tree construction process begins at the so called root node, which is simply the complete learning sample and is continued until a stopping criterion is met. A node for which no further splitting is performed is known as a terminal node (or leaf). In the context of survival data, one can generally associate a discrete value of the predicted relative risk with each node. Every patient with complete data can be classified at each split (followed down the tree) until the appropriate terminal node is located. In this way, a unique relative risk or incidence can be assigned to each patient, as described by Dannegger [9], [10].

Splits are selected to maximize a measure of "goodness of split," such as homogeneity within a node or heterogeneity compared to other nodes. These criteria often utilize common test statistics. Splitting measures, stopping criteria, pruning strategies and performance evaluation procedures, in particular for censored survival data as applied here, were discussed in detail and implemented by Dannegger [10]. The splitting criterion is a log-rank test (p=0.05). A minimum of 10 patients per node is enforced, and all splits are binary. This algorithm was applied as a scoring procedure for validation by Kates *et al.* [30].

2.4   Intelligent Systems as Statistical Models

The performance of a statistical model is mainly related to the accuracy and the validity (generalization capability) of its output, whether the emphasis is on classification, scoring, forecasting, or some other application. One of the typical attributes of a statistical analysis framework is that it is customary to provide not only expectation values, but also estimates of variance and bias. Such estimates are sometimes, but not always provided in neural nets and related intelligent systems.

In a clinical context, characterization of patients may often be viewed as a kind of scoring problem, in which one or more scores are to be assigned to each patient on the basis of factors (individual data patterns) available at some initial time. These scores can be used for decision support, e.g., for stratification of patients with respect to their risk of relapse or their probability of response to available treatments.

In recent years there have been numerous claims concerning the capabilities of adaptive systems such as neural nets for scoring problems. However, a closer look at these claims reveals that the performance has not always been analyzed objectively. In some of these cases commercial interests are involved: A typical commercial application of a scoring procedure is in the rapidly expanding field of "data mining," where, for example, customer data bases may be analyzed with regard to buying or cancellation probability. There are clear mathematical similarities to the problem of decision support in a medical context, but also several important differences:

- In commercial applications, large data bases with 20 000 or more entries are typical, making it easier to find even a weak "signal" above the "noise" of random statistical variations. In clinical studies, data are often expensive to collect, and collectives with more than a few hundred patients are rare.

- In commercial applications, the cost (e.g., losing a customer) associated with an occasional "miss" can often be compared to the cost of a moderate number of "false alarms" (e.g., superfluous cancellation avoidance measures). In medical applications, the consequences of a "miss" (omitting treatment for a patient who could have benefited) may be unacceptable.

- In commercial applications, it may be acceptable to measure the performance (e.g., forecasting error) after implementation. However, potential users in a medical decision making environment need to be more sensitive to the problem of error estimates before decisions are made due to the potential risks involved.

When applied in the context of bio-medical applications, it is often quite enlightening to re-formulate an intelligent system if possible as a statistical model. In particular, this re-formulation may aid in investigating the question of confidence intervals, or more generally, the distributions of parameters or output quantities compared to the corresponding "true" values. The general problem of interpreting neural networks in the context of a statistical approach has begun to attract considerable interest [16], [39], [46], [49]. In particular, the literature has been characterized by a moderation of what some regard as exaggerated expectations [40], [43], [47]. If the risks in a disease are truly described by a standard (say, linear) statistical model, then the performance of this model (including generalization) is likely to be better than that of a neural network, especially if only limited data are available from clinical studies.

Nonetheless, intelligent systems such as neural nets offer an important potential advantage over traditional statistical models in their ability to represent and also identify a broad spectrum of nonlinear effects such as arbitrary factor interactions. Representation and identification of nonlinearities are two distinct properties: Indeed, it may happen that a statistical approach is capable of representing some nonlinear relationships, but that the estimation procedure does not identify a key nonlinear relationship, even if present. Hence, the answer to the question of whether neural networks can improve our ability to extract prognostic and predictive information from measured factors depends in practice on the disease under consideration. In the following section, we will see that existing empirical results provide some clues that breast cancer is indeed a sufficiently complex disease to require a nonlinear model for optimal prognosis and prediction.

3 Breast Cancer as a Complex Disease

3.1 A Representative Study

Tumor biology involves complex, interacting processes such as invasion, metastasis, and neo-vascularization. The potential severity of these and other key processes manifests itself to a certain degree in invasion and metastasis markers such as PAI-1, uPA, and cathepsin D, in proliferation factors such as MIB1 or S-phase fraction, as well as in established histomorphological factors.

Three-hundred and sixteen consecutive patients with primary breast cancer were enrolled between 1987 and 1991 in a prospective study performed at the Dept. of Obstetrics and Gynecology of the Munich Technical University, Germany. Of these patients, 147 were node-negative, i.e., they had no axillary lymph node involvement. A sub-group of 125 node-negative patients received no adjuvant systemic therapy and are of particular interest, as discussed below. Established and tumor-biological factors known to be related to the risk of relapse and/or death in primary breast cancer were determined for each patient. Details of the determinations and assessments of their impact were reported in [21], [22], [26], [27]. Those factors considered in our discussion may be classified as follows:

- established prognostic factors: number of affected lymph nodes, tumor size, patient age, steroid hormone receptor status, grading
- invasion and metastasis markers: uPA, PAI-1, and cathepsin D
- proliferation markers SPF (S-phase fraction), MIB1 (Ki-67), and ploidy.

In particular, the urokinase-type plasminogen activator uPA and its inhibitor PAI-1 are tumor-biological markers related to invasion and metastasis. In the above cited papers, it was established that PAI-1 in particular plays an important role in prognosis among many patient groups (including both node-positive and node-negative patients) and continues to do so even after a long follow-up. Its prognostic impact can be enhanced by that of uPA. PAI-1 also gives valuable information on survival after first relapse. Based to a large extent on these results, serious efforts towards international standardization of the determination methods for both PAI-1 and uPA have been undertaken within the last few years under the auspices of the BIOMED 1 program of the European union. A prospective multi-center therapy trial was begun in Germany in 1993 [28]. This trial includes internal and external quality control and emphasizes standardized methods.

Some biological processes may leave their signature in more than one factor. Moreover, there is evidence that some factors (such as PAI-1) are involved in multiple processes. Hence, an important research focus in recent years has been to study just what independent information is provided by each factor in a multivariate setting. The use of intelligent knowledge engineering systems such as advanced statistical methods represents a logical extension of this research.

3.2 Node–Negative Breast Cancer: A Multivariate Proportional Hazards (Cox) Prognostic Model

The treatment of node-negative breast cancer patients varies rather widely from country to country. One can attribute this variation to differing policies with respect to the priority of therapeutic security compared to therapeutic efficiency. As discussed above, one of the main goals of modeling is to stratify this group with respect to risk of relapse. In countries where high therapeutic security is emphasized, this stratification could help to avoid unnecessary treatment for a low-risk sub-group that should ideally include as many as possible of the 70 % of patients cured by surgery alone.

Therapy clearly has an influence on relapse-free and overall survival and thus may act as a confounding factor. It is therefore especially enlightening to examine a sub-collective of 125 node-negative patients from the study described above (Department of Obstetrics and Gynecology, Munich Technical University) who received *no* adjuvant systemic therapy (referred to in what follows as "untreated") [21]. Hence, the follow-up information until first relapse represents the natural course of the disease. In these patients, established histomorphological prognostic factors as well as invasion markers uPA and PAI-1 were prospectively determined. Additional tumor-biological factors (cathepsin D, S-phase fraction, ploidy, MIB1, HER-2/neu, p53) were retrospectively determined in all cases with a sufficient amount of tumor tissue left for analysis. Measured factor values were assigned to categories as described in [21]. Cutoffs for continuous variables had been established or optimized in previous studies [20], [27], [28], [42].

Tumor-biological as well as established factors were then related to patient outcome with a median follow-up period of 76 months. The following table summarizes the relative risk for relapse according to univariate and multivariate analysis.

Table 1. Results of univariate (Kaplan-Meier) and multivariate[1] (Cox) analysis for disease-free survival in untreated node-negative breast cancer patients.

factor	univariate p-value	multivariate p-value	relative risk	95 % confidence interval
PAI-1	< 0.001	< 0.001	6.2	2.3-16.4
cathepsin D	0.004	n.s.		
uPA	0.008	n.s.		
S-phase fraction	0.023	n.s.		

In the above table, n.s. means not significant in multivariate analysis. The factors DNA ploidy, hormone receptor status, menopausal status and grading, which were not significant in univariate analysis, were excluded from the multivariate Cox model.

3.3   Univariate Risk Assessment in Subgroups

In clinical routine it is customary to define patient subgroups according to traditional prognostic factors. Here we consider clinically relevant binary subgroups defined by:

- post-menopausal vs. pre/peri-menopausal
- hormone receptor positive vs. negative
- tumor size ≤ 2 cm vs. > 2 cm
- G 1/2 vs. G 3/4.

---

[1] Since the multivariate analysis was carried out on the basis of complete cases, only 96 of the untreated 125 patients could be included.

In each case, the first of the two categories listed is generally associated with more favorable prognosis.

Table 2. Dependence of relapse rates on proliferation and invasion factors in subgroups defined by established factors in node-negative breast cancer patients without adjuvant systemic therapy (n=125).

	menopausal status		hormone receptor status		tumor size		grading	
	post	pre/peri	pos.	neg.	≤ 2cm	> 2cm	G 1/2	G 3/4
uPA low (≤ 3 ng/mg protein)	7/49	3/34	10/69	0/14	3/42	7/41	8/67	2/16
uPA high (> 3 ng/mg protein)	7/30	6/12	8/30	5/12	6/23	7/19	7/26	6/16
p value	0.31	**0.002**	0.17	**0.008**	**0.04**	0.067	0.08	0.12
PAI-1low (≤ 14 ng/mg protein)	7/61	4/38	10/83	1/16	6/56	5/43	7/80	4/19
PAI-1high (> 14 ng/mg protein)	7/18	5/8	8/16	4/10	3/9	9/17	8/13	4/13
p value	**0.004**	**<0.001**	**<0.001**	**0.04**	**0.016**	**0.0002**	**<0.0001**	0.49
cath. D low (≤ 41 pmol/mg prot.)	1/34	4/26	4/49	1/11	2/35	3/25	3/48	2/12
cath. D high (> 1 pmol/mg prot.)	12/42	5/19	13/46	4/15	7/28	10/33	11/41	6/20
p value	**0.003**	0.39	**0.007**	0.28	**0.017**	0.09	**0.007**	0.36
SPF low (≤ 6 %)	2/29	4/26	6/48	0/7	2/29	4/26	4/42	2/13
SPF high (> 6 %)	10/35	3/11	9/33	4/13	4/18	9/28	8/31	5/15
p value	**0.03**	p=0.44	p=0.07	p=0.12	**p=0.05**	p=0.12	p=0.065	p=0.23
MIB1 low (≤ 25 %)	10/62	5/34	13/80	2/16	4/50	11/46	10/77	5/19
MIB1 high (> 25 %)	4/12	2/8	3/11	3/9	3/7	3/13	3/8	3/12
p value	0.14	0.45	0.41	0.21	**0.01**	0.93	0.07	0.97

In order to illustrate the complexity of the relationship between factors and disease, one may observe that in several cases the discrimination provided by the invasion and proliferation factors occurs much more strongly in only one of the two subgroups defined by an established factor. Moreover, this subgroup is sometimes the more favorable one, and sometimes the less favorable one. For example, cathepsin D was significant for disease-free survival in post-menopausal and hormone receptor positive patients. In contrast, uPA was significant in pre-menopausal and hormone receptor negative patients. MIB1 was significant for small tumors, but not for large tumors, despite relatively similar case numbers.

For clinical application of prognostic factors, an especially important characteristic is the ability of a factor to distinguish very-low-risk subgroups among a group that already has a low risk, because it is these very-low-risk subgroups that could be candidates for receiving no adjuvant systemic therapy, even in countries where high therapeutic security is emphasized. For this reason, it is instructive to take a closer look at the factor PAI-1. As the following figure shows, even within the low-risk groups defined by established factors, PAI-1 turned out to be an important prognostic factor for disease-free survival (Figure 1).

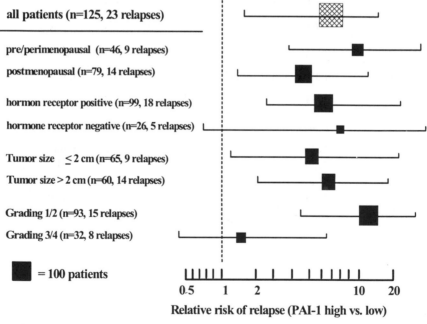

Figure 1. Dependence of relative risk for relapse on PAI-1 in node-negative breast cancer patients without adjuvant systemic therapy. In each subgroup, the risk for the group with high PAI-1 levels in the primary tumor (compared to the low-PAI-1 group) is shown as a box (size adjusted to patient number) surrounded by the nominal 95 % confidence interval.

Summarizing, the dependence of breast cancer patient prognosis on available factors is complex, and there exist clinical requirements for good discrimination that might be available using new factors. These characteristics strongly underline the need for advanced modeling techniques.

3.4   Analysis of Time-Varying Effects

As discussed above, the proportional hazards assumption is not always satisfied in a complex disease. A time-varying impact of axillary lymph node and steroid hormone receptor status on prognosis in breast cancer patients was first shown by Gray [17]. Schmitt *et al.* [42] applied this modified Cox model (see Section 2.2) to study the time-varying impact on prognosis of the new tumor-biological factors uPA and PAI-1 and also included the established prognostic factors axillary lymph node status and steroid hormone receptor status in this analysis. Their results illustrate the necessity of non-proportional-hazards modeling in any advanced statistical model.

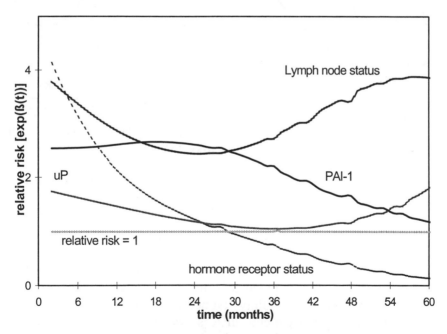

Figure 2. Statistical estimate of the time dependence of the hazard (relative risk) associated with lymph node status, steroid hormone receptor status, uPA and PAI-1 in patients with primary breast cancer (n=316). Near the end of the observation period, error ranges (not shown) are large.

Figure 2 shows an estimate of the time dependence of the estimated relative risk associated with the factors nodal status, hormone receptor status, uPA, and PAI-1.

For the node-negative group, the remaining three factors show time dependence as follows (Figure 3).

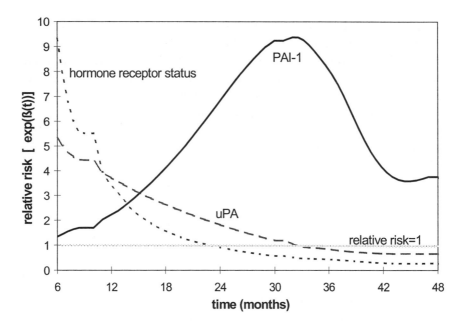

Figure 3. Time dependence of the prognostic strength of uPA, PAI-1 and hormone receptor status in patients with node-negative breast cancer (n=147). The hazard (relative risk) associated with initially elevated levels of these factors is shown as a function of time following surgery. The hazards associated with different factors are far from being proportional.

Specific interpretation of time dependence is complicated by the fact that these curves are computed in a multivariate setting and are also subject to statistical uncertainty. Nonetheless, it appears that in the subset of node-negative patients, uPA is associated with a higher risk of relatively early relapses, independently of all other factors. At later times, either uPA is not associated with a higher risk of relapse, or its prognostic power is not independent of the remaining factor(s). In the case of hormone receptor status, a similar statement can be made both for node-negative patients and for the sample of all patients.

Among all patients, the estimated strength of lymph node status actually declines briefly to about the same level as that of PAI-1. In node-negative patients, the estimated independent prognostic impact of PAI-1 rises initially and persists longer than that of uPA.

Several biological mechanisms have been advanced [42] that could account for the observed time dependence. Note that a proportional hazards model could severely underestimate or even completely miss a time-varying influence that changes sign during the course of the disease. Hence, these results illustrate the necessity of non-proportional-hazards modeling in any advanced statistical model.

3.5 Classification and Regression Trees (CART)

Another indication of the complexity of the relationships between factors and outcome in breast cancer is provided by a CART – analysis of these data as illustrated in Figure 4.

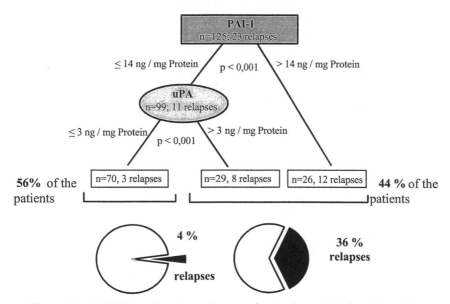

Figure 4. CART (classification and regression tree) analysis for relapse-free survival time, carried out in the subgroup of 125 node-negative patients who received no adjuvant systemic therapy, following a median follow-up of 76 months.

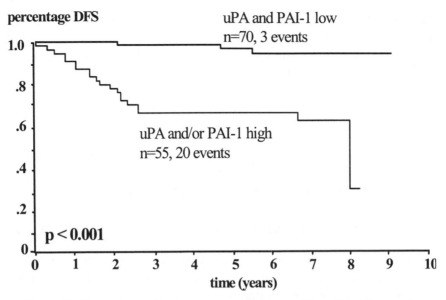

Figure 5. Dependence of relapse free survival on uPA and PAI-1 in node-negative breast cancer patients not receiving adjuvant systemic therapy. Upper curve: relapse-free survival for very-low-risk group (leftmost node in the tree of Figure 4). Lower curve: relapse-free survival for combination of other nodes.

If the relapse rate on this collective were generalizable, the patients with low uPA and PAI-1 levels would constitute a group for which one could argue that exclusion from adjuvant systemic therapy is justified without sacrificing therapeutic security.

In node-positive patients, patients with high PAI-1 had a 68 % relapse rate compared to 47 % in patients with low PAI-1 [22]. However, in contrast to node-negative patients, uPA did not contribute any significant information in node-positive patients selected by PAI-1. Therapy may of course have played a role in this result. Nonetheless, this behavior gives a hint that complex factor interactions could indeed be present in the risk structure of breast cancer.

4   Neural Survival Models

4.1   Neural Nets and Prognosis in a Clinical Setting

Statistical modeling of clinical data using artificial neural networks has the *potential* advantage that a broad class of nonlinear relationships, such as multiple interactions among factors, can be represented. However, one of the main challenges for nonlinear statistical models, especially neural nets, is posed by the often sparse and "noisy" nature of the data available for learning in a clinical context: First, collectives are often relatively small (a few hundred patients). Second, survival data in most clinical studies is censored. Third, some risk factors are unknown, and their effects can only be modeled as "noise." Moreover, the explanatory factors are often highly correlated with one another (multicollinearity).

These typical features of clinical data may result in *overlearning* and hence poor generalization capability in any nonlinear statistical model. As a consequence, parsimonious use of modeling parameters is a key to success, particularly in applying neural nets. Hence, the focus of our research on neural survival models has involved complexity reduction techniques appropriate for clinical data.

4.2   Previous Approaches to Survival Modeling Using Neural Nets

Survival forecasting using neural networks has been investigated by a number of workers. The practical application of neural networks for analysis of prognostic factors in breast cancer including comparison with the Cox proportional-hazards model [8] and the analysis of nonlinear 3-way interactions were studied by Ravdin and colleagues in a series of papers [11], [37], [38]. However, this approach did not include a statistically unbiased method for treating censored data.

Liestol *et al.* [35] formulated a survival model with different nodes for each time interval where an individual is at risk. However, smoothed estimates of the hazard function are not directly obtained from the network. The problems of redundant inputs and irrelevant hidden nodes were discussed.

Faraggi and Simon [13] formulated proportional hazards neural survival models appropriate for censored data using a multilayer perceptron architecture and applied these models to sample data. Several useful indices for judging performance were also introduced. The treatment of censored data is patterned after the proportional hazard model and is similar to one of the approaches reported here. In particular, a likelihood function was given, with network training (optimization) corresponding to maximization of the likelihood.

As noted above, "violations" of the proportional hazards assumption, which were not included in the formulation, may be important in medical applications such as breast cancer prognosis [42]. Faraggi *et al.* [14] refined their approach using a Bayesian formulation to reduce over-fitting. However, even in this refined approach, no prescription was given for dynamic complexity reduction, e.g., pruning of individual weights.

Biganzoli *et al.* [2] recently described have recently published a partial logistic regression approach to analysis of censored survival data ("PLANN"). Complexity is regulated by weight decay and by adjustment of the number of hidden nodes according to a particular heuristic information (complexity) criterion. However, here as well there is no prescription for the dynamic pruning of individual weights.

The problem of statistical error estimates for perceptron regression models (no censoring) has been investigated by Tibshirani [45].

4.3   Neural Topology Used for Survival Modeling

In this section we would like to summarize a neural network representation of the survival problem and an algorithm for network optimization recently developed in our group. Mathematical details will be described in specialized publications.

Suppose one has a vector of observed independent variables (covariates) **x** and seeks an estimate of the dependent variable y given that **x** has been observed. In a statistical context, one may regard an output of a neural network NN(**x**) as providing an estimate of the expectation value $E(y|\mathbf{x})$ of the random variable y. As we will see, within a properly defined statistical framework, specification of a neural network including all connectors with their weights, activation functions, and auxiliary parameters represents a statistical model for y. There may be several such functions y required to specify a phenomenon of interest. In this case, one can consider multiple outputs $NN_1(\mathbf{x})$, $NN_2(\mathbf{x})$, ... The neural network architecture considered here is a multi-layer perceptron with direct connectors from input to output layer as illustrated in the following diagram:

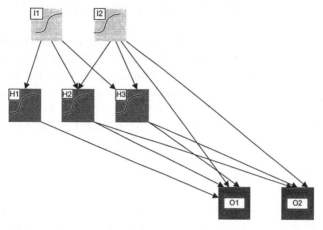

Figure 6. Multi-layer perceptron architecture including linear connectors. I, H, and O stand for input, hidden, and output, respectively.

The connectors from the input layer directly to the output layer represent linear relationships between the (transformed) input variables and the output. These are not necessarily required in a feed-forward architecture, but they are useful as a basis for comparison with ordinary linear statistical models and will be preferred if a factor has a truly linear effect on the output. The most important structure allowing nonlinear modeling is the hidden layer. Connectors from the input to the hidden layer are weighted, summed and then passed to a monotonic but nonlinear function such as the hyperbolic tangent to produce a response from each hidden neuron. The hidden responses are passed to the output layer via connectors and are weighted to produce the stimulus to the output layer, whose response is interpreted within the framework of the statistical model as discussed below. Finally, certain additional parameters such as a global time constant may be optimized as part of the statistical model, though they are not pictured in the neural network.

4.3.1   Transformations and Input Neurons

For proper interpretation of weights in a neural network, it is convenient to work with variables of order unity. Moreover, many of the variables have quite skewed distributions. For these reasons, the inputs $x_i(j)$ are usually transformed before being passed to following layers of the network. Here, the index i refers to the ith input (independent variable), and the index j refers to the jth pattern. The transformation used in the results reported here is performed as follows:

For a each component i, the median $x_{Median,i}$ is first computed and subtracted from each $x_i(j)$ value (j^{th} pattern). A scaling factor $x_{Q,i}$ is then defined component by component depending on whether the resulting value is positive or negative. Components above the median are scaled by the 75 % quartile, values below the median by the 25 % quartile. The results are then "squashed" by a hyperbolic tangent function. This procedure can be summarized by the formula

$$X_i\,(j) = \tanh[(x_i\,(j) - x_{Median,i})/x_{Q,i}] \tag{5}$$

describing the response of the input neurons. Hence, the procedure amounts to defining the hyperbolic tangent function as the activation function of the input layer, which is applied to the transformed input value. Here, x_{Median} plays the role of a bias, and the scaling factor $(1/x_{Q,i})$ that of a weight. However, these "weights" and "biases" are static, as they depend only on the univariate distribution of x_i.

It is of course possible to bypass the transformation (4). This may be preferable for input factors that already have a desired distribution, or are categorical or binary-valued.

4.3.2   Hidden Neurons

The signal to hidden neuron h due to pattern j is a weighted sum of inputs of the form

$$z_h(j) = \sum_i w_{ih} X_i(j), \tag{6}$$

where w_{ih} is the weight associated with the connector from input neuron i to hidden neuron h and $X_i\,(j)$ is the scaled response of the ith input. The response of hidden neuron h is given by

$$Y_h(j) = F_h(z_h(j) - b_h), \tag{7}$$

where b_h is the bias of hidden neuron h, which is treated as one of the weights of the network. The squashing (nonlinear activation) function F_h is usually taken to be the hyperbolic tangent as discussed above.

4.3.3 Output Nodes

The computation of output o for a presented pattern j proceeds as follows: First, the activation status of output o is checked. The output can be active due to active connectors from either the hidden or the input layer. A signal (denoted here z_o) is first constructed; the bias of the neuron (denoted here b_o) is subtracted, and the activation function for the output neuron o is applied to this difference, resulting in an output O_o (j):

$$z_o(j) = \sum_i w_{io}(X_i(j) - c_i) + \sum_h w_{ho}Y_h(j)$$
$$O_o(j) = F_o(z_o(j) - b_o) \tag{8}$$

The first summation in Eq. (4) represents a linear regression model on the transformed inputs. The activation function F_o of the output layer is chosen for most of the applications discussed here (survival models) as the identity (no squashing). There is no reduction in the space of functions that can be represented due to this choice of activation.

In many applications, such as survival analysis, addition of an overall constant to an output (say z_1) is equivalent to re-normalization of another parameter in the model. Hence, to avoid redundant parameters, the bias b_o of each output neuron o is generally not optimized freely as in the case of the hidden layer biases b_h, but is subject to a constraint. A convenient constraint is to require that the median response over the training set from all output neurons be zero.

4.4   A Survival Model Using Neural Nets to Define the Time-Dependent Risk Structure

Assume that we are given a censored patient data set with explanatory factors as in Section 2.2. Eqs. (1)-(3) defined the survival functions of interest, and Eq. (4) gave the Cox proportional hazards model, which models the log of the hazard ratio as a linear combination of explanatory factor values. The role of the neural network is analogous, in that it must supply an estimate of the hazard function $\lambda(t|\mathbf{x})$ for a patient with covariates $\mathbf{x}$ at time t. Here, the hazard is modeled by writing

$$\lambda(t \mid \mathbf{x}) = \lambda_0(t)h(t \mid \mathbf{x}) \tag{9}$$

with

$$h(t \mid \mathbf{x}) = \exp\left[\sum_{k=1}^{K} B_k(t)NN_k(\mathbf{x})\right] \tag{10}$$

Here, the $B_k(t)$ are a set of functions of t that are bounded at t=0 and that may be chosen a priori on the basis of favorable properties in the problem at hand. An example is the case of "fractional polynomials", i.e., functional dependence $B_k = t^p$ is allowed with p not necessarily restricted to integer values. The time dependence of the hazard function now resides in the functions B_k (t). In case $B_1=1$ and only one term is included in the sum (coefficients of all other B_k vanish) this model obeys the assumption of proportional hazards. Deviations from proportional hazards thus arise from terms with k>1.

The quantity λ_0, which acts as an overall normalization factor for the hazard, is taken to be a constant (independent of t). One then obtains from Eqs. (1)-(3) and (10)

$$\lambda_0 \exp\left[\sum_k NN_k(\mathbf{x})B_k(t)\right] = -\frac{d}{dt}\log(S(t)). \tag{11}$$

Hence, for a known neural net and known values of the remaining constants, Eq. (11) can be integrated to obtain the desired functions S(t) and f(t).

The objective function for neural optimization is the likelihood function

$$L(\mu;\{\mathbf{x},t\}) = \prod_{j=1}^{n} \left[f_{NN(\mathbf{x})}(t_j)\right]^{\delta_j} \left[S_{NN(\mathbf{x})}(t_j)\right]^{1-\delta_j} \tag{12}$$

In this equation, the functional dependence of the likelihood on the statistical model (here, the neural net) is denoted by the vector μ. The parameters included in μ are the survival time scale λ_0 and the weights of the neural net.

4.5   Net Optimization

The input data is allocated at random to training and validation sets according to percentages specified by the user. Net optimization includes initialization, training, and complexity reduction phases.

4.5.1   Initialization

As part of the initialization phase, linear statistics (such as regressions of each input variable on all the others) are tabulated for further use, and univariate neural net models (one input, one hidden, and one output node) are constructed. These univariate neural net models are then taken into account in ranking the factors and in finding a preferred class of initial configurations, among which a random realization is chosen.

4.5.2   Training

For a fixed neural net topology, the goal of training is to locate a minimum of the objective function (e.g., negative log likelihood) with respect to the data of the training set. The n-dimensional parameter space for this search consists of the n-1 active weights in the net together with the global time constant λ_0. The algorithm implemented here is based on the method of Nelder and Mead [36]. The search requires construction of a n-dimensional *simplex* in parameter space. A simplex is determined by specifying n+1 non-degenerate vertices. It surrounds an n-dimensional point set in parameter space. The optimization search proceeds in epochs. During each epoch, the objective function on the training set is evaluated at the current position in weight space and at vertices of one or more simplexes defined by combinations of the operations reflection, expansion, and contraction in parameter space. Directions for these operations are chosen on the basis of function evaluations at the vertices of the preceding epoch.

This iteratively determined optimization procedure results in a monotonically decreasing sequence of values of the objective function (here the negative log likelihood) corresponding to the iteration epochs. The procedure is continued either until it converges to a local minimum of the function (to within a stated accuracy) or some other stopping criterion is satisfied.

In contrast to gradient descent methods such as the well-known back propagation algorithm, the simplex optimization method implemented here does not require an analytic formula for the derivatives of the objective function with respect to the weights of the network. Note that these derivatives depend mathematically on the activation functions implemented. Hence, this property of the optimization method offers the practical advantage that arbitrary activation functions appropriate for different applications may be inserted without rewriting large portions of the code.

In addition to evaluating the objective function on the training set, the algorithm evaluates the objective function on the validation set periodically (say every 50 epochs). Whereas the objective function decreases strictly monotonically on the training set, the value on the *validation* set is unconstrained and provides an indication of the degree of learning of underlying structures that has taken place. A steady worsening of the performance (as measured by, say, the average value of the objective function per pattern) on the validation set is an indication that training is producing over-learning and that simplex optimization should be stopped. (At this point, complexity reduction should be attempted, as described below.) However, temporary "stochastic" fluctuations of the performance on the validation set are possible even when the overall trend is monotonic.

Hence, appropriate conditions for stopping need to be flexible enough to tolerate small stochastic fluctuations but still strict enough to allow the program to enforce stopped training when required. A satisfactory automatic stopping criteria may be obtained by considering the exponentially smoothed performance characteristic on the validation set. Training is stopped if the smoothed performance characteristic exceeds its most recent minimum by a fixed percentage. A percentage increase of about 1 % was estimated for typical training set sizes (300 or more patients) by trial and error. At this level, stopping due to reaching a minimum on the training set occurs more often than stopping due to worsening of the performance on the validation set if the validation and training sets are of roughly comparable size. This desirable property of the algorithm represents an indication that true learning is taking place, because the performance on the validation set can only improve if the neural net has recognized underlying structure as opposed to noise.

4.5.3　Complexity Reduction

Training results in a set of weights $\{w_{[1]}, \ldots w_{[n]}\}$ that locally minimize the objective function (negative log-likelihood). (Here, it is convenient to use a notation for the weight numbering $[1] \ldots [n]$ which does not refer to the topological role played by the weight.) This minimum refers to a fixed complexity as characterized by n and fixed topology. In order to minimize over-learning, it is desirable to reduce the complexity by *pruning* the network if it is possible to do so without significantly degrading performance.

Pruning in this context refers to deactivation of connectors, whose corresponding weights are frozen at a fixed value (usually zero in the context of a multilayer perceptron architecture). It is possible to prune individual weights or entire nodes (neurons), in which case all weights entering and leaving the node are deactivated. The result is a reduction in complexity, i.e., the number of parameters in the model. Complexity reduction is achieved by weight pruning as well as a variety of other internal transformation procedures designed to reduce the number of parameters in the model.

In the models presented below, a complexity reduction step is carried out if possible following each training phase. Pruning decisions are made on the basis of statistical testing taking into account validation and training sets. A variety of hypotheses for redundancy of various forms in the representation of the relationship between explanatory factors and output are tested.

Weight pruning may result in isolation of a neuron from input, output, or both (in the case of a hidden neuron). In this case, it is advantageous to associate a deactivation flag with the neuron. Due to the various topology checks, additional connectors may be recognized as functionally inactive or redundant, and additional neurons may be recognized as isolated.

If changes have been made in the complexity reduction step, the network is retrained, otherwise the network optimization algorithm records the network configuration, computes various statistics, and exits.

5   Simulated Follow-Up Data

5.1   Simulation Technique

Simulation is an effective method of testing the performance of different nonlinear statistical tools. It allows direct comparison of the "true" (i.e., simulated) and predicted risk on training and generalization sets according to each statistical tool evaluated.

Synthetic (normalized) values of "risk factors" X were generated by a tool developed in our group [30] using the clinically measured distributions of risk factors as described in Section 3.1 as input. (The follow-up information was not used.) The multivariate distributions (in particular, the covariance matrix) of the randomly generated patient data were close to those of the measured distributions.

The simulator assigns a synthetic risk to each simulated patient on the basis of the normalized risk factors according to a freely specifiable set of rules, which in the present case represent a nonlinear risk structure. Given a risk, the actual survival time is generated randomly according to an appropriate distribution (here exponential). The data are then (right) *censored*; i.e., the status of patients surviving beyond the duration of the study is unknown to the statistical modeling program.

5.2   Simulated "Nonlinear Diseases"

Models of two simulated "diseases" are reported here. In both "diseases," patients were divided into two equally sized groups according to the number of positive lymph nodes. In the first disease, the high-lymph-node group was assigned a synthetic risk using the values of factors X_{upa} and X_{pai}. These were used to determine a hazard h according to

$$h=\exp(\max(Z_{pai},Z_{upa})),\qquad\qquad(13)$$

where

$$Z_{pai} = 4*(X_{pai} - Median(X_{pai})) \tag{14}$$
$$Z_{upa} = X_{upa} - Median(X_{upa}) \tag{15}$$

In the "low lymph-node" group, the hazard was assigned according to tumor size:

$$h = exp(Z_{tum}), \tag{16}$$

where

$$Z_{tum} = X_{tum} - (C + Median(X_{tum})) \tag{17}$$

The constant C was chosen to include about 1/4 of these patients in the higher-risk group.

In the second "disease," the definition of Z_{upa} was replaced by

$$Z_{upa} = -4* (X_{upa} - Median(X_{upa})), \tag{18}$$

all other factors remaining unchanged.

The above risks are typical in magnitude for breast cancer. However, we emphasize that the nonlinear risk structures assumed here are purely fictitious. Note also that X_{upa} and X_{pai} are significantly correlated (0.36) as are X_{tum} and X_{lymph} (0.46). X_{upa} and X_{pai} are not significantly correlated with X_{lymph}. This will be important in what follows.

On the basis of the above nonlinear risk structure, the actual survival time of each simulated patient was generated randomly according to an exponential distribution. The data were then (right) *censored* by specifying a hypothetical "study" of finite duration with a typical pattern of inclusion of patients. Time constants were chosen for the "study" and for "censoring" such that about 1/3 of the patients were censored. For each disease, two data sets of 500 patients each were generated, one each for training and optimization.

5.3   Statistical Tools

Four statistical tools were used to analyze the above simulated data:

1. An ordinary multivariate Cox [8] model using the 7 risk factors
    $\{..., X_{tumor}, X_{upa}, X_{pai}, ...\}$ as linear factors.
2. A quadratic Cox model including products of the X's.
3. Classification and regression trees for censored data as formulated
    by Dannegger [9], [10].
4. The neural network system described in this chapter.

Variables were included in the Cox models as reported here by the
forward stepwise method. However, similar results were obtained by
backward elimination. All 500 patterns were used.

The CART models were computed using maximized log-rank for
binary splitting and a maximum of 10 patients per end leaf. All 500
patterns were used for training.

In the case of the neural network tool, the original configuration for
training contained 7 input nodes, 7 hidden nodes, and one output node.
The *first* trained network was used in both "diseases". Each of these
cases had 3 remaining hidden nodes at the end of training. Of the 500
patterns, 400 were used for training and the remaining 100 for
validation in each "disease." All statistical testing was performed at the
5 % level.

5.4   Performance

For each patient in the four simulated data sets, a record was kept of the
"true" relative risk. From each statistical tool considered, it was
possible to extract a quantity interpretable as the modeled relative risk
for each patient. Here, we analyze the performance of the statistical
tools for survival data by considering the squared correlation r^2 between
the true and modeled risk. For the first disease, the results on the
training and generalization sets are summarized in Table 3.

The linear Cox model included three parameters: the coefficients of the
variables X_{lymph}, X_{tumor}, and X_{pai}. In addition to linear terms with these
three variables, the nonlinear Cox model included quadratic terms of
the form $(X_{grading} * X_{pai})$, $(X_{lymph} * X_{tumor})$, and $(X_{lymph} * X_{pai})$. The
regression tree contained 42 end leaves. The neural net contained 26
weights, including biases.

Table 3. Squared correlation coefficient between true risk and score assigned by model for the training and generalization sets in the first disease.

Technique	Training r^2	Generalization r^2
Linear Cox	.548	.507
Quadratic Cox	.756	.692
CART	.581	.489
Neural Net	.688	.638

In this disease, the Cox model with quadratic terms had the highest correlation between true and predicted hazard, followed rather closely by the neural net. A close look at the risk structure of this "disease" (which is high in the high-lymph-node group if either X_{pai} or X_{upa} is high) together with the correlation between X_{pai} and X_{upa}, implies that a quadratic interaction $(X_{lymph}*X_{pai})$ provides a reasonably good representation of the risk structure, at least in part. Hence, the Cox model with quadratic terms would be expected to perform well.

For the second disease, the results on the training and generalization sets are summarized in the following table:

Table 4. Squared correlation coefficient between true risk and score assigned by model for the training and generalization sets in the second disease.

Technique	Training r^2	Generalization r^2
Linear Cox	.564	.446
Quadratic Cox	.690	.669
CART	.698	.691
Neural Net	.785	.761

The linear Cox model included four parameters: the coefficients of the variables X_{lymph}, X_{tumor}, and X_{pai} and X_{upa}. The relationship between true and modeled risk on the generalization set for the linear Cox model is shown in Figure 7.

In addition to linear terms with these four variables, the nonlinear Cox model included quadratic terms of the form $(X_{grading} * X_{upa})$, $(X_{lymph}*X_{tumor})$, $(X_{lymph}*X_{pai})$ $(X_{lymph}*X_{upa})$, $(X_{lymph}*X_{hormone})$, $(X_{tumor}*X_{upa})$, and $(X_{pai}*X_{upa})$. The relationship between true and modeled risk on the generalization set for the quadratic Cox model is shown in Figure 8.

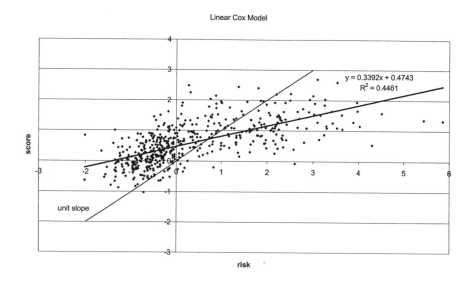

Figure 7. Plot of relationship between true risk and score assigned by the linear Cox model for the second disease on the generalization set (n=500). Also shown are a least-squares regression and a line of unit slope through the origin representing the ideal relationship.

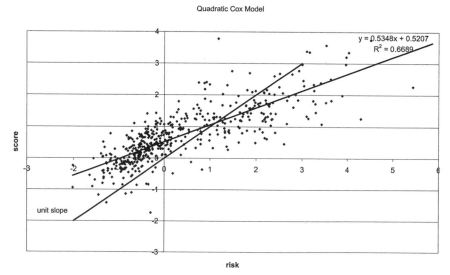

Figure 8. Plot of relationship between true risk and score assigned by the quadratic Cox model for the second disease on the generalization set (n=500). Also shown are a least-squares regression and a line of unit slope as above.

The regression tree contained 26 end leaves. The relationship between true and modeled risk on the generalization set for the CART model is shown in Figure 9.

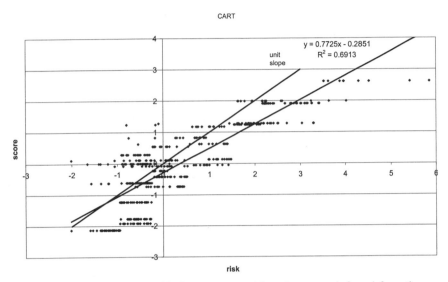

Figure 9. Plot of relationship between true risk and score as inferred from the CART for the second disease on the generalization set (n=500). Least-squares regression and line of unit slope as above.

The distribution of CART scores is of course discrete. Most of the variance seems to come from inhomogeneity within classes.

The neural net contained 14 weights, including biases. The relationship between true and modeled risk on the generalization set for the neural network is shown in Figure 10.

In this problem, the neural network had the highest correlation between true and predicted hazard, followed by the CART method and the Cox model with quadratic terms. The standard linear Cox model performed poorly as expected.

The superior performance of the neural network in this case seems quite reasonable in view of the risk structure of the second "disease", in which high values of X_{pai} *or* low values of X_{upa} were associated with high risks in the high lymph node group. Here, the positive correlation of X_{pai} and X_{upa} implies that a quadratic interaction does not provide a good representation of the risk structure.

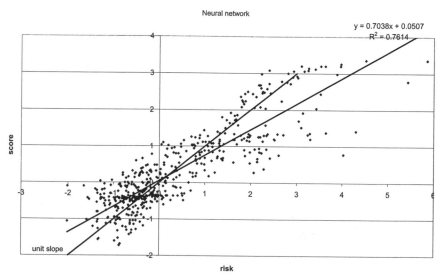

Figure 10. Plot of relationship between true risk and score assigned by the neural network for the second disease on the generalization set (n=500). Least-squares regression and line of unit slope as above.

The differences in the performance of the CART models in these two "diseases" could be related to the overall stronger effect of the risks associated with X_{upa} in the second disease.

An important measure of performance in the clinical context is the number of misclassified patients, since the precise value of the score is not important as long as the correct decision is made. Taking score=0 as a classification threshold in each of the above figures allows one to obtain a rough qualitative picture of the discrimination capability: the upper right and lower left quadrants (log-risk and score both positive or both negative) represent correctly classified patients; the lower right quadrant (risk positive and score negative) represents "misses"; and the upper left quadrant (risk negative and score positive) represents "false alarms." All four methods, even the linear Cox method, manage to avoid misses. However, the medians of the distributions of scores obtained from the two Cox models are evidently positive. Hence, the low number of misses in these models is achieved at the expense of a large number of false alarms. In a hypothetical clinical context, if patients with positive scores were treated (high therapeutic security), then the therapeutic efficiency would be low, i.e., many would be unnecessarily treated. (In the quadratic Cox model, taking an appropriately chosen positive score as the threshold would reduce the false alarms while hardly affecting the misses, but choosing a new threshold represents a new estimation problem.) There is a strong visual impression that the classification tree and the neural net classify most patients correctly and thus achieve high therapeutic security and therapeutic efficiency at the same time in this example.

Of course, one can not make a general statement about the relative performance of different statistical models on the basis of a few examples. Nonetheless, one sees that a suitable neural network approach to modeling of survival data can significantly outperform other statistical models with respect to generalization, even if only relatively small data sets (500 patients) are available. This superior forecasting performance of the neural network tools in the second example seems to be attributable to the complex interactions present in the second simulated "disease."

6   Conclusions and Outlook

The use of knowledge based systems for prognosis and prediction offers potentially substantial benefits for application to decision support in breast cancer: At least some breast cancers are curable; identification of the most appropriate therapy concept for each patient requires analysis of the individual manifestation of the disease. Some patients will survive without any adjuvant systemic therapy and should if feasible be spared the ensuing risks or harmful side effects. Tumor-associated proteolytic factors representing the plasminogen activation system (uPA and PAI-1) are now available that provide new information on invasion capacity and metastatic potential of the tumor for each individual patient. Hence, whether intelligent learning systems such as neural networks or more traditional statistical methods are used for forecasting, they will have an improved and complementary information basis for their predictions compared to what would have been possible by measurement of "established" factors only.

One should recognize, however, that reliable and accurate forecasting of the course of a complex disease at time of primary therapy is one of the most challenging problems in bio-mathematics: Several lines of evidence point to the need for a multivariate approach that includes factor interactions. Underlying tumor biological processes also give rise to a time-varying risk structure that must also be modeled. Hence, there is an intrinsic level of complexity in the problem that should be properly represented for good performance.

At the same time despite the improved quality of prognostic factors, there still may be tumor-biological processes important for the course of the disease that simply do not reveal themselves in markers that can be measured clinically with current technology at the time of primary therapy. Moreover, as the simulations of the preceding section illustrated, even with "complete" knowledge of risks, there is an intrinsic level of randomness associated with the time of system failures. This randomness implies that substantial data resources are required for a learning system to distinguish among the multitude of possible distinct nonlinear relationships among factors that have similar consequences. The presence of censoring in the data serves to aggravate this problem. Hence, if neural networks are to be used in the context of medical decision support, they must be designed to avoid overlearning but still capture the essential interactions in an environment in which uncertainties are substantial and data resources are relatively scarce.

This chapter has presented encouraging evidence that a statistical mode of neural net operation emphasizing the avoidance of *unnecessary* complexity can recognize and represent the complicated dependence of the disease on factors and distinguish this dependence from the "noise." The time dependence of underlying risk structures was also taken into account in the neural net formulation described here. Of course, simulation studies do not prove that the potential advantages of neural nets compared to other nonlinear statistical approaches will play a role in the case of actual breast cancer data. However, preliminary investigations based on the breast cancer data discussed in Section 3 and other patient data suggest that scoring using the neural network approach of Section 4 will indeed provide a very high level of risk-group discrimination: As a measure of this discrimination, if the patient collective is divided into two groups of equal size, the low-risk half turns out to exhibit at least a 40 % higher 10-year survival rate than the high-risk half. It seems to be possible to discriminate low-risk and high-risk groups much more effectively than with conventional methods. (The improvement in discrimination depends on the factors available for analysis.) Investigations are currently underway to validate and quantify this performance advantage using a variety of breast cancer data sets.

Neural nets are not the only advanced statistical methods available for modeling nonlinear interactions. Techniques such as recursive partitioning (CART) or nonlinear generalizations of the Cox proportional hazards model also provide improvement over linear modeling if used in the proper context. Indeed, there are almost certainly problem domains in which such nonlinear models offer superior performance compared to neural nets. However, in clinical decision support for treatment of a disease, we generally do not have *a priori* information on the risk structure of the disease, including possible factor interactions. Hence, proper modeling requires a statistical tool capable of representing and identifying *arbitrary* predictive relationships. The ability to represent arbitrary relationships is a well known property of neural networks and constitutes one of the strongest arguments for applying them to decision support.

One of the main requirements in using intelligent systems of any kind to provide support for therapy decisions in a clinical context is the need for a *high level of confidence* in the predictions of such a model on the part of physicians and patients. One way of improving confidence would be a interpretation of the representation of risk as being "reasonable," that is in conformity with a biological paradigm of the underlying disease. Indeed, the representation of a complex risk structure by a nonlinear method such as CART or neural nets could potentially provide new insight into the underlying nature of a disease. However, ease of interpretation is not always a typical feature of the neural network representation of a complex relationship. In the case of CART, ease of interpretation is related to the number of splits in the tree representation. While this number was rather low in the breast cancer data of Section 3.5, quite a large number of splits were required in the simulations (Section 5), and the resulting trees gave no obvious clues to the underlying logic of the "diseases" being modeled. A challenge for research into intelligent systems as applied to disease modeling is therefore to improve the interpretability of the representation.

However, in most advanced statistical methods, including both CART and neural nets, *stability* of the internal representation of the explanatory structure is not guaranteed, because small random changes in the data sample can result in important qualitative changes in the representation of risk (though *not* in risk *prediction*). These qualitative changes are closely related to features such as multicollinearity (more generally, redundancy) of the available information, because small random changes in the data sample can obviously affect the relative ranking of factors with similar predictive characteristics. Hence, any attempt to improve interpretability for the clinical context will probably need to address the issues of representation stability and information redundancy. It could well be that appropriate fusion of different representations of knowledge could be useful in this context.

The ability to provide reliable *uncertainty estimates* is clearly facilitated by embedding neural networks in a statistical framework, as described here. Plausible uncertainty estimates are essential for clinical confidence in the decision support provided by intelligent systems, all the more considering that the internal representation of knowledge by intelligent systems is usually difficult for most users to interpret. Hence, further improvement in estimation and characterization of uncertainties is likely to constitute an important direction for fundamental research in this area.

Acknowledgments

We are very grateful to Dr. Felix Dannegger for useful insights into recursive partitioning and for making his CART analysis program available to us. Our thanks to Ursula Berger for help in statistical analyses. The neural network research reported here was supported by the Wilhelm Sander Foundation.

References

[1] Andreasen, P.A., Kjöller, L, Christensen, L., and Duffy, M.J. (1997), "The urokinase-type plasminogen activator system in cancer metastasis: a review," *Int. J. Cancer*, vol. 72, pp. 1-22.

[2] Biganzoli, E., Boracchi, P., Mariani, L., and Marubini, E. (1998), "Feed Forward Neural Networks for the Analysis of Censored Survival Data: A Partial Logistic Regression Approach," *Statistics in Medicine*, vol. 17, p. 1169.

[3] Bouchet, C., Spyratos, F., Martin, P.M., Hacène, K., Gentile, A., and Oglobine, J. (1994), "Prognostic value of urokinase-type plasminogen activator (uPA) and plasminogen activator inhibitors PAI-1 and PAI-2 in breast carcinomas," *Br. J. Cancer*, vol. 69, pp. 398-405.

[4] Box, G., Jenkins, G., and Reinsel, G. (1994), *Time Series Analysis, Forecasting and Control*, Prentice Hall.

[5] Breiman, L., Friedman, J., Olshen, R. and Stone, C. (1984), *Classification and Regression Trees,* Chapman and Hall, New York.

[6] Clark, G.M., and McGuire, W. (1988), "Steroid receptors and other prognostic factors in primary breast cancer," *Semin Oncol*, vol. 15, pp. 20-25.

[7] Clark, G. (1996), "Prognostic and predictive factors," in Harris, J.R., Lippmann, M.E., Morrow, M., and Hellmann, S. (Eds.), *Diseases of the Breast*, Lippincott-Raven Publishers, Philadelphia, pp 461-485.

[8] Cox, D. (1972), "Regression models and life tables," *J R Stat Soc* [B] 34, pp. 187-200.

[9] Dannegger, F. (1998), "Improving prediction of tree-based models," in Marx, B. and Friedl, H. (Eds.), *Statistical Modeling*, Proceedings of the 13th International Workshop on Statistical Modeling, pp. 155-161.

[10] Dannegger, F. (1999), *Improving Predictions of Tree-Structured Algorithms*, Dissertation, Technische Universität München, Germany.

[11] De Laurentiis, M. and Ravdin, P. (1994), "Survival analysis of censored data: neural network analysis detection of complex interactions between variables," *Breast Cancer Res. Tr.*, vol. 32, p. 113.

[12] Duffy, M.J., Reilly, D., O'Sullivan, C., O'Higgins, N., Fennelly, J.J., and Andreasen, P. (1990), "Urokinase-plasminogen activator, a new and independent prognostic marker in breast cancer," *Cancer Res.*, vol. 50, pp. 6827-6829.

[13] Faraggi, D. and Simon, R. (1995), "A neural network model for survival data," *Statistics in Medicine*, vol. 14, p. 73.

[14] Faraggi, D., Simon, R., Yaskil, E., and Kramar, A., (1997), "Bayesian neural network models for censored data," *Biometrical Journal*, vol. 39, p. 519.

[15] Foekens, J.A., Schmitt, M., van Putten, W.L.J., Peters, H.A., Kramer, M.D., Jänicke, F., and Klijn, J.G.M. (1994), "Plasminogen activator inhibitor-1 and prognosis in primary breast cancer," *J. Clin. Oncology*, vol. 12, pp. 1648-1658.

[16] Golden, R. (1996), *Mathematical Methods for Neural Network Analysis and Design*, MIT.

[17] Gray, R. (1992), "Flexible methods for analyzing survival data using splines, with applications to breast cancer prognosis," *J. American Statistical Association*, vol. 87, p. 942.

[18] Grøhndahl-Hansen, J., Christensen, I.J., Rosenquist, C., Brünner, N., Mouridsen, H.T., Danø, K., and Blichert-Toft, M. (1993), "High levels of urokinase-type plasminogen activator and its inhibitor PAI-1 in cytosolic extracts of breast carcinomas are associated with poor prognosis," *Cancer Res.*, vol. 53, pp. 2513-2521.

[19] Grøhndahl-Hansen, J., Hilsenbeck, S.G., Christensen, I.J., Clark, G.M., Osborne, C.K., and Brünner, N. (1997), "Prognostic significance of PAI-1 and uPA in cytosolic extracts obtained from node-positive breast cancer patients," *Breast Cancer Res. Treat*, vol. 43, pp. 153-163.

[20] Harbeck, N., Dettmar, P., Thomssen, C., Henselmann, B., Kuhn, W., Ulm, K., Jänicke, F., Höfler, H., Graeff, H., and Schmitt, M. (1998), "Prognostic impact of tumor biological factors on survival in node-negative breast cancer," *Anticancer Res.*, vol. 18, pp. 2187-2198.

[21] Harbeck, N., Dettmar, P., Thomssen, C., Berger, U., Ulm, K., Kates, R., Jänicke, F., Höfler, H., Graeff, H., and Schmitt, M. (1999a), "Risk-group discrimination in node-negative breast cancer using invasion and proliferation markers: six-year median follow-up," *Br. J. Cancer*, vol. 80, no. 3/4, pp. 419-426.

[22] Harbeck, N., Thomssen, C., Berger, U., Ulm, K., Kates, R., Höfler, H., Jänicke, F., Graeff, H., and Schmitt, M. (1999b), "Invasion marker PAI-1 remains a strong prognostic factor after long-term follow-up both for primary breast cancer and following first relapse," *Breast Cancer Res. Treat*, vol. 54, pp. 147-157.

[23] Harris, J.R., Lippman, M.E., Veronesi, U., and Willett, W. (1992), "Medical progress: Breast cancer (third of three parts)," *New Engl. J. Med.*, vol. 327, pp. 473-490.

[24] Hastie, T. and Tibshirani, R. (1990), *Generalized Additive Models*, Chapman & Hall.

[25] Hilsenbeck, S.G. and Clark, G.M. (1996), "Practical p-value adjustment for optimally selected cutpoints," *Statistics in Medicine*, vol. 15, pp. 103-112.

[26] Jänicke, F., Schmitt, M., and Graeff, H. (1991), "Clinical relevance of the urokinase-type and tissue type plasminogen activators and of their type 1 inhibitor in breast cancer," *Sem Thromb Hemostasis*, vol. 17, pp. 303-312.

[27] Jänicke, F., Schmitt, M., Pache, L., Ulm, K., Harbeck, N., Höfler, H., and Graeff, H. (1993), "Urokinase (uPA) and its inhibitor PAI-1 are strong, independent prognostic factors in node-negative breast cancer," *Breast Cancer Res. Treat*, vol. 24, pp. 195-208.

[28] Jänicke, F., Thomssen, C., Pache, L., Schmitt, M., and Graeff, H. (1994), "Urokinase (uPA) and PAI-1 as selection criteria for adjuvant chemotherapy in axillary node-negative breast cancer patients," in Schmitt, M, Graeff, H, and Jänicke, F. (Eds.), *Prospects in Diagnosis and Treatment of Cancer*, Elsevier Science, the Netherlands, pp. 207-218.

[29] Kalbfleisch, J. and Prentice, R. (1980), *The Statistical Analysis of Failure Time Data*, Wiley.

[30] Kates, R., Berger, U., Ulm, K., Harbeck, N., Graeff, H., and Schmitt, M. (1999), "Performance of neural nets, CART, and Cox models for censored survival data," in Jain, L.C. (Ed), *Proceedings of Third International Conference on Knowledge-Based Intelligent Information Engineering Systems (KES '99)*, Adelaide, p. 309.

[31] Knoop, A., Andreasen, P.A., Andersen, J.A., Hansen, S., Laenkholm, A.V., Simonsen, A.C.W., Andersen, J., Overgaard, J., and Rose, C. (1998), "Prognostic significance of urokinase-type plasminogen activator and plasminogen activator inhibitor-1 in primary breast cancer," *Br. J. Cancer*, vol. 77, no. 6, pp. 932-940.

[32] Kute, T.E., Grohndahl-Hansen, J., Shao, S.M., Long, R., Russell, G., and Brünner, N. (1998), "Low cathepsin D and low plasminogen activator type 1 inhibitor in tumor cytosols defines a group of node negative breast cancer patients with low risk of recurrence," *Breast Cancer Res. Treat*, vol. 47, pp. 9-16.

[33] Lauffenburger, D. (1996), "Making connections count," *Nature*, vol. 383, pp. 390-391.

[34] LeBlanc, M., and Crowley, J. (1992), "Relative risk trees for censored data," *Biometrics*, vol. 48, pp. 411-425.

[35] Liestol, K., Anderson, P., and Anderson, U. (1994), "Survival analysis and neural nets," *Statistics in Medicine*, vol. 13, p. 1189.

[36] Nelder, J.A. and Mead, R. (1965), "A simplex method for function minimization," *Computer Journal*, vol. 7, p. 308.

[37] Ravdin, P. and Clark, G. (1992), "A practical application of neural network analysis for predicting outcome of individual breast cancer patients," *Breast Cancer Res. Tr.*, vol. 22, p. 285.

[38] Ravdin, P., Clark, G., Hilsenbeck, S., *et al.* (1992), "A demonstration that breast cancer recurrence can be predicted by neural network analysis," *Breast Cancer Res. Tr.*, vol. 21, p. 47.

[39] Ripley, B. (1993), "Statistical aspects of neural networks," in Barndorff-Nielsen, O., Jensen, J., and Kendall, W. (Eds.), *Networks and Chaos – Statistical and Probabilistic Aspects*, Chapman & Hill.

[40] Sauerbrei, W., Blettner, M., and Schumacher, M. (1997), "The importance of basic statistical principles for the interpretation of epidemiological data," *Onkologie*, vol. 20, p. 455.

[41] Schmitt, M., Harbeck, N., Thomssen, C., Wilhelm, O., Magdolen, V., Reuning, U., Ulm, K., Höfler, H., Jänicke, F., and Graeff, H. (1997), "Clinical impact of the plasminogen activation system in tumor invasion and metastasis: prognostic relevance and target for therapy," *Thrombosis Haemostasis*, vol. 78, pp. 285-296.

[42] Schmitt, M., Thomssen, C., Ulm, K., Seiderer, A., Harbeck, N., Höfler, H., Jänicke, F., and Graeff, H. (1997), "Time-varying prognostic impact of tumor biological factors urokinase (uPA), PAI-1, and steroid hormone receptor status in primary breast cancer," *Br. J. Cancer*, vol. 76, no. 3, pp. 306-311.

[43] Schumacher, M., Rossner, R., and Vach, W. (1996), 'Neural networks and logistic regression," *Computational Statistics & Data Analysis*, vol. 21, p. 661 (Part I).

[44] Slamon, D., Leyland-Jones, B., Shak, S., Paton, V., Bajamonde, A., Fleming, T., Eiermann, W., Wolter, J., Baselga, J., and Norton,

L. (1998), "Addition of Herceptin (Humanized anti-HER2 antibody) to first line chemotherapy for HER2 overexpressing metastatic breast cancer (HER2+/MBC) markedly increases anticancer activity: a randomized, multinational controlled phase III trial," *ASCO Proc.*, p. 377.

[45] Tibshirani, R. (1996), "A comparison of some error estimates for neural network procedures," *Neural Computation*, vol. 8, p. 152.

[46] Tu, J. (1996), "Advantages and disadvantages of using artificial neural networks versus logistic regression for predicting medical outcomes," *J. Clin. Epidemiol.*, vol. 49, p. 1225.

[47] Vach, W., Rossner, R., and Schumacher, M. (1996), "Neural networks and logistic regression," *Computational Statistics & Data Analysis*, vol. 21, p. 683 (Part II).

[48] Wagenpfeil, S., Hennig, M., Kates, R., and Neiss, A. (1999), "Analysis of repeated measurements in clinical studies: departures from study design," in Jain, L.C. (Ed.), *Proceedings of Third International Conference on Knowledge-Based Intelligent Information Engineering Systems (KES '99)*, Adelaide, p. 313.

[49] Warner, B. and Misra, M. (1996), "Understanding neural networks as statistical tools," *The American Statistician*, vol. 50, p. 284.

Chapter 4

MammoNet: a Bayesian Network Diagnosing Breast Cancer

L.M. Roberts

A woman has a 1 in 8 chance of developing breast cancer in her lifetime. Screening mammography effectively detects early breast cancers and can increase the likelihood of cure and long-term survival. Differentiating between benign and malignant mammographic findings, however, is difficult, with the majority of mammograms classified "indeterminate." Computer technology in the form of a clinical decision-support tool can be employed to improve the diagnostic accuracy and cost-effectiveness of screening mammography. Automated classification of mammographic findings using discriminant analysis and artificial neural networks has already indicated the potential usefulness of computer-aided diagnosis. Bayesian network technology can be used as the formalism to construct such a decision support tool. This tool would provide accurate, reliable, and consistent diagnoses. One can use a Bayesian network to perform a differential diagnosis by specifying the observed symptoms and computing the posterior probability of the various diagnoses using standard probability formulas.

1   Introduction

In 1999, an estimated 175,000 women in the United States will be newly diagnosed with breast cancer, and 43,300 will die of the disease [32]. According to the National Cancer Institute (NCI), between 1973 and 1989, the rate of breast cancer cases rose 1.7% per year. A lifetime estimate of 1 in 8 to 9 women developing breast cancer indicates every woman is at risk [28, NCI]. Screening mammography effectively detects early breast cancers and can increase the likelihood of cure and long-term survival [8].

Differentiating between benign and malignant mammographic findings, however, is difficult. A suspicious or indeterminate mammographic finding can lead the attending physician to perform a breast biopsy. But in a large study it was found that as many as 75% of certain mammograms fall into indeterminate grades of radiological suspicion [1]. One would like to avoid recommending unnecessary biopsy because of the costs and discomfort to the patient and because biopsy can confound later mammographic testing by producing radiographic abnormalities which can be mistaken for cancer [23]. Using biopsies in excess for benign conditions also increases the costs of mammographic screening and represents a barrier to the effective utilization of this resource [3]. Only 15%-30% of biopsies performed on nonpalpable but mammographically suspicious lesions prove malignant [15].

Automated classification of mammographic findings using discriminant analysis and artificial neural networks has indicated the potential usefulness of computer-aided diagnosis [11], [32]. Thus, we were motivated to develop a decision support tool to aid in the evaluation of mammographic findings.

2   Bayesian Networks

We explored the use of Bayesian networks as a diagnostic decision aid in mammography. Bayesian networks—also called belief networks or causal probabilistic networks—use probability theory as a formalism for reasoning under conditions of uncertainty [2], [22]. Bayesian networks can express the relationships between diagnoses, physical findings, laboratory test results, and imaging study findings. Physicians can determine the *a priori* ("pre-test") probability of a disease, and then incorporate laboratory and imaging results to calculate the *a posteriori* ("post-test") probability. In radiology, Bayesian networks have been applied to the diagnosis of liver lesions on MR images [31] and to the selection of imaging procedures for patients with suspected gallbladder disease [12].

A Bayesian belief network—a graphical representation of probabilistic information—is a directed acyclic graph. The graph is "directed" in that the links between nodes have directionality, that is, they are "one way." The graph is "acyclic" in that it cannot contain cycles or "feedback" loops. The nodes of the network represent random variables (stochastic)—uncertain quantities—which take on two or more possible values. Each state is associated with a probability value; for each node, these probability values sum to one. The states for any node are mutually exclusive and completely exhaustive. The states of a node define the set of possible values a node can be in at any one time. The directed links signify the existence of direct causal influences between the connected nodes. The strengths of these nodes are quantified by conditional probabilities. The connections between variables represent direct influences, expressed as conditional probabilities such as sensitivity and specificity. The links represent causal influences or class-property relationships. In this formalism, variables are given numerical probability values signifying the degree of belief accorded them, and the values are combined and manipulated according to the rules of standard probability theory.

A Bayesian network contains two types of nodes: nodes with parents and nodes without. A node with at least one parent is represented graphically with a directed link from the parent node to the child node. In Bayesian terminology the parent node influences the child node. A node with a set of parents is conditioned on that parent set. A node with no parents is represented graphically with no directed links coming into the node. This type of node represents a prior probability assessment and is represented by an unconditioned probability.

The strengths of influences between the nodes are represented with conditional-probability matrices associated with the connecting links. For example, if node Z has two parent nodes X and Y, the conditional-probability matrix specifies the probabilities of the possible values that Z can assume given all possible combinations of values that X and Y can assume. Nodes without parents are quantified by prior probabilities representing prior knowledge. The prior and conditional probability values used to build a Bayesian network can be derived directly from published values of sensitivity and specificity and collected from expert opinion.

The primary operation of a Bayesian network is the computation of posterior probabilities. A posterior probability of a variable is the probability distribution for this variable given all its conditioning variables. This inference operation consists of specifying values for observed variables, e.g., setting a node state to one, and computing the posterior probabilities of the remaining variables.

2.1   Probability Notation

Let X be a variable with n states, $x_1,\ldots,x_n$. Let Y be a variable with m states, $y_1,\ldots,y_m$.

The **probability P** of any variable X being in state x_i is denoted by

$P(X = x_i) = p,$

where p is the degree of belief accorded to X being in state x_i. The probability value p is a real number in the interval [0..1].

The **conditional probability** of any variable X being in state x_i given a context Y being in state y_j is denoted by

$P(X = x_i | Y = y_j) = p,$

where p is the degree of belief accorded to $X = x_i$ given context $Y = y_j$.

The **joint probability** of any variables X being in state x_i and Y being in state y_j is denoted by

$P(X = x_i, Y = y_j) = p,$

where p is the degree of belief accorded to $X = x_i$ and $Y = y_j$.

The **probability distribution** of any variable X with states $x_1,x_2,\ldots,x_n$, is denoted by

$P(X) = (x_1,x_2,\ldots,x_n)$, given $x_i \; 0 \geq 0$ and $\sum x_i = 1,$

where x_i is the probability of X being in state x_i.

The **probability distribution** of any variable X can be **calculated** from the joint probability distribution P(X,Y). Let x_i be a state of X where X has states has states $x_1,x_2,\ldots,x_n$. Let y_i be a state of Y where Y has states $y_1,y_2,\ldots,y_m$. There are exactly m different events for which variable X is in state x_i: $(x_iy_1),(x_iy_2),\ldots,(x_iy_m)$. The probability of $X = x_i$ is calculated by summing over these partitions and is denoted by

$$P(X = x_i) = \sum_{j=1}^{m} P(X = x_i, Y = y_j).$$

The probability distribution $P(X = x_1,\ldots,X = x_n) = (p_1,\ldots,p_n)$ is denoted by

$$P(X) = \sum_Y P(X,Y).$$

This calculation is referred to as the **summation rule**.

The **inversion formula** (Bayes Theorem) is denoted by

$$P(Y \mid X = e) = P(X = e|Y) \cdot P(Y) / P(X = e),$$

where e is evidence.

The **product rule** in probability is denoted by

$$P(X|Y) \cdot P(Y) = P(X,Y).$$

2.1.1 Conditional Probability

A conditional probability distribution is all combinations of the variable X conditioned on its conditioning variable Y. The distribution will contain (number of states in X) $\cdot$ (number of states in Y) entries. For example, if X is a node with three states x_1, x_2, x_3 and Y is a node with three states y_1, y_2, y_3, then $P(X|Y)$ is the conditional probability table of size $3 \cdot 3 = 9$ containing the real numbers $P(X=x_i|Y=y_j)$ denoted as:

Table 1. Conditional Probability Distribution $P(X \mid Y)$.

$P(X|Y)$	Y_1	y_2	y_3
x_1	$P(X = x_1|Y = y_1)$	$P(X = x_1|Y = y_2)$	$P(X = x_1|Y = y_3)$
x_2	$P(X = x_2|Y = y_1)$	$P(X = x_2|Y = y_2)$	$P(X = x_2|Y = y_3)$
x_3	$P(X = x_3|Y = y_1)$	$P(X = x_3|Y = y_2)$	$P(X = x_3|Y = y_3)$

For each state y_j of Y, where $i = 1,\ldots,n$ and $j = 1,\ldots,m$

$$\sum_{i=1}^{n} P(x_i \mid y_j) = 1.$$

2.1.2   Joint Probability

A joint probability distribution is all combinations of the variable X and the variable Y. The distribution will contain (number of states in X) • (number of states in Y) entries. The joint probability distribution P(X,Y) is calculated using the fundamental product rule P(X|Y) • P(Y) = P(X,Y) as:

Table 2. Joint Probability P (X, Y) Distribution.

P(X,Y)	Y_1	y_2	y_3
x_1	$P(X = x_1, Y = y_1)$	$P(X = x_1, Y = y_2)$	$P(X = x_1, Y = y_3)$
x_2	$P(X = x_2, Y = y_1)$	$P(X = x_2, Y = y_2)$	$P(X = x_2, Y = y_3)$
x_3	$P(X = x_3, Y = y_1)$	$P(X = x_3, Y = y_2)$	$P(X = x_3, Y = y_3)$

where each value $P(X = x_i, Y = y_j)$ is $P(X = x_i, Y = y_j) \cdot P(Y = y_j)$, for $i = 1, \ldots, n$ and $j = 1, \ldots, m$.

The sum of all the joint combinations equals 1.

$$\sum_{i=1}^{n} \sum_{j=1}^{m} P(X = x_i, Y = y_j) = 1.$$

2.2   Benefits of Bayesian Networks

Bayesian networks provide a number of powerful capabilities for representing uncertain knowledge. Their flexible representation allows one to specify dependence and independence of variables in a natural way through the network topology. Because dependencies are expressed qualitatively as links between nodes, one can structure the domain knowledge qualitatively before any numeric probabilities need be assigned. The graphical representation also makes explicit the structure of the domain model: a link indicates a causal relation or known association.

The encoding of independencies in the network topology admits the design of efficient procedures for performing computations over the network. A Bayesian network compactly represents all the information in the joint probability distribution of the variables. Let $U = \{X_1, \ldots, X_n\}$ be a universe of variables. If we have access to the joint probability table $P(U) = P(X_1, \ldots X_n)$, we can calculate $P(X_i)$. The size of the joint probability table P(U) is the product of number of states for all the variables. For X_1 with m states, and X_n with p states, the joint probability is an m × ... × p table. This table can become quickly intractable.

Using the Chain Rule–a generalization of the product rule–the probability distribution of the joint table $P(X_1,...X_n)$, can be rewritten as a product of the conditional probabilities

$$P(X_1,...X_n) = P(X_n|X_{n-1},...,X_2,X_1)...P(X_2|X_1)P(X_1)$$

The number of calculations is considerably simplified by exploiting the conditional independencies of the network. The model in Figure 1 reflects a network with five variables.

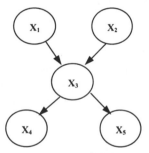

Figure 1. Bayesian network with five variables.

If we do not explicitly specify dependencies, we are assuming all variables are dependent on each other. In this case, the computations for the network in Figure 1 are:

$$P(X_1,X_2,X_3,X_4,X_5) =$$
$$P(X_5|X_4,X_3,X_2,X_1){\bullet}P(X_4|X_3,X_2,X_1){\bullet}P(X_3|X_2,X_1){\bullet}P(X_2|X_1){\bullet}P(X_1)$$

However, the unlinked nodes in Figure 1 are the conditional independencies of the network and the computations are simplified to:

$$P(X_1,X_2,X_3,X_4,X_5) = P(X_5|X_3){\bullet}P(X_4|X_3){\bullet}P(X_3|X_2,X_1){\bullet}P(X_2){\bullet}P(X_1)$$

A further advantage of the graphical representation is the perspicuity of the resulting domain model. Finally, since Bayesian networks represent uncertainty using standard probability, one can collect the necessary data from the domain model by drawing directly on published statistical studies.

3   Breast Cancer Problem Overview

Mammography is an important tool in early detection of breast cancer. Indeterminate mammographic findings often challenge the physician to distinguish between a malignant or benign condition. Successful diagnosis depends on the ability of a physician to recognize and evaluate a mammographic abnormality, as well as integrate the information from multiple clinical aspects (e.g., risk factors and physical findings) to determine the likelihood of breast cancer [9].

The node domain used in this model integrates predictive factors deemed significant to breast cancer diagnosis by clinical resources and other artificial intelligence systems (neural networks and discriminate analysis systems). Functionally this network is close to if not already optimal both in the sense of structure and information. This is to say that the addition of more nodes will not significantly increase the network's performance and may in fact hinder its manageability in a clinical setting.

3.1   Risk Factors and Physical Symptoms

Recent demographic investigations as described by Gail *et al.* [10] and Colditz [4] have reported several risk factors considered to increase a woman's chance of developing breast cancer. Breast cancer incidence rates increase with age. Breast cancer is uncommon for a woman less than age 40, though this group shows the fastest rate of increase of the disease. Positive diagnoses occur with greater frequency in post-menopausal women. An early menarche, with its associated early onset of regular menstrual cycles, is another accepted risk factor. A late child bearing age, that is giving birth after age 30 or never giving birth, raises the risk. Women with a first-degree relative (mother or sister) who has had breast cancer double their chances of developing breast cancer.

Symmonds in [28] studied the correlation between physical symptoms and breast cancer. Breast pain, nipple discharge, and skin thickening are reported by women during clinical exam. These indicators detect few early-stage cancers. The risk factors and physical findings alone are not sufficiently sensitive for malignancy determinations; thus, the use of mammography is an important screening tool.

3.2   Mammographic Findings

None of the established risk factors practically translates into preventive measures, making mammography an important screening tool. Mammographers group breast cancer findings into direct and indirect signs. Direct mammographic indications are calcified or noncalcified masses or calcifications[1] alone. Indirect mammographic signs include architectural distortion, asymmetry, dilated duct, and developing density.

3.2.1   Direct Mammographic Findings: Mass Analysis

Benign and malignant masses are differentiated through mass attributes of margin, density, location, and the presence of the Halo[2] sign [27]. Certain breast masses are identified as benign because their characteristics are accepted as benign. Round, low-density masses with smooth, sharply defined margins are considered benign. The presence of the Halo sign is considered a strong indicator of benignity. Other breast masses are deemed malignant based on characteristics associated with malignancy. Stellate or star-shaped, high density masses with poorly defined margins are considered malignant. Spiculated masses, masses characterized by sharp margins with needlelike points, also fall into this category [25].

Frequently, though, masses are classified as indeterminate, not clearly benign or malignant. Improved mammography and increased screening of asymptomatic women have increased the number of cancerous masses detected not displaying the characteristic radiographic features of malignancy. Instead of spiculated masses, many masses display as nondescript lesions having poorly defined or irregular margins [25].

---

[1] deposits of calcium salts in tissues.
[2] complete or partial radiolucent ring surrounding the periphery of a breast mass.

3.2.2   Direct Mammographic Findings: Calcification Analysis

Similarly, the attributes of size, shape, density, distribution pattern, and number are examined when differentiating between benign and malignant calcifications. Benign and malignant calcifications can occur with or without a mass. Benign calcifications are typically large (1 to 4 mm in diameter) and coarse, round or oval, and monomorphic[3]. Their distribution pattern is typically scattered or diffuse. If the calcifications are clustered, they number less than five per cluster. Some benign calcifications display bizarre, irregular shapes, but because of their large size are considered noncancerous [3], [21], [25].

Malignant calcifications are typically microscopic (< 0.5 mm in diameter) and fine, linear branching or rod-shaped, punctate-[4] or stellate-shaped, and pleomorphic[5]. Their distribution pattern is grouped or clustered, and they are innumerable. A "rule of thumb" is the greater the number of calcifications in a cluster (usually greater than 5), the greater the likelihood of malignancy [3], [21], [25]. As was the case with breast masses, calcifications can display indistinct characteristics making the determination of malignancy difficult. Both benign and malignant calcifications can appear tiny and clustered in mammographic appearance [25]. Typically malignant calcifications present with a wide range in size, shape, and density [7].

3.2.3   Indirect Mammographic Findings

Sickles in [24] notes that almost 20% of cancers present with neither mass nor calcifications, but with subtle or "indirect" signs of malignancy. Architectural distortion is a frequent indicator of breast cancer. However, a woman who has undergone a breast biopsy can present with this indication. Developing density, an enlarging area of glandular tissue density, is a strong indicator of cancer. Dilated ducts and breast asymmetry (increased density as compared with mirror-image location in the opposite breast) are less effective indicators.

---

[3] uniform in size and shape.
[4] pointy, sharp.
[5] varying in size and shape.

4 *MammoNet:* Bayesian Network Diagnostic Tool for Breast Cancer

We created a Bayesian network model of breast cancer diagnosis, called *MammoNet*, which incorporates one hypothesis node, five patient-history features, three physical findings, and sixteen mammographic findings. Refer to Figure 2. The model assumes that all of the evidence pertains to one particular site identified by mammography. *MammoNet* infers the posterior probability of breast cancer at that site based on the available evidence. Given each case's constellation of

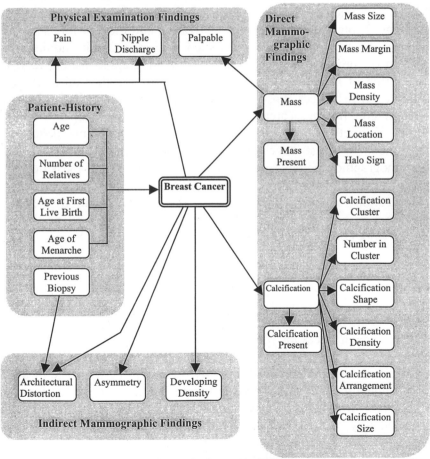

Figure 2. Topology of *MammoNet* Bayesian network.

demographic, clinical, and mammographic features, a posterior probability is calculated using standard probability. *MammoNet* uses a probability of threshold for breast cancer of 15% (which approximates the positive predictive value of mammographic suspicion) to determine the presence of breast cancer.

4.1   *MammoNet* Network Topology

Employing standard breast cancer classification methodology, we categorized the random variables in our domain into three primary areas: demographic features (also referred to as patient history), mammographic indications, and physical examination findings. Mammographic findings are further subdivided into direct and indirect findings. Table 3 presents this categorization and the possible states of each of the twenty-five nodes depicted in Figure 2. The noninferred portion of the network incorporates five demographic factors (age in years, age of menarche, age of first live birth, number of first order relatives with cancer, previous biopsy at same site), three physical examination findings (breast pain, nipple discharge, palpable mass), three indirect mammographic findings (architectural distortion, asymmetry in breast, developing density in breast), and thirteen direct mammographic findings (mass, mass size, mass margin, mass density, mass location, halo sign, calcification, calcification cluster shape, calcification number, calcification shape, calcification density, calcification arrangement, calcification size). The inferred portion of the network consists of the single hypothesis node, breast cancer.

Mammographically detectable mass and calcification are modeled as conditionally independent manifestations of malignancy. The Mass and Calcification nodes have three states: "malignant," "benign," and "none". If no mass is evident, for example, the Mass Present node is set to "no", which forces the Mass node to the state "none" and nodes such as Mass Margin to the state "not applicable" (NA). The Mass Present node allows one to express uncertainty regarding the presence of mass independently of the descriptive features. The mammographic features of a mass (Mass Size, Mass Margin, Mass Density, etc.)—although conditionally independent of Breast Cancer given Mass—affect the diagnosis by their influence on the Mass node's "malignant" and "benign" states. The model treats Calcification and its related nodes in similar fashion.

Table 3. Definitions of *MammoNet*'s nodes and their states. NA = not applicable.

Category	Node	States
DIAGNOSIS	Breast Cancer	present, absent
PATIENT-HISTORY	Age (years)	20 - 24, 25 - 29 ,..., 75 - 79
	Age at Menarche (years)	< 12, 12 - 13, ≥ 14
	Age at First Life Birth (years)	< 20, 20 - 24, 25 - 29, ≥ 30
	Number of First Degree Relatives with Breast Cancer	0, 1, ≥ 2
	Previous Biopsy	yes, no
PHYSICAL EXAMINATION FINDINGS	Pain	present, absent
	Nipple Discharge	present, absent
	Palpable Mass	present, absent
INDIRECT MAMMOGRAPHIC FINDINGS	Architectural Distortion	present, absent
	Asymmetry	present, absent
	Developing Density	present, absent
DIRECT MAMMOGRAPHIC FINDINGS	**Mass**	malignant, benign, none
	Mass Present	yes, no
	Mass Size	inSitu, ≤5, 6-10, 11-20, multiFocal, none
	Mass Margin	spiculated, irregular, relatively well-defined, NA*
	Mass Density	high, low, NA
	Halo Sign	present, absent, NA
	Mass Location	upper outer, upper inner, lower outer, lower inner, retroareolar, NA
	Calcification	malignant, benign, none
	Calcification Present	yes, no
	Calcification Cluster Shape	punctate, round, linear, variable, NA
	Number of Calcifications in Cluster	< 5, 6 - 10, 16 - 25, 26 - 50, > 50, NA
	Calcification Shape	linear branching, irregular, indeterminate, round, NA
	Calcification Density	1 - 2, 1 - 3, 2 - 3, 3 - 4, NA
	Calcification Arrangement	scattered, clustered, scattered & clustered, single, NA
	Calcification Size (mm.)	0.05 - 0.1, 0.05 - 0.2, 0.001 - 1, 0.01 - 2, 1 - 3, NA

4.1.1 *MammoNet* Network Terminology

Wherever possible, we used standardized terminology as proposed in the American College of Radiology's Breast Imaging Reporting and Data Systems (BIRADS) lexicon [5] to describe the nodes and their states (Table 3). BIRAD is a collection of standardized breast imaging terms and classifications (Table 4). In other cases, the terminology of the consulted expert was used.

Table 4. BIRAD classification and terminology for breast masses.

BIRAD Category	BIRAD Terms
Calcification Cluster Shape	Punctate
	Round
Calcification Arrangement	Scattered
	Scattered & Clustered
Mass Margin	Well-defined
	Spiculated
Mass Density Modifier	High density
	Low density

4.1.2 *MammoNet* Data Acquisition

Statistical studies published in radiology journals provided most of the data for *MammoNet's* knowledge base. When required probability data were unavailable or the sample size too small, we consulted a mammographic expert at the Medical College of Wisconsin. She provided subjective estimates of the probabilities for architectural distortion, previous biopsy at the same site, and the Halo sign.

Prior probabilities are assigned to the demographic nodes. Age statistics were obtained from the National Cancer Institute and the U.S. Census Bureau, Population Division, release PPL-8. Statistics for age of menarche were acquired from the Department of Health, Education, and Welfare, Vital and Health Statistics. Population and Vital Statistics, Statistical Record of Women Worldwide provided statistics for age of first live birth. The remaining demographic feature, number of first-degree relatives with a known history of breast cancer, was estimated based on information from Colditz [4].

Conditional probabilities for the physical findings given breast cancer were obtained from Symmonds *et al.* [28], for the mammographic findings given breast cancer from Sickles [24], [25], Egan *et al.* [7], and Jackson *et al.* [18], and for the indirect mammographic findings given breast cancer from Sickles [24].

4.2   *MammoNet* Demographic Features

Demographic features consist of variables for the established risk factors, age, age of menarche, age at first live birth, and number of first degree relatives with breast cancer. These four patient-history features influence the presence of breast cancer, which in turn influences the presence of the physical findings and mammographic findings. The fifth patient-history feature, previous biopsy at same site, influences the indirect mammographic finding, architectural distortion.

4.2.1   Demographic Feature: Age

The incidence of breast cancer is influenced by age. Breast cancer is uncommon for a woman less than age 40 and positive diagnoses occur with greater frequency in post-menopausal women. The age node is divided into twelve states, each state encompassing a 5-year period. The age node covers a 60-year span, beginning at age 20 and ending at age 79. Refer to Table 5.

Table 5. Probability distribution for 12 age intervals.

Age Interval	Probability Distribution
20-24	0.01025
25-29	0.1107
30-34	0.1235
35-39	0.1185
40-44	0.1067
45-49	1.0874
50-54	0.0706
55-59	0.0616
60-64	0.0610
65-69	0.0612
70-74	0.0536
75-79	0.0428

Source: U.S. Bureau of the Census, Population Division, release PPL-8, United States Population Estimates, by Age, Sex, Race, and Hispanic Origin, 1990 to 1993.

4.2.2   Demographic Feature: Age of Menarche

An early menarche is another accepted risk factor for breast cancer. The age of menarche node is partitioned into three states. These states are younger than 12, 12 to 13, and 14 and older.

Table 6. Probability distribution for age of menarche.

Age at Menarche (in years)	Probability Distribution
younger than 12	0.136
12 to 13	0.514
14 and older	0.350

Source: Age at Menarche United States, Vital and Health Statistics, 1973, U.S. Department of Health, Education, and Welfare.

4.2.3   Demographic Feature: Child Bearing Age

A late child bearing age, that is giving birth after age 30, or never giving birth is an accepted risk factor for breast cancer. The age of first live birth node is divided into four states. These states are younger than 20, 20 to 24, 25 to 29 and ages 30 and older. Table 7 shows this.

Table 7. Probability distribution for first live birth.

Age at First Live Birth (in years)	Probability Distribution
younger than 20	0.2595
20 to 24	0.374
25 to 29	0.255
30 and older	0.1115

Source: Population and Vital Statistics, Statistical Record of Women Worldwide.

4.2.4   Demographic Feature: Number of First Degree Relatives with History of Breast Cancer

The number of first degree relatives with a known history of breast cancer is an accepted risk factor for breast cancer. This node is divided into three states. These states are 0, 1, and 2 or more first degree relatives with a history of breast cancer. See Table 8.

4.2.5   Demographic Feature: Previous Biopsy at Same Site

A previous biopsy at the same site of the abnormality under examination is an accepted risk factor. This binary node is divided into two states, yes and no. Refer to Table 9.

Table 8. Probability distribution for number of first degree relatives.

Number of First Degree Relatives	Probability Distribution
0	0.6
1	0.3
2	0.1

Source: estimate from mammography expert.

Table 9. Probability distribution for previous biopsy at same site.

Previous Biopsy at Same Site	Probability Distribution
yes	0.2
no	0.8

Source: estimate from mammography expert.

One of the patient-history factors, that of a prior biopsy at same site, serves as a competing cause of the mammographic finding of architectural distortion. Architectural distortion without a previous biopsy at the same site is "an automatic request for a biopsy" according to mammographic experts. However, a previous biopsy at the same site is a reasonable explanation for an architectural distortion. Both breast cancer and previous biopsy at the same site are causes of architectural distortion. Positive evidence for a previous biopsy at the same site explains away breast cancer as a cause of architectural distortion.

4.3   *MammoNet* Hypothesis Node

The hypothesis node, disease breast cancer, is the node of interest in *MammoNet*. It is influenced by demographic features, and in turn, it influences the mammographic findings and physical findings. The binary node Breast Cancer consists of two states, present and absent. Its conditional table consists of 432 entries, all combinations of the states of the demographic nodes and the hypothesis node. Table 10 shows a portion of this table. We calculated the initial values for this table. Using data retrieved from the National Cancer Institute's Surveillance Program, we determined the probability of developing breast cancer in a specific time interval. We multiplied the Relative Risk (RR) factors computed in [10] by the base risk factor for a specific age group to obtain an adjusted probability. A 50-year old woman with no history of breast cancer runs a 2% baseline risk of developing cancer. An age of menarche in the 12 to 14 year range, adds a RR factor of 1.099.

Similarly, a first birth in the range of 20 to 24 years, and no history of
breast cancer in first degree relatives, adds a RR factor of 1.244. The
adjusted probability for developing breast cancer is computed by
multiplying the base factor by a product of the additional risk factors.
Sample computation of risk factors for breast cancer:

$$(\text{BASE\_RISK}) \times (\text{RELATIVE\_RISK}) = \text{ADJUSTED\_RISK}$$
$$0.02 \quad \times \quad (1.099 \times 1.244) \quad = \quad 0.02734312$$

Table 10. Probability distribution for breast cancer given age, age of menarche, age
of first live birth, and number of relatives w/history of breast cancer; partial table.

breast cancer present	breast cancer absent	age	age of menarche	age of first live birth	number of relatives with breast cancer
0.00005100	0.99994900	20 to 24	14 and older	younger than 20	0
0.00013296	0.99986704	20 to 24	14 and older	younger than 20	1
0.00034670	0.99965330	20 to 24	14 and older	younger than 20	2
0.00006344	0.99993656	20 to 24	14 and older	20 to 24	0
0.00013673	0.99986327	20 to 24	14 and older	20 to 24	1
0.00029452	0.99970548	20 to 24	14 and older	20 to 24	2
0.00007895	0.99992105	20 to 24	14 and older	25 to 29	0
0.00014055	0.99985945	20 to 24	14 and older	25 to 29	1
0.00025025	0.99974975	20 to 24	14 and older	25 to 29	2
0.00009828	0.99990172	20 to 24	14 and older	30 and older	0
0.00014453	0.99985547	20 to 24	14 and older	30 and older	1
0.00021262	0.99978738	20 to 24	14 and older	30 and older	2

4.4   *MammoNet* Physical Examination Symptoms

Breast cancer can cause several physical symptoms. The symptoms we
included in our model are breast pain, nipple discharge, and palpable
mass. Physical symptoms skin thickening and vein dilation, were
eliminated from the model because the probabilities were insignificant
as malignancy indicators. Unfortunately, the cancers were in an
advanced stage when these symptoms were evident, making
mammographic decisioning irrelevant.

The nodes representing pain, nipple discharge, and palpable mass
contain two states, present and absent. As breast pain and nipple
discharge are both directly influenced by breast cancer and palpable
mass is directly influenced by mass, their probability vectors are

conditional distributions. For the breast pain variable, the probability distribution is defined by all combinations of:

Probability (Breast Pain = Present or Absent |
          Breast Cancer = True or False)

Table 11. Conditional probability of breast pain given breast cancer.

Breast Pain State		Breast Cancer State
present	absent	
3/65	62/65	True
9/379	370/379	False

4.5   *MammoNet* Mammographic Indirect Findings

The nodes representing the indirect signs contain two states, present or absent. Architectural distortion can be influenced by the presence of breast cancer and can also be influenced by a previous biopsy at the same site. The node representing a previous biopsy at the same site consists of two states, present and absent. A finding of architectural distortion without a previous biopsy at the site is a certain cause for a breast biopsy. Asymmetry and developing density nodes are influenced solely by the breast cancer node.

For node Architectural Distortion, the probability vector is conditioned on the nodes breast cancer and previous biopsy at same site. Its probability distribution is defined by all combinations of:

Probability (Architectural Distortion = Present or Absent |
          Breast Pain = Present or Absent,
          Previous Biopsy Same Site = True or False)

Table 12. Conditional probability of architectural distortion given breast cancer and previous biopsy at same site.

Architectural Distortion State		Breast Cancer State	Previous Biopsy State
present	absent		
99/100	1/100	True	True
26/300	274/300	True	False
99/100	1/100	False	True
1/1000	999/1000	False	False

4.6   *MammoNet* Mammographic Direct Indications

The nodes representing the direct, observable signs of breast cancer, mass and calcifications are influenced by the breast cancer node. Breast cancer can produce a mass with or without calcifications or calcifications alone. The model is designed to treat these two symptoms independently. The mammography expert consulted in this study indicated that the reasoning she uses treats each symptom separately. In the case of a calcified mass, the mass is reasoned about and the calcification is reasoned about, with the results considered together for a determination of malignancy or benignity. The mass and calcification nodes are divided into three states, benign, malignant, and absent.

4.6.1   Mammographic Direct Indication: Mass

The node mass influences several nodes representing characteristics used in differentiating between a malignant or benign tumor mass. Mammographers categorize the malignancy or benignity of breast masses by considering size, shape, clarity of margin, and density.

Certain breast masses are identified as benign because their characteristics are accepted as benign. Round, low-density masses with smooth, sharply defined margins are considered benign. A very large sized mass usually suggests a benign mass. Other breast masses are deemed malignant based on characteristics associated with malignancy. High density, stellate-shaped, spiculated-knobby masses with poorly defined margins are thought to be malignant [25]. Most malignant masses are not larger than 10 mm.

Frequently, though, masses are classified as indeterminate, not clearly benign or malignant. Improved mammography and increased screening of asymptomatic women have increased the number of cancerous masses detected not displaying the characteristic radiographic features of malignancy. Instead of spiculated masses, many masses display as nondescript lesions having poorly defined or irregular margins [25].

Density assessment of breast masses is the comparison of the mass to an equal volume of normal parenchyma [18]. Nonfatty, low-density masses are widely believed to be benign and high-density masses, malignant.

Other radiographic features in determining the state of a breast mass are mass location and the presence of the Halo sign. Mass location is considered an ineffective determination of breast malignancy. Most malignant breast masses are found in the upper outer quadrant of the breast. At the same time, most benign breast masses are found in this same quadrant [25]. The Halo sign, long considered a sign of certain benignity, has in recent studies appeared in malignant breast masses.

4.6.1.1 Mass Characteristics

The node representing mass margin is divided into 4 states: spiculated, irregular, relatively well defined, and not applicable (NA) [24].

The node representing mass size is divided into seven states: in situ (in site or precancerous), ≤5 mm, 6-10 mm, 11-20 mm, >20 mm and multifocal (numerous masses scattered through the breast.

The node representing mass density is divided into three states; high density, low density, and NA. Low density expresses density less than or equal to the density of normal parenchymal structures and high density expresses density greater than the density of the normal parenchymal structures [18], [25].

The node representing mass location in the breast is divided into 6 states: "upper outer" UO, "upper inner" UI, "lower outer" LO, "lower inner" LI, "retroareolar" RA, and NA [18], [25].

The node representing the Halo sign is divided into three states: present, absent, and NA [25].

For node Mass Location, the probability vector is conditioned on the node mass. Its probability distribution is defined by all combinations of:

Probability (Mass Location = UO, UI, LO, LI, RA, NA |
Mass = Malignant, Benign, None)

Table 13. Conditional probability of mass location given mass.

Mass Location State						Mass State
UO	**UI**	**LO**	**LI**	**RA**	**NA**	
0.52	0.143	0.143	0.05	0.144	0.00	Malignant
0.54	0.14	0.10	0.07	0.15	0.00	Benign
0.00	0.0	0.00	0.00	0.00	1.00	None

4.6.2   Mammographic Direct Indications: Calcifications

The calcifications node influences several nodes representing characteristics used in differentiating between malignant or benign breast calcifications. Mammographers categorize the malignancy or benignity of breast calcifications by considering size, shape, density, distribution pattern, and number. Benign and malignant calcifications can occur with or without the presence of a mass.

Benign calcifications are typically large (1-4 mm in diameter) and coarse, round or oval and monomorphic. Their distribution pattern is typically scattered or diffuse. If the calcifications are clustered, they number less than 5 per cluster. Some benign calcifications display bizarre, irregular shapes, but because of their large size are considered noncancerous [3], [21], [25].

Malignant calcifications are typically microscopic (<0.5 mm in diameter) and fine, linear branching or rod-shaped, punctate- or stellate-shaped, and pleomorphic. Their distribution pattern is grouped or clustered, and they are innumerable. A rule of thumb is the greater number of calcifications in a cluster (usually greater than 5), the greater likelihood of malignancy [3], [18], [21].

As was the case with breast masses, calcifications can display indistinct characteristics making the determination of malignancy difficult. Both benign and malignant calcifications can appear tiny and clustered in mammographic appearance [18]. Certain benign calcifications can display bizarre and random shapes. Typically malignant calcifications present with a wide range in size, shape, and density [7].

4.6.2.1 Calcification Characteristics

The node representing number of calcifications in a cluster is divided into 7 possible states (expressed as 3 or more calcifications in an area no larger than 0.5x0.5 cm.): ≤5, 6-10, 11-15, 16-25, 26-50, >50, and NA. The number ranges from few to innumerable [7].

The node representing calcification size is divided into 6 states (expressed in mm.): 0.05-0.1, 0.05-2, 0.01 -1, 0.01-2, 1-3, 2-3 and NA. The size varies from very fine to rather coarse [7].

The node representing calcification density is divided into 5 possible states (expressed as density increasing from 1 to 4): 1-2, 1-3, 2-3, 3-4, NA.

Density ranges from very faint (almost imperceptible) to very dense [7].

The node representing calcification shape divides into 5 possible states: punctate, round, linear, variable, and NA [7].

The node representing calcification distribution or arrangement is divided into 5 states: scattered, clustered, scattered & clustered, single, and NA [7].

For node Calcification Cluster Shape, the probability vector is conditioned on the node calcification. Its probability distribution is defined by all combinations of:

Probability (Calcification Cluster Shape =
      Punctate, Round, Linear, Variable, None |
      Calcification = Malignant, Benign, None)

Table 14. Conditional probability of cluster shape given calcifications.

Calcification Cluster Shape State					Calcification State
Punctate	**Round**	**Linear**	**Variable**	**None**	
0.36	0.08	0.02	0.54	0.0	Malignant
0.64	0.14	0.04	0.18	0.0	Benign
0.0	0.0	0.0	0.0	1.0	None

5   Decision Support System

A shortcoming of Bayesian networks in automated medical reasoning is the difficulty of users understanding and trusting the systems. The users' trust in these systems depends on their ability to interact with the system and their ability to obtain understandable explanations [30]. Bayesian networks are composed of large numbers of numeric relationships that interact in non-intuitive ways and do not provide information about their origin. Explanation of probabilistic data must explain the numeric relations that comprise the probabilistic model and the probabilities that are derived from the model. Hence, an effective explanation relates its numerical information to the world knowledge it underlies.

Bayesian Networks provide good models for representing uncertainty, however, the reasoning they support differs significantly from how people think about uncertainty. Users have different information needs. Users interested in the model structure will be concerned with *How* the system justifies its answers. Users interested with how the model relates its conclusions to their own view of the problem will be concerned with *Why* the system answered as it did.

Explanation generation in this system is an interactive, multimodal process that allows users without expertise in Bayesian network technology understand the decision system. The system incrementally produces multimodal explanations that use natural language, text, and graphics in an ongoing dialog adapting the interaction to the users' needs and concerns. Users express themselves through direct manipulation and natural language description. The system responds to the users by presenting synchronized graphical and verbal replies that clarify and reinforce its answers. Users concerned with the underlying structure of the model can view a graphical depiction of the model's overall topology enhanced with a natural language summary of important results. Users can interact with the system by selecting a node for further description. Users interested in how the results of the system relate to their concerns can interact with the systems by questions.

5.1   System Architecture

The decision support system, *MammoNet*, is implemented in C++ and designed using an object-oriented model. The system architecture is designed to provide an effective method for communicating explanations to its users. Major components of the system are the multimodal user interface, the knowledge representation module, the multimodal discourse module, and the Bayesian network inference engine. The schematic overview of *MammoNet* is depicted in Figure 3.

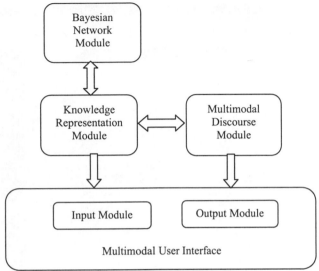

Figure 3. *MammoNet* block diagram.

5.1.1   User Interface

MammoNet is implemented as a Windows™-based program, and the user interface makes use of standard graphical devices (controls, menus, icons). Users can interactively explore the workings of a Bayesian network for mammographic diagnosis of breast cancer. Evidence for the Bayesian network is entered through a series of data entry selections. Model explanation—information about states, parents, and children of model nodes, causation links, and probabilities—is offered for users interested in *how* the model works. Probability elucidation—information on how each piece of evidence affects the breast cancer diagnosis—is made available for users interested in *why* the model works as it does.

5.1.1.1 Diagnosis Data Entry

A user is presented with a sequence of tabbed property sheets. Data entry of relevant patient-history information, physical examination findings, and mammographic data is achieved through an easy point and click selection. Refer to Figure 4 for an example of a data entry screen that a user might use to enter data corresponding to *MammoNet's* patient-history (demographic factors) nodes (age, age of menarche, etc.).

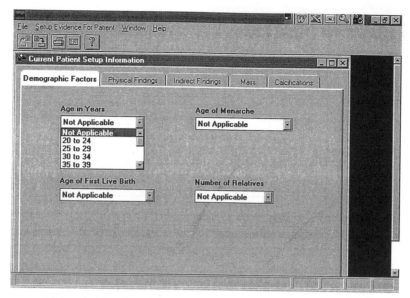

Figure 4. User interface: demographic factors data entry screen.

From a simple point-and-click interface, users can enter diagnostic data for mammographic diagnosis of breast cancer.

5.1.2 Knowledge Representation Module

The knowledge representation module serves a two-fold purpose. To support discourse processing, it parses and encodes the multimodal input objects (natural language strings, text, mouse gestures, and graphical presentation objects) it receives from the user interface into representations of the user's actions. These representations comprise the multimodal discourse module's discourse history. To support explanation generation of probabilistic data, it acts as an interface between the multimodal discourse module and the back-end of the Bayesian network inference engine. During a dialog with a user, it processes inquires from the multimodal discourse module and interrogates the Bayesian network inference engine for probability calculations.

The knowledge representation module is made up of a breast cancer specific lexicon and parser for natural language interpretation, a semantic structure which encodes the meaning of the system, and logic to process data and commands between the user interface, the multimodal discourse module, and the Bayesian network inference engine.

5.1.2.1 Parser Output as Abstract Statements

The natural language parser outputs abstract conceptual statements that comprise the discourse history and are used in the on-going dialog between system and user. These statements consist of four components: statement type, statement origin, statement modality, and statement context. Statement type classifies an utterance into categories describing the action of the system or the request of the user.

Statement origin indicates the origin of the utterance (user or system). Statement modality indicates the modality that statement is issued in. Statement context assigns a contextual meaning to an utterance relating the utterance to the domain (Breast Cancer Diagnosis). Refer to Tables 15, 16, and 17 for samples of statement types, modalities and contexts.

Table 15. Sample of statement types and system descriptions.

Statement Type Token	Statement Type Description
GENERAL_EXPLAIN_COMMAND	System identified general request for explanation
SPECIFIC_CONCERN_QUERY	System identified specific request for concern
SPECIFIC_DEMO_COMMAND	System identified specific request for demo
CONCEPT_NOUN_AGE_MENARCHE	System identified topic Age at Menarche
CONCEPT_NOUN_NIPPLE_DISCHARGE	System identified topic Nipple Discharge
CONCEPT_NOUN_MASS_MARGIN	System identified topic Mass Margin
CONCEPT_NOUN_CALCIFICATION_DENSITY	System identified topic Calcification Density

Table 16. Sample of modality types and system descriptions.

Modality Type	Modality Type Description
TYPED_KEYBOARD	User typed utterance at keyboard
RIGHT_MOUSE_CLICK	User single-clicked right mouse button
LEFT_MOUSE_CLICK	User single-clicked left mouse button
DOUBLE_CLICK	User double-clicked mouse button
DISPLAYED_GRAHPICS	System displayed graphics on screen
DISPLAYED_TEXT	System displayed text on screen

Table 17. Sample of context types and system descriptions.

Statement Context	Statement Context Description
GENERAL_EXPLAIN	System participants engaged in general explanation processing
SPECIFIC_CONCERN	System participants engaged in specific concern processing
SPECIFIC_DEMO	System participants engaged in specific demo processing
SPECIFIC_CONCERN_AGE_MENARCHE	System participants engaged in age of menarche processing
SPECIFIC_CONCERN _NIPPLE_DISCHARGE	System participants engaged in nipple discharge processing
SPECIFIC_CONCERN _MASS_MARGIN	System participants engaged in mass margin processing
SPECIFIC_CONCERN _CALCIFICATION_DENSITY	System participants engaged in calcification density processing

5.1.2.2 Semantic Encoding of Bayesian Network

Semantic encoding of the Bayesian network provides the decision support system with a central repository of information to draw from when constructing explanations for users. Information about the network includes node attributes (name, states, associated probability distributions, and parent/child relationships), classifications of nodes (e.g., node age is classified as demographic factor or patient-history, node nipple discharge is classified as physical examination symptoms), node importance or ordering (e.g., in node mass margin, probability of state spiculated is stronger than probability of state relatively well-defined), and user-entered evidence.

Ordering information about patient-history, physical examination findings, and mammographic indications is based on a user's entered evidence. It is presented as an ordered bar graph, indicating the strengths of the entered evidence in the determination of breast cancer.

5.1.3 Multimodal Discourse Module

The multimodal discourse module is central to the architecture of the system. Discourse processing is the task of creating a dynamic representation of the multimodal interaction that defines the relations between the system's and a user's actions. The discourse module, which represents the content and structure of an ongoing dialog, supports statements of facts and questions about the domain, commands to provide an explanation, and referring expressions (indicate a focus of interest to the system). The system is capable of providing explanations to a wide range of users: users who are concerned with the "*how*" of the system and users who are concerned with the "*why*" of the system.

5.1.3.1 *"How"* the System Works: *The Professor*

How does the system work? *What* are its components? *What* are the nodes? *What* are the node states? *How* are the nodes related? Users concerned with the underlying model of the system ask questions of this sort. *The Professor* is the component of the multimodal discourse module that manages how-the-system-works explanations.

The Professor is implemented as a display of clickable buttons, labeled according to the primary areas of the domain variables (demographic factors, physical examination findings, and mammographic indications). A button click opens a graphical chart of the nodes that comprise that primary area. The user can learn the name, node states, node dependencies (which set of nodes influences the current node), and node influences (which set of nodes the current node influences). Right-clicking with a mouse on the node name displays further information on that node. See Figures 5, 6, and 7.

5.1.3.2 "Why" the System Works: *The Explainer*

Unlike users who are concerned with the mechanics or structure of the system, there are users who are concerned with how the system relates its conclusions to their specific situation. This system is capable of providing explanations to users concerned with questions about their likelihood of breast cancer as it relates to their specific situation. The system provides these explanations using a combination of modalities, including text displays, and graphics. These are questions and statements of the kind: "I am worried about my health." "Tell me why my risk is such." "Yes, I'd like more information on what I can do to improve my situation." "Tell me why the mass in my left breast is likely cancerous," and so forth. The component of the multimodal discourse module that manages this type of discourse is "The Explainer."

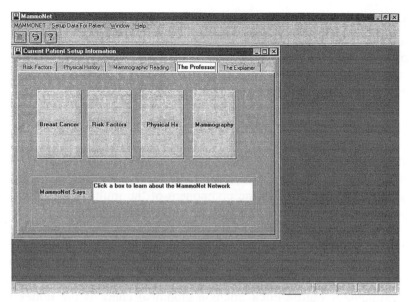

Figure 5. *The Professor*: clickable boxes.

NODE	STATES	INFLUENCES	DEPENDS ON
Age in 5-year intervals	20 to 24, 25 to 29 . . . 65 to 69,70 to 75	Risk of Breast Cancer	
Age of Menarche (in years)	Younger than 12; 12 to 13; Older than 13	Risk of Breast Cancer	
Age of First Live Birth	Younger than 20; 20 to 30, Older than 30	Risk of Breast Cancer	
Family History of Breast Cancer: Number of Relatives	0 , 1, 2 or more	Risk of Breast Cancer	

Right click on one of the Risk Factor (Age, Age of Menarche, Age of First Live Birth, Family History of Breast Cancer) boxes for detailed information.

OK

Help

Figure 6. *The Professor*: open clickable box.

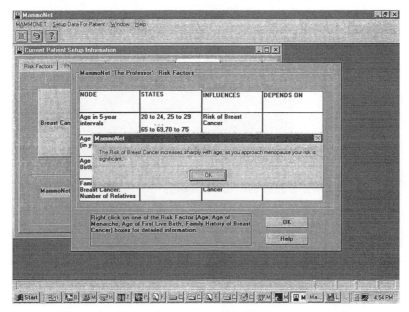

Figure 7. *The Professor*: open clickable boxes with detail.

"The Explainer" encapsulates the information necessary to provide the user and the system with information to carry on a dialog with questions, statements, and answers. The user is presented with a type-in text box, though which the user can type in questions. The mouse can be used for pointing and referring, and selection options. "The Explainer" supports two modalities: mouse clicks and typed text input. The Parser in the knowledge representation module processes the typed input, parsing and encoding the utterance into an abstract concept which is then stored as dialog entries in dialog table. The evidence vector from the Bayesian network provides the semantic structure of the knowledge representation module with information for the particular user. The semantic structure provides "The Explainer" with information on the network structure, and the specific entered evidence for the current user session.

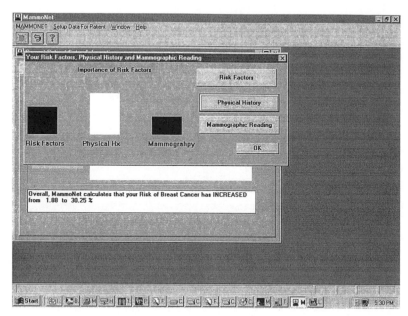

Figure 8. *The Explainer*: bar chart for specific patient data.

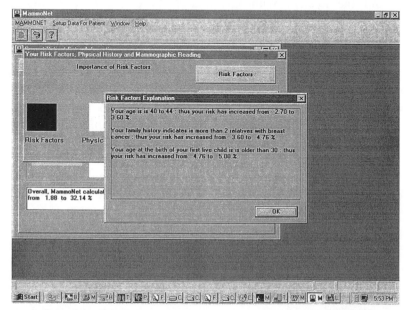

Figure 9. *The Explainer*: detailed information for specific pateint data.

A user can enter evidence through the graphical interface, and then enter "*The Explainer*." This component provides the processing to support the ongoing dialog of questions, statements, and answers between the system participants. The user can request further information on how the system calculates her risk; the system provides graphical and typed-text display responses by sending the explanations and the presentation specifications to the output module. In turn, the output module interprets the presentation specifications and supports the actual display of the explanations. See Figures 8 and 9.

5.1.4   Bayesian Network Inference Engine

The reasoning component of the decision support system is implemented as a Bayesian network inference engine. The inference engine computes the posterior probability of breast cancer given a configuration of observable evidence. The basic calculations used to perform the evidence propagation and belief update of all network nodes are standard probability formulas as detailed in Section 2.1.

We used an object oriented approach to design and implement the inference engine. The basic classes (data structures) include node, clique, and Bayesian network. At program startup, the inference engine is initialized First, the member components—nodes and cliques—of the Bayesian network are created and initialized. Second, the Bayesian network, composed of nodes and cliques, is constructed. Third, the joint probability tables (for every conditional probability distribution) and initial prior probability vectors (for each node) are calculated and stored. Finally, an evidence vector (for each node) is created and initialized with no evidence and the system then waits for user input.

5.1.4.1 Class Node Implementation

Class Node represents a domain variable of the Bayesian network (e.g., age, age of menarche, etc.) Each node is an instantiation of this class. Class Node stores information relating to node attributes: number of states, textual name, unique identifying node number, number of parent and children nodes, parent and children nodes, joint probability table size, member clique, and vectors for prior and conditional probabilities. Table 18 shows how information is stored for a node without parents (age), a hypothesis node (breast cancer), and a node with parents (mass location).

5.1.4.2 Class Clique Implementation

To ensure a controlled evidence propagation (updating of the network nodes with evidence), the network or graph of nodes is triangulated into a tree of cliques. The network divides into twenty cliques, and each clique holds the joint probability distribution table of its member nodes. The inversion formula (Bayes Theorem) is applied to these tables during evidence propagation.

Table 18. Class Node instantiation examples.

Class Node Information	Node *Age*	Node *Breast Cancer*	Node *Mass Location*
number of states	12	2	6
textual name of node for reports	"Age"	"Breast Cancer"	"Mass Location"
node number for identification	0	4	14
number of parent nodes	0	4	1
number of children nodes	1	8	0
parent nodes	none	Age, Menarche, Birth, Relatives	Mass
children nodes	Breast Cancer	Mass, Calcification, Asymmetry, Developing Density, Pain, Nipple Discharge, Architectural Distortion	none
joint probability table size	0	864	18
member clique	0	0	8
prior probability vector	{0.1025, ..., 0.0427}	calculated by software	calculated by software
conditional probability vector	none	{(0.00005100, 0.99994900), ..., (0.50319830, 0.49680170)}	{(0.52, 0.143, 0.143, 0.05, 0.144, 0.00), (0.00, 0.00, 0.00, 0.00, 0.00, 1.00)}

Class Clique stores information relating to the attributes of a clique: number of node members, unique identifying clique number, root clique indicator, number of links to other cliques, list of links to other cliques, number of common nodes (nodes that a clique has in common with another clique), member nodes referenced by node number, common nodes referenced by node number, and a base node (conditioned variable).

Figure 10 shows the cliques of *MammoNet* and Table 19 details the cliques and their member nodes.

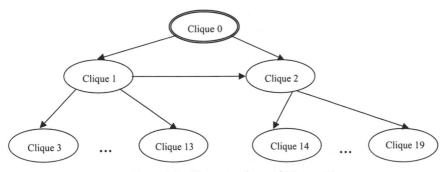

Figure 10. Clique topology of *MammoNet*.

Table 19. Cliques and their member nodes.

Clique Number	Member Nodes
0	Breast Cancer, Age, Age of Menarche, Age at First Life Birth, Number of Relatives
1	Mass, Breast Cancer
2	Calcification, Breast Cancer
3	Asymmetry, Breast Cancer
4	Developing Density, Breast Cancer
5	Pain, Breast Cancer
6	Nipple Discharge, Breast Cancer
7	Architectural Distortion, Breast Cancer, Previous Biopsy
8	Mass Location, Mass
9	Mass Margin, Mass
10	Mass Density, Mass
11	Halo Sign, Mass
12	Mass Size, Mass
13	Palpable Mass, Mass
14	Calcification Shape, Calcification
15	Calcification Number, Calcification
16	Calcification Cluster Shape, Calcification
17	Calcification Density, Calcification
18	Calcification Size, Calcification
19	Calcification Arrangement, Calcification

Table 20. Class clique instantiation examples.

Class Clique	Clique 0	Clique 1	Clique 14
number of node members	5	2	2
unique clique number	0	1	15
root clique Boolean	TRUE	FALSE	FALSE
number of links to cliques	2	12	2
links	null, clique 11	cliques 0, 2, 3, 4, 5, 6, 7, 8, 9, 10, 11, 12, 13, 14	clique 2, null
number of common nodes	1	2	1
member nodes	Breast Cancer, Age, Age of Menarche, Age at First Life Birth, Number of Relatives	Mass, Breast Cancer	Calcification Shape, Calcification
common nodes	Breast Cancer	Breast Cancer, Mass	Calcification
base node	Breast Cancer	Mass	Calcification Shape

Table 20 contains an example of information stored for the root clique (Clique 0), and two non-root cliques (Cliques 1 and 14).

5.1.4.3 Initialization of Bayesian Inference Engine

After the nodes and cliques are created and initialized, the Bayesian network is constructed. For each of its nodes, an initial probability distribution is computed. Nodes without parents (e.g., age, age of menarche, etc.) initially have probability distributions associated with them. Nodes with parents (e.g., breast cancer, mass margin, etc.) initially have conditional probability distributions. A prior probability vector is calculated for each variable in the network. For each conditional table, the product rule computes a joint distribution. Application of the summation rule to the joint distribution produces prior probabilities (unconditional probability) distributions for each variable in the joint distribution. The cliques enforce an ordering in the calculation of the initial prior probabilities. A tree traversal—starting at the root clique and following the left links—of the clique tree is performed, and at each clique the prior probabilities are calculated by applications of the product rule and the summation rule. (Clique traversal order: 0, 1, 2, 12, 13, 14, 15, 16, 17, 18, 19, 3, 4, 5, 6, 7, 8, 9, 10, 11.)

To calculate the initial prior probability distribution for node Calcification, the product rule is applied using the conditional probability distribution associated with node Calcification and the newly computed probability distribution of node Breast Cancer. Node Calcification has three states (malignant, benign, and absent). Node

Breast Cancer has two states (present, absent). Node Calcification is conditioned on Node Breast Cancer:

$$P(\text{Calcification} = c_i \mid \text{Breast Cancer} = b_j), \quad i = 0, 1, 2 \text{ and } j = 0, 1.$$

The conditional distribution {0.2, 0.0, 0.8, 0.0, 0.1, 0.9} for P(Calcification = c_i | Breast Cancer = b_j) and the initially computed prior probability distribution {0.0598131, 0.940187} for P(Breast Cancer = b_j) are element-wise multiplied according to the product rule to produce the joint probability distribution P(Calcification = c_i, Breast Cancer = b_j). Application of the summation rule to the joint probability distribution, sums out the initial prior probability distributions for nodes Calcification and Breast Cancer. The calculations for the initial probability distribution of node Calcification {0.0119626, 0.0940187, 0.894019} are detailed in Tables 21 and 22. Table 23 shows the summation rule applied to the joint table to extract the prior probability distribution of node breast cancer.

Before presenting any evidence, the probability of breast cancer calculated by *MammoNet* is 0.0598131. Introducing a single piece of evidence, for instance a mass margin that is spiculated, raises the probability of breast cancer to 0.99193. A mass margin which is spiculated is a feature of a mass which is malignant, and a malignant mass is caused by breast cancer. The following illustrates how a piece of evidence propagates through the network.

Table 21. Calculation of joint probability distribution by product rule:
P(Calcification = c_i | Breast Cancer = b_j) • P(Breast Cancer=b_j) =
= P(Calcifiction=c_i, Breast Cancer=b_j).

Calcification = state$_i$	Breast Cancer = state$_j$	Breast Cancer = state$_j$	Product Rule Calculation
Malignant	Present	Present	0.2 • 0.0598131 = 0.0119626
Malignant	Absent	Absent	0.0 • 0.940187 = 0.0
Benign	Present	Present	0.0 • 0.0598131 = 0.0
Benign	Absent	Absent	0.1 • 0.0940187 = 0.0940187
Absent	Present	Present	0.8 • 0.0598131 = 0.0478505
Absent	Absent	Absent	0.9 • 0.940187 = 0.846168

Table 22. Calculation of prior probability distribution of node calcification using summation rule.

Calcification = state$_i$,	Breast Cancer = state$_j$	Joint Probability Value	ΣP(Calcification = c$_i$, Breast Cancer = b$_j$)
Malignant	Present	0.0119626	0.0119626 0.0000000 +
Malignant	Absent	0.0000000	0.0119626
Benign	Present	0.0000000	0.0000000 0.0940187 +
Benign	Absent	0.0940187	0.0940187
Absent	Present	0.0478505	0.0478505 0.846168 +
Absent	Absent	0.846168	0.894019

Table 23. Calculation of prior probability distribution of node breast cancer using summation rule.

Calcification = state$_i$,	Breast Cancer = state$_j$	Joint Probability Value	ΣP(Calcification = c$_i$, Breast Cancer = b$_j$)
Malignant	Present	0.0119626	0.0119626 0.0 0.0478505 +
Benign	Present	0.0	
Absent	Present	0.0478505	0.0598131
Malignant	Absent	0.0	0.0 0.0940187 0.846168 +
Benign	Absent	0.0940187	
Absent	Absent	0.8461680	0.940187

A piece of evidence entered into the network by the user causes the prior probability of the corresponding node to be set such that one state becomes certain (set to 1) and the other states become impossible (set to 0). The node representing mass margin contains four states spiculated, irregular, rwdefined and Not Applicable. The prior probability vector associated with node mass margin changes from (0.00981001, 0.0116527, 0.0962701, 0.882267) to (1, 0, 0, 0).

As node mass margin is a member of clique 9, which contains the joint probability distribution for P(mass margin = s$_i$, mass = s$_j$) where i = 0,1,2,3 and j = 0,1,2, this table is updated using the inversion formula. From the updated table, the summation rule is used to compute new prior probability distributions for member nodes.

In Table 24, the joint probability distribution is element-wise multiplied by the prior probability vector for node mass margin with state spiculated set to 1.

Table 24. Multiply joint probability distribution by prior probability vector of mass margin = spiculated: $P(\text{Mass} = c_i, \text{Mass Margin} = b_j) \bullet P(\text{Mass Margin} = b_j)$.

Mass = state$_i$,	Mass Margin = state$_j$	Mass Margin = state$_j$	Multiplication Calculation
Malignant	Spiculated	Spiculated	$0.00971364 \bullet 1.0 = 0.00971364$
Benign	Spiculated	Spiculated	$9.40187e\text{-}05 \bullet 1.0 = 9.40187e\text{-}05$
Absent	Spiculated	Spiculated	$0.00000000 \bullet 1.0 = 0.0$
Malignant	Irregular	Irregular	$0.0115559 \bullet 0.0 = 0.0$
Benign	Irregular	Irregular	$9.40187e\text{-}05 \bullet 0.0 = 0.0$
Absent	Irregular	Irregular	$0.00000000 \bullet 0.0 = 0.0$
Malignant	RW-defined	RW-defined	$0.00241645 \bullet 0.0 = 0.0$
Benign	RW-defined	RW-defined	$0.09383070 \bullet 0.0 = 0.0$
Absent	RW-defined	RW-defined	$0.00000000 \bullet 0.0 = 0.0$
Malignant	Not applicable	Not applicable	$0.00000000 \bullet 0.0 = 0.0$
Benign	Not applicable	Not applicable	$0.0\ 000000 \bullet 0.0 = 0.0$
Absent	Not applicable	Not applicable	$0.8820560 \bullet 0.0 = 0.0$

Then, this result is divided by the prior probability of node mass margin, before it received evidence. See Table 25.

The final step is to perform the summation rule to extract the prior probability distributions for the members of the clique that was updated. Since node mass margin is no longer uncertain, node mass is the only clique member to have its updated prior probability computed.

The values in Table 26 are normalized and the newly updated prior probability distribution for node mass is (0.990414, 0.00958625, 0). Compare this to node mass's prior probability distribution before the evidence was applied, (0.0239252, 0.0940187, 0.882056). The piece of evidence, mass margin is spiculated, greatly increases the probability that the mass is malignant.

Table 25. Divide modified joint probability distribution by prior probability vector of mass margin: $P(\text{Mass} = c_i, \text{Mass Margin} = b_j) / P(\text{Mass Margin} = b_j)$.

Mass = state$_i$,	Mass Margin = state$_j$	Mass Margin = state$_j$	Division Calculation
Malignant	Spiculated	Spiculated	0.00971364 / 0.00981001 = 0.990177
Benign	Spiculated	Spiculated	9.40187e-05 / 0.00981001 = 0.00958395
Absent	Spiculated	Spiculated	0.000000 / 0.00981001 = 0.0
Malignant	Irregular	Irregular	0.000000 / 0.0116527 = 0.0
Benign	Irregular	Irregular	0.000000 / 0.0116527 = 0.0
Absent	Irregular	Irregular	0.000000 / 0.0116527 = 0.0
Malignant	RW-defined	RW-defined	0.000000 / 0.0962701 = 0.0
Benign	RW-defined	RW-defined	0.000000 / 0.0962701 = 0.0
Absent	RW-defined	RW-defined	0.000000 / 0.0962701 = 0.0
Malignant	Not applicable	Not applicable	0.000000 / 0.882267 = 0.0
Benign	Not applicable	Not applicable	0.000000 / 0.882267 = 0.0
Absent	Not applicable	Not applicable	0.000000 / 0.882267 = 0.0

Table 26. Summation rule to extract prior probability vector for node mass.

Mass = state$_i$,	Mass Margin = state$_j$	Joint Probability Value	$\Sigma P(\text{Mass} = c_i, \text{Mass Margin} = b_j)$
Malignant	Spiculated	0.990177	0.990177
Malignant	Irregular	0.0	0.0
Malignant	RW-defined	0.0	0.0
Malignant	Not Applicable	0.0	0.0 +
			0.990177
Benign	Spiculated	0.00958395	0.00958395
Benign	Irregular	0.0	0.0
Benign	RW-defined	0.0	0.0
Benign	Not Applicable	0.0	0.0 +
			0.00958395
Absent	Spiculated	0.0	0.0
Absent	Irregular	0.0	0.0
Absent	RW-defined	0.0	0.0
Absent	Not Applicable	0.0	0.0 +
			0.0

The remainder of the network is updated in a similar fashion. The order of the clique updates is determined by the node link. Clique 1 is updated next. Cliques 0, 2, 12, 13, 14, 15, 16, 17, 18, 3, 4, 5, 6, 7, 8, 10, 11, and 12 are then updated and new prior probability distributions calculated. Each piece of additional evidence is propagated through the network as described above. Suppose our patient was a 74-year old woman, with a RA-located mass with margins that are spiculated and a density classified as high density. *MammoNet* computes a final probability distribution for the hypothesis node, breast cancer. It changes from the original distribution (0.0598131, 0.940187) to (0.99892, 0.00108), with all pieces of evidences propagated. Refer to Table 27.

Table 27. Comparison of prior probability distribution of breast cancer before and after evidence.

	P(Breast Cancer = Present)	P(Breast Cancer = Absent)
Before Evidence	0.0598131	0.940187
After Evidence	0.99892	0.00108

6   Results

To test *MammoNet*, we encoded 67 cases from a mammography atlas [29] and 10 cases from a clinical teaching file. Each case included clinical data, the mammographic findings, the expert mammographer's diagnosis, and the histological diagnosis based on clinical follow-up and/or biopsy results. The atlas provided a set of relatively straightforward cases; the clinical teaching file contained cases considered diagnostically challenging. Of the 77 cases, 25 were positive for breast cancer. Table 28 offers a sampling of our test cases.

MammoNet computed the posterior probability of breast cancer given each case's constellation of demographic, clinical, and mammographic features. For example, case #32 from the atlas described a known malignancy in a 65-year-old woman with an irregular, low-density mass, no halo sign, and no calcifications; *MammoNet* calculated a probability of breast cancer of 99.6%.

Analysis using the LABROC1 program [20] yielded an estimated area under the receiver operating characteristic (ROC) curve of 0.881 ±0.045 (Figure 11). Sensitivity and specificity relate to the indices "true positive fraction" and the "false positive fraction" and measure the accuracy of a diagnostic test based on some arbitrarily selected decision threshold. The ROC curve is an empirical description of this threshold. The true positive and false positive decisions are used for plotting the ordinate and abscissa, respectively of the ROC curves.

Table 28. *MammoNet* text cases.

Physical Exam	Mammo-graphy Analysis	Radiologist's Analysis	Histology	*MammoNet* Coding	*Mammo-Net*'s Result
age 65	no halo sign mass circumscribed irregular low density	"though the circumscribed tumor is low density, it is irregular and there is no halo sign"	mucinous carcinoma with no axillary metastases	Age = 65-69 MassMargin = irregular HaloSign = absent MassDensity: = LowDensity Calcification = none	Breast Cancer = Present at 99.6017%
age 74 menarche at age13 first pregnancy at age 29	LI quadrant, lobulated mass, asymmetric density, few scattered punctate calcifications	"if biopsy is not performed, follow-up mammogram is suggested in 6 months: possible breast disease"	atypical epithelial hyperplasis	Age = 70-74 AgeofFLB = 25-29 AgeMenarche = 12-13 Asymmetry = present MassLoct = LI MassMargin = Rwdefined Calc arrangement = scattered CalcShape = round	Breast Cancer = Absent at 1.0 absent
age 50 menarche at age 13 first pregnancy at age 25 no family history	solid mass UI quadrant no calcifications well-defined margin skin unremarkable no malignant characteristics	benign-appearing mass on ultrasound appears solid. needle or open biopsy suggested	breast biopsy fibroadenoma fibrocystic disease	Age = 50-54 AgeofFLB = 25-29 AgeMenarche = 12-13 MassMargin = rwdefined Calcification = none MassLoct = UI	Breast Cancer = Absent at 0.0020074887 Present 0.9979925112 absent
age 52	small tumor UO quadrant sharply outlined, low density	probably benign	benign	Age = 50-54 MassMargin = rwdefined MassLoct = UO MassDensity: = LowDensity	Breast Cancer = Absent at 1- 0.00195%

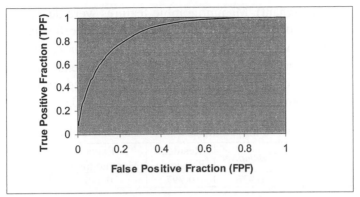

Figure 11. Receiver operating characteristic (ROC) curve for *MammoNet*.

At a probability threshold for breast cancer of 15% (which approximates the positive predictive value of mammographic suspicion), *MammoNet* correctly identified 23 of the 25 actually positive cases (sensitivity, 92.0%; 95% confidence interval [CI], 75.0% to 97.8%). *MammoNet*'s specificity at this threshold was 88.5% (95% CI, 77.0% to 94.6%). Three benign lesions that *MammoNet* falsely identified as positive were considered suspicious by the mammographers and were referred for biopsy.

MammoNet compares favorably in a comparison with a neural net in an evaluation of radiologists with varying levels of expertise reviewing mammograms at ACR-accredited mammography sites. The mammograms were selected from Tabar's *Teaching Atlas of Mammography*. Table 29 shows the ROC curve of *MammoNet*, a neural network, and varying levels of physicians.

Table 29. Statistics on the performance of radiologists and computer-aided tools in evaluating mammograms.

Model	*MammoNet*	Neural Net	Resident Physician	Attending Physician	Expert Mammographer
Az Value	0.881	0.89	0.80	0.84	0.845

In addition, *MammoNet* was evaluated in a clinical test at the Medical College of Wisconsin. Mammograms of 58 diagnostically challenging cases with known biopsy results (27 malignant) were presented with relevant clinical data. *MammoNet*, three experienced mammographers, and six radiology residents rated each case from 0 (definitely benign) to

100 (definitely malignant). Mammographic features were described for *MammoNet* by one of the authors. ROC analysis was performed. Area under the ROC curve (Az) was 0.926 ±0.03 for *MammoNet*, 0.840 ±0.04 for mammographers, and 0.771 ±0.04 for residents (see Table 30). At any value of sensitivity, *MammoNet* achieved significantly better specificity than experienced mammographers (P<0.01).

Table 30. Statistics on the performance of *MammoNet* and physicians.

Model	*MammoNet*	Resident Physician	Expert Mammographer
Az Value	0.926	0.797	0.840

In conclusion, computer-aided tools such as *MammoNet* can exceed human observers in integrating clinical and mammographic features for the diagnosis of breast cancer. The improved specificity could help reduce the number of patients unnecessarily referred to biopsy.

7   Conclusion

Bayesian networks represent a promising technique for clinical decision support and provide a number of powerful capabilities for representing uncertain knowledge. They provide a flexible representation that allows one to specify dependence and independence of variables in a natural way through the network topology. Because dependencies are expressed qualitatively as links between nodes, one can structure the domain knowledge qualitatively before any numeric probabilities need be assigned. The graphical representation also makes explicit the structure of the domain model: a link indicates a causal relation or known association. The encoding of independencies in the network topology admits the design of efficient procedures for performing computations over the network. A further advantage of the graphical representation is the perspicuity of the resulting domain model. Finally, since Bayesian networks represent uncertainty using standard probability, one can collect the necessary data for the domain model by drawing directly on published statistical studies.

MammoNet's performance—as measured by its area under the ROC curve (A_z)—compares very favorably with that of artificial neural network (ANN) models and expert mammographers. An ANN with 14 input features achieved an A_z value of 0.89 (vs. 0.84 for attending radiologists) [33] on cases from the same mammography atlas as used in this study [29]. ANNs learn directly from observations, but cannot meaningfully explain their decisions. Their knowledge consists of an "impenetrable thicket" of numerical connection values. The ability of Bayesian networks to explain their reasoning [16], [17] in an important advantage over ANNs; physicians generally will not accept and act on a computer system's advice without knowing the basis for the system's decision.

This design attempts to open Bayesian networks to a wider audience of users by providing an interactive multimodal explanation system. This asserts that the system participants, the user and the software, are able to carryon an ongoing dialog in which both participants are able to question, state about, and explain their actions and concerns. The system additionally is designed to be usable by two levels of users, a user who is concerned about the underlying structure of the model (i.e., a physician) and a user who is concerned with why a system is reaching a certain conclusion (i.e., a patient).

Another computer-assisted decision aid for mammographic interpretation included a checklist of 12 features determined to have particular diagnostic value [6]. Given a quantitative assessment of the 12 features, the decision aid estimated the probability of malignancy using weighting factors obtained from discriminant analysis. ROC analysis of this model showed a gain of about 0.05 in sensitivity or specificity when the other value remained constant at 0.85.

The ongoing refinement of *MammoNet* includes adding variables and states to the mode, acquiring conditional-probability data from large case series, and rigorous testing and evaluation. We are considering the addition of demographic features such as race and geographic location, and patient-history features such as diet, body habitus, history of hormone therapy, and previous cancers. The granularity of the model's variables could be increased by partitioning the Breast Cancer node into more than the current two states to represent the numerous types of cancer and benign conditions. We are developing links between *MammoNet* and a database to allow collection and analysis of a large set of clinical cases. Our goal is to create a decision support tool to improve the diagnostic accuracy and cost-effectiveness of screening mammography. Such a decision aid must be reliable, integrated with a clinical database and reporting system, and able to generate explanations to the physicians who use it.

Acknowledgments

We thank Nancy Louise Vasy-Dal Besio (1953-1998) who provided the inspiration for this work. She worked the hardest of us all. We thank Peter Haddawy and Charles E. Kahn, Jr., M.D. for the support and encouragement. We also thank Robert Krieger and Katherine A. Shaffer, M.D. for many helpful discussions and Olvi Mangasarian for the breast cancer information. A heartfelt "thank you" to Kun Wang who diligently helped calculate probabilities, enter data, and test the network. Thank you to Melinda Ruth Roberts who kept the fire of interest burning. We thank Charles E. Metz, Ph.D., for use of the LABROC software. This work was facilitated by a grant from the National Institutes of Health (USPHS G08 LM05705) to the Medical College of Wisconsin for Integrated Advanced Information Management Systems (IAIMS) planning.

References

[1] Albertyn, L.E. (1991), "Mammographically indeterminate micro-calcifications – can we do better?" *Australian Radiology*, vol. 35, no. 4, pp. 350-357.

[2] Andreassen, S., Jensen, F.V., and Olesen, K.G. (1991), "Medical expert systems based on causal probabilistic networks," *International Journal of Biomedical Computing*, vol. 28, pp. 1-30.

[3] Bassett, L.W. (1992), "Mammographic analysis of calcifications," *Radiologic Clinics of North America*, vol. 30, pp. 93-105.

[4] Colditz, G.A. (1993), "Family history, age, and risk of breast cancer prospective data, from the nurses' health study," *JAMA*, vol. 270, pp. 338-343.

[5] D'Orsi, C.J. and Kopans, D.B. (1993), "Mammographic feature analysis," *Sem Roentgenol*, vol. 28, pp. 204-230.

[6] D'Orsi, C., et al. (1992), "Reading and decision aide for improved accuracy and standardization of mammographic diagnosis," *Radiology*, vol. 184, pp. 619-622.

[7] Egan, R.L., *et al.* (1980), "Intramammary calcifications without an associated mass in benign and malignant diseases," *Radiology*, vol. 137, pp. 1-7.

[8] Feig, S.A. (1988), "Decreased cancer mortality through mammographic screening: results of clinical trials," *Radiology*, vol. 167, pp. 659-665.

[9] Feig, S.A. (1992), "Breast masses, mammographic and sonographic evaluation," *Radiologic Clinics of North America*, vol. 30, pp. 67-92.

[10] Gail, M.H., *et al.* (1989), "Projecting individualized probabilities of developing breast cancer for white females who are being examined annually," *ARTICLES*, vol. 81, pp. 1879-1886.

[11] Getty, D.J., Pickett, R.M., D'Orsi, C.J., and Swets, J.A. (1988), "Enhanced interpretation of diagnostic images," *Investigative Radiology*, vol. 23, pp. 240-252.

[12] Haddawy, P., Kahn Jr., C.E., and Butarbutar, M. (1994), "A bayesian network model for radiological diagnosis and procedure selection: work-up of suspected gallbladder disease," *Medical Physics*, vol. 21, pp. 1185-1192.

[13] Haddawy, P. and Krieger, R.A. (1995), "Principled construction of minimal bayesian networks from probability logic knowledge bases," *J Artif Intel Res*: (under review).

[14] Haddawy, P. (1994), "Generating Bayesian networks from probability logic knowledge bases," *Uncertainty in Artificial Intelligence:Proceedings of the Tenth Conference* San Mateo, CA., pp. 262-269.

[15] Hall, F.M., Storella, J.M., Silverstone, D.Z., and Wyshak, G. (1988), "Nonpalpable breast lesions: recommendations for biopsy based on suspicion of carcinoma at mammography," *Radiology*, vol. 167, pp. 353-358.

[16] Heathfield, H.A., *et al.* (1990), "Computer assisted diagnosis of fine needle aspirate," *Journal of Clinical Pathology*, vol. 43, pp. 168-170.

[17] Heathfield, H.A., *et al.* (1991), "Knowledge-based computer system to aid in the histopathological diagnosis of breast cancer," *Journal of Clinical Pathology*, vol. 44, pp. 502-508.

[18] Jackson, V.P., *et al.* (1991), "Diagnostic importance of the radiographic density of noncalcified breast masses: analysis of 91 lesions," *American Journal of Roentgenology*, vol. 157, pp. 25-28.

[19] Jensen, F. (1996), *Introduction to Bayesian Networks*, New York, SpringerVerlag Inc.

[20] Metz, C.E. (1978), "Basic principles of ROC analysis," *Seminars in Nuclear Medicine*, vol. 4, pp. 283-298.

[21] Muir, B.B., *et al.* (1983), "Microcalcification and its relationship to cancer of the breast: experience in a screening clinic," *Clinical Radiology*, vol. 34, pp. 193-200.

[22] Pearl, J. (1988), *Probabilistic Reasoning in Intelligent Systems: Networks of Plausible Inference*, CA: Morgan Kaufmann Publishers.

[23] Sickles, E.A. (1981), "Mammograph of the postsurgical breast," *American Journal of Roentgenolog*, vol. 136, pp. 584-588.

[24] Sickles, E.A. (1986), "Mammographic features of 300 consecutive nonpalpable breast cancers," *American Journal of Roentgenology*, vol. 146, pp. 661-663.

[25] Sickles, E.A. (1986), "Breast calcifications: mammographic evaluation," *Radiology*, vol. 160, pp. 289-293.

[26] Srinivas, S. and Breese, J. (1995), "IDEAL: a software package for analysis of influence diagrams," *Proceedings of the Sixth Conference on Uncertainty in Artificial Intelligence*, pp. 212-219.

[27] Swann, C.A. *et al.*, (1987), "The halo sign and malignant breast lesion," *American Journal of Roentgenology*, vol. 149, pp. 1145-1147.

[28] Symmonds, R.E., *et al.* (1987), "Management of nonpalpable breast abnormalities," *Annals of Surgery*, vol. 205, pp. 520-528.

[29] Tabar, L. and Dean, P.B. (1985), *Teaching Atlas of Mammography*. New York: Theime-Stratton.

[30] Teach, R. and Shortliffe, E. (1984), *Rule-based Expert Systems: The MYCIN Experiments of the Stanford Heuristic Programming Project*, Massachusetts: Addison-Wesley.

[31] Tombropoulos, R., Shiffman, S., and Davidson, C. (1993), "A decision aid for diagnosis of liver lesions on MRI," *Proceedings of the 17th Annual Symposium of Computer Applications in Medical Care*, pp. 439-443.

[32] Wingo, P.A., Tong, T., and Bolden, S. (1995), "Cancer statistics," *Ca Cancer J Clin*, vol. 45, pp. 8-30.

[33] Wu, Y. *et al.* (1993), "Artificial neural networks in mammography: application to decision making in the diagnosis of breast cancer," *Radiology*, vol. 187, pp. 81-87.

Chapter 5

Predicting Prognosis and Treatment Response in Breast Cancer Patients

M.G. Daidone and **D. Coradini**

In clinical breast cancer, the contribution of biological variables to segregate patients into low- and high-risk subsets and, more recently, to identify tumors susceptible or resistant to clinical treatments has been extensively investigated. Steroid hormone receptors and tumor proliferative activity represent biofunctional markers able to identify patients destined to develop specific relapse types and responsive to specific treatments, in terms of type of drugs and/or scheduling. Despite the most widely diffuse use of an "*a priori* assessed" single cut-point to define slowly or rapidly proliferating as well as receptor-positive or negative tumors, the recent availability of statistical approaches able to investigate the relation between quantitative biomarkers and prognosis or clinical outcome following specific treatments proved to significantly contribute to understanding the biological complexity of clinical breast cancer by using all the prognostic and predictive information obtained from the variables under investigation. In the near future, the use of flexible regression techniques in survival analysis and of measurements of the predictive ability of the variables under investigation will favor an optimal use of the information derived from translational studies. These powerful statistical tools, together with the development of guidelines for designing, conducting, analyzing and reporting biomarker studies and with the increasing attitude to include the measurement of biofunctional markers in clinical protocols, will provide valuable means to state the clinical impact of biological markers and to help clinicians in patient management and treatment decision making.

1   Introduction

In the last two decades, the object of translational studies in breast cancer has been the search for markers to be used as a complement to clinico-pathologic staging in order to identify patients destined to relapse or progress independent of treatment, and to predict those likely to respond or to develop resistance to a specific treatment [1]. The contribution of factors related to functional aspects of the cells, such as hormone and growth factor receptors, cell proliferation, invasiveness or angiogenic properties, DNA ploidy and alterations or deregulation of oncogenes and tumor-suppressor genes, has been defined for the identification of patients at high risk of relapse (who need aggressive, systemic treatments) and of patients with an indolent disease (who are potentially curable by local-regional treatment alone) [2]. However, following an initial emphasis on reducing the gap from the bench to the bedside with the clinical application of laboratory research, a growing skepticism regarding the actual usefulness of biological markers led to a progressive reduction of their use in clinical practice. Such a finding, in addition to the lack of methodological issues regarding evaluation of the clinical utility and criteria for the design of studies to assess the prognostic or predictive significance of biomarkers, has produced varied results and widely differing conclusions from individual studies. Recently, interest in biomarkers has been renewed, and biomarker determination is now foreseen within clinical treatment protocols: (1) to biologically characterize individual patient tumors, for an appropriate tailored therapeutic approach; (2) to provide intermediate end points to quickly differentiate responders from non-responders to conventional treatments (i.e., neoadjuvant therapy, by measuring early changes induced in biological profiles); (3) to possibly detect the presence of biological targets of innovative treatments, such as those employing anti-angiogenic agents.

Twenty-five years after the introduction of the first biological marker in clinical management of human breast cancer (estrogen receptor, ER, initially considered as an indicator of endocrine responsiveness, then as a predictor for early recurrence), recent interest in assessing the clinical impact of prognostic and predictive biological markers has emphasized the need for guidelines for an appropriate and standardized use [1] as well as for designing, conducting, analyzing and reporting biomarker studies [3]-[5]. In the latter area of guidelines, a critical problem is represented by the optimal modeling of the information provided by putative prognostic variables, as well as by the measurement scale of biomarkers, determining both the quantity and the quality of clinically relevant information. The application of regression modeling techniques (which can interpolate mathematical functions with complex shapes) in survival analysis [6] and the availability of substantial case series of patients with biologically characterized breast cancer, homogeneous for pathologic stage and clinical treatment and with a long-term follow-up, have allowed us to thoroughly investigate the functional and time-dependent relationship between the risk of unfavorable events and biological variables. In the present chapter, we will mainly present results from our studies in which we tried to extrapolate the biological complexity of breast cancer from the information provided by quantitative biomarkers by applying flexible statistical models.

2   Patients and Methods

Our laboratory has been involved since 1974 in the determination of tumor proliferative activity (evaluated as the fraction of cells in the S-phase which incorporates ^{3}H-thymidine, and quantified by the ^{3}H-thymidine labeling index, TLI) and steroid hormone receptor status (evaluated using the dextran-coated charcoal technique) on tumor specimens from breast cancer patients undergoing surgery at the Istituto Nazionale per lo Studio e la Cura dei Tumori of Milan (INT). At present, the availability of unique resources, such as a biological database with cell kinetic characterization for more than 13,000 breast cancers, hormone receptor status and content for about 30,000 specimens, tumor banks from paraffin-embedded specimens (more than 10,000 cases), frozen cytosols and nuclei pellets (about 5,000 cases) from women who underwent local-regional and systemic treatments at our Institute, and of an updated database of clinico-pathologic findings has allowed us to integrate biological information with clinically useful prognostic indices using different statistical techniques. All the studies have been possible for the close collaboration with the Surgical, Pathology, Medical Oncology and Radiotherapy Departments, and with the Unit of Biostatistics.

2.1 Case Series

The case population entering the present overview consisted of 3,535 women with unilateral primary resectable breast cancer, and no radiologic or clinical evidence of distant metastasis, who underwent radical or conservative surgery plus radiotherapy and lymph node axillary dissection followed by histological assessment at INT during the period 1974 to 1992. All the patients had no previous diagnosis of carcinoma (except basal cell carcinoma of the skin and stage I cervical cancer) and were followed and/or received local or systemic treatments in the outpatient clinic, in the Medical Oncology or in the Radiotherapy Departments of our Institute. Information on their follow-up (generally longer than 1 year, with a median duration of 10 years) was available in patient records.

In particular, the series under investigation included:
- 3000 women with histologically node-negative primary cancer who received no systemic postoperative therapy until new disease manifestation was documented. The patients entered three partially overlapping studies, in which the prognostic role of cell proliferation, p53 expression and steroid receptors was analyzed on the different unfavorable events;
- 250 postmenopausal women with histologically node-positive primary cancer who received different postoperative adjuvant treatments (tamoxifen or cyclophosphamide, methotrexate and 5-fluorouracil (CMF));
- 285 women with histologically node-positive primary cancer who entered a prospective randomized clinical trial comparing sequential or alternating doxorubicin and CMF regimens [7].

2.2 Laboratory Determinations

Immediately after surgery, part of the tumor material was incubated with [^{3}H]thymidine and then processed for conventional histoautoradiographic procedures for the determination of TLI [8] and p53 expression [9]. The rest of the tumor material was frozen in liquid nitrogen and stored at -80°C for estrogen (ER) and progesterone receptor (PgR) determination [10]. The determination of proliferation index and steroid receptors was performed within National Quality Control Programs [8], [11].

2.3 Clinico-Biological Database

Identification of patients eligible for translational studies is a two-step process that involves the tumor tissue banks (frozen and paraffin-embedded) and the clinico-biological database. In the tumor bank database, for each tumor specimen that reaches the laboratory the following information is recorded: laboratory code number, hospital record number, date of surgery, type of tissue, fixation procedure, results of the biological characterization (including, among the several markers under investigation, TLI [as the percentage of ^{3}H-thymidine–labeled cells], ER and PgR content [in terms of fmol/mg cytosolic protein], p53 expression [as the percentage of immunoreactive cells]), the amount of remaining tissue (frozen, paraffin-embedded), cytosol and nuclear pellet. In the clinico-biological database, a limited amount of information, besides laboratory code number and hospital record number, described the patient (age and menopausal status), tumor (pTNM, number of positive nodes, number of examined nodes, histology, histologic grade, type and site of the lesion), local-regional treatment (date and type of surgery, radicality, radiotherapy), systemic treatment (type of chemotherapy regimen, type and duration of hormonal treatment, combined treatments), and follow-up (date and type of the first adverse event [local, regional, distant, contralateral, secondary malignancy], location, treatment, type of the second adverse event, survival status, date of the last contact or of death, and cause of death).

2.4 Statistical Approaches

TLI, ER and PgR contents and p53 expression were generally considered on a continuous scale. Since ER and PgR distributions were markedly positively skewed, a natural logarithmic transformation was adopted. To avoid the problem of 0 value in receptor determinations, all values under the detection limit of the assay (2 fmol/mg of cytosolic protein) were arbitrarily considered as 1. The role of each prognostic variable (univariate analysis) and their joint effect (multivariate analysis) were investigated by the Cox multiple regression model.

A flexible model technique based on restricted cubic splines [12], [13] was adopted to study the relationship between the variables and the logarithm of the hazard of unfavorable events. A cubic spline function is a smoothly joined piecewise polynomial of degree three. Smoothly joined means that the function and its first two derivatives are constrained to be continuous at the junction points (knots). The spline functions constrained to be linear in the tails are called restricted. The approach allows quantitative data to be fitted by the Cox regression model without assuming a log-linear prognostic relationship [6]. The most complex model tested was a 4-knot spline. Since the shape of the spline is generally insensitive to the location of the knots, we placed them at the values corresponding to the 5%, 50%, 75% and 95% percentiles of the frequency distribution of the biomarker under investigation. A full model with a 4-knot restricted spline function is given by the sum of three terms: the linear term and two cubic transformations of the variable. Models with less than three terms (4-knot splines without the linear term, 3-knot splines with and without the linear term, and the linear term only) were also fitted. However, models with the same number of knots but with a different knot location could not be hierarchical owing to the linearity constraints. To compare them and identify the most appropriate, an information criterion proposed by Akaike (Akaike Information Criterion, AIC) was used [14]. The model identified by such criteria represents the best compromise between the minimization of the error over the training data and the degree of complexity, represented by the number of estimated parameters. Moreover, since the spline functions were linear in the regression coefficients, standard methods of inference (likelihood ratio test) were used to test the significance of the contribution of each variable or of the biologically relevant interaction terms. P values of less than 0.05 were considered statistically significant. Even though the spline approach is flexible, it has the disadvantage that the corresponding regression coefficients are not easily interpreted. From a clinical viewpoint, the information provided by a spline function requires a graphic representation of the prognostic relationship. A graphic representation of such an approach is reported in Section 5.1.

The predictive capability of regression models was measured by Harrell's c statistic [13]. The statistic, which is a generalization of the area under the receiver operating characteristic (ROC) curve for censored data, can assume values ranging between 0.5 and 1.00. If the model has no predictive ability (i.e., the variables are not useful discriminators for the outcome), the statistic c is expected to be 0.5, whereas it tends to be 1.00 in the case of a high prognostic ability. The contribution of each variable to the predictive ability of the model was investigated by computing the c statistic on the model without the variable itself. In order to aid clinical interpretation, we suggested that a value of 0.6 to 0.7 be considered a weak predictor, a value of 0.71 to 0.8 a satisfactory predictor, and a value greater than 0.8 a good predictor. To help interpretation of the multivariate model results, we have provided, for selected values of continuous predictors, the estimates of the hazard ratio (HR) of relapse and the corresponding confidence intervals calculated by the coefficients of the regression model.

When the time-dependent relevance of variables was investigated, time-dependent covariates were included in the Cox regression model, and nonproportional effects were modeled in a flexible way as the product of the restricted cubic spline of time and the pertinent terms of the considered variables [15]. HRs were plotted as a function of covariate values and time.

For the identification of distinct prognostic subgroups for adverse events, recursive partition and amalgamation analyses were used [16], and graphic representations of such an approach are reported in Section 4.3. The analysis began on the whole sample, and the best split into two groups for any variable was determined by the likelihood ratio test based on the Cox model. Each subgroup was further split into two, until a minimum size (50 patients and 15 events) was reached. Then, a subtree was chosen by pruning the large tree, i.e., by discarding branches that contained negligible information on relative hazards. The final tree contained terminal nodes (some of which may have similar event-free survival rates), which were then combined to form the final prognostic subgroups. The HR for each subgroup was estimated by the Cox proportional hazard regression model that considered the best-prognosis group as a reference.

3   Continuous versus Categorical Biological Variables

In the last two decades, the use of traditional clinical prognostic factors, measured or considered in most cases on a qualitative basis (histologic type, pathologic stage, axillary lymph node involvement), has been complemented by an increasing number of biological variables, measured in tumor tissue by means of quantitative analytical techniques (i.e., protein levels quantified, according to the determination method, as fmol/mg cytosolic protein if detected by binding assays, or as fraction of immunoreactive cells if detected by immunocytochemistry, etc.). Notwithstanding the frequent availability of biological information whose experimental values are expressed on a continuous scale, the dichotomization of such measurements into two subsets (high versus low, or positive versus negative) on the basis of a threshold value is a frequently used approach. However, such a dichotomization, which is artificial and often unnecessary, often discards potentially important quantitative information, thus reducing the power to detect a real association with tumor progression and clinical end points [6].

A common strategy for analyzing the clinical predictivity of a continuous variable is to convert it into a categorical variable by grouping patients mainly into two or more subsets. Different criteria, based on retrospective or prospective approaches, have been used to categorize continuous variables (Table 1). Among the former approaches, the search of the "best cutoff" became very popular in the last few years. Such an approach, called the "minimal P value approach" since it relies on the selection of the cut-point which minimizes the P value relating the biological factor to clinical outcome, enhances the separation between subsets at different prognosis and is based on the computation of the statistical significance level for all the possible cut-points.

Although the approach shares with other approaches using a single cut-point the advantage of an easy interpretation of results and use of multivariate methods, there are several problems associated with it [16] (including biased estimates of P values, survival curves, etc.) due to data overfitting. In addition, it is markedly data-dependent, does not allow inference about the population of breast cancer patients, and implies a possible loss of information on the relation between the biological variable and clinical outcome (in terms of prognosis and treatment response). Notwithstanding the possibility of P value adjustment for multiple testing, the false positive (type I) error rate associated with the procedure is markedly higher than the nominal 5%.

Table 1. Categorizing continuous variables.

Criterion	Cut-point(s)	Pro	Contra
Retrospective	Best cutoff	Interpretation of results	Data dependency
		Multivariate analysis	False-positive error rate
			Loss of information
Prospective	Mean, median	Interpretation of results	Assumption of linearity
		Multivariate analysis	Loss of information
	Percentiles	Retained information	Interpretation of results
		Nonlinear trends	Multivariate analysis
		Intra- and inter-groups comparison of results	

The prospective utilization of cut-points defined on the frequency distribution of the biomarker, assessed on an independent data set and generally corresponding to mean or median values was an approach frequently used in the past, with fewer biases compared to the minimal P value approach. However, besides the likely loss of prognostic or predictive information, it implies assumptions of linearity between the marker and the risk of unfavorable events, which are not always proven, and of an *a priori* attribution of high risk of unfavorable events to about 50% of the cases.

Finally, the use of multiple cut-points, prospectively defined on the basis of the percentiles of the frequency distribution of the biomarker, is preferable since it retains most information on clinical outcome and allows the detection of nonlinear trends in the prognostic or predictive relationship. In addition, it allows comparison of results with those obtained in the same laboratory on successive, independent case series, or reported by other authors in the literature. However, interpretation of results and the use of multivariate models are sometimes difficult when using the approach, which represents a compromise between dichotomizing data or treating them on a continuous scale.

4   Biomarkers and Prediction of Prognosis

Since the late 1970s, when the identification of ER and PgR as biological markers associated with breast cancer progression and susceptibility to hormonal treatment induced clinicians to use laboratory information to complement clinicopathologic features for patient management, a number of markers associated with specific cellular functions (such as proliferation, apoptosis, invasion, metastasis and tumor vascularization) have been proposed, assessed and validated as prognostic factors. In theory, minimal guidelines for a prognostic assessment of biomarkers before their routine use for clinical decision making should include [18]:

1) a methodological validation of the assay(s), which should be standardized and reproducible within and among laboratories, relatively cheap and available when needed to help in patient management;
2) pilot studies to identify the clinical end points on which the biomarker is able to provide specific information;
3) confirmatory studies, performed to validate the clinical impact of a biomarker on independent internal or external case series, in which the reproducibility of continuous or categorical values associated with favorable or unfavorable clinical outcome is assessed and the prognostic contribution in multivariate analyses, in the presence of previously validated prognostic markers, is defined;
4) an assessment of the clinical usefulness to discriminate patients in subsets with a markedly different prognosis.

Much effort has already been spent in translational studies, but few markers have proved to fulfill completely the aforementioned guidelines. The way biomarkers have been studied seems to be questionable, since sufficient evidence for a valuable contribution to guideline preparation has not been provided, except for ER and PgR [1]. However, it is conceivable that the development of several methodological approaches and criteria for a proper design of studies focused on evaluating and grading the clinical usefulness of putative prognostic factors [4], [19] as well as their laboratory and clinical effectiveness [5] will make order among biomarkers and in the related literature, which is overwhelmed by often redundant studies. Such a process will benefit from the recent availability of statistical approaches able to adequately model the prognostic information provided by putative prognostic variables, with an integration of methodologies of biological, clinical and statistical research.

4.1 Proliferation-Related Variables

Tumor proliferative activity represents one of the cellular functions most thoroughly investigated for its association with neoplastic progression and metastatic potential. In the last two decades, several proliferation markers have been proposed [20]. The initial quantitative measurement of cells in the S-phase of the cell cycle (i.e., in the DNA-synthesizing phase) by evaluating the fraction of tumor cells actively incorporating ^{3}H-thymidine (^{3}H-thymidine labeling index, TLI) has been successively paralleled by the evaluation of cells with a DNA-synthesizing content by flow cytometry. More recently, the availability of an antibody raised against an antigen expressed by cycling cells (Ki67/MIB-1) has made it possible to evaluate the putative entire fraction of proliferating cells (i.e., the growth fraction). In general, cell proliferation proved to be associated with breast cancer prognosis [21], [22], with sensitivity and specificity rates slightly varying as a function of the different proliferation indices.

Mean or median values have been generally used as cut-points to discriminate slowly and rapidly proliferating tumors, which were respectively associated with a favorable or unfavorable prognosis. In particular, for TLI the value of 3% of labeled cells has been independently identified by several laboratories as the median value of frequency distribution in breast cancer [8], and by using such a cut-point a significant association has been observed with the hazard of overall relapse, local-regional recurrence and distant metastasis, and death [10], and such findings held true for short and long-term follow-up over a period of 20 years [23]. In a recent study on 1400 patients with node-negative resectable breast cancer, treated with radical or conservative surgery plus radiotherapy until relapse, we comparatively analyzed the prognostic power at a 10-year follow-up of TLI and of p53 expression, considered as dichotomous or continuous variables [9], on distant metastasis, which represents the most frequent unfavorable event in breast cancer. TLI and the expression of p53 (a protein coded by the TP53 gene and involved in controlling cell proliferation, apoptosis and response to DNA damage in different models of experimental and clinical tumors [24]) provided significant prognostic information. However, the consideration of TLI as a dichotomous variable (based on the median value) or as a continuous variable (even by using a linear regression model or polynomial models with splines) gave similar results in terms of predictivity, as indicated by the chi square values obtained by the likelihood ratio test (Table 2). Conversely, for p53 expression, the maximum predictivity, with a twofold chi square value and two-log different P values, was obtained by considering it as a continuous variable and by applying modeled regression functions with splines.

Thus, the use of p53 as a dichotomous variable could lead to a biased interpretation of results since the prognostic relation between the appearance of metastases and p53 expression is not monotonic [9]. In fact, the risk of metastases increases to its highest value with increasing percentages of p53-positive cells up to a value of 15%, but it decreases thereafter with further increases in the fraction of p53-immunoreactive cells, thus suggesting a protective role of p53 in tumors highly expressing the protein. Such a complex, non-monotonic prognostic relation, which became evident only considering p53 as a continuous variable, at further analysis showed a significant (P=0.0004), protective interaction between p53 and TLI, which had already emerged when dichotomous variables were considered [9].

Table 2. Univariate analysis of 10-year distant metastasis in 1400 node-negative breast cancers as a function of proliferation-related variables.

Variable	Model	Chi square	Degrees of freedom	P value
TLI				
Cutoff: 3% (median value)	Threshold	12.12	1	0.0005
Continuous	Linear	10.37	1	0.0013
	Polynomial with splines	13.86	3	0.0031
p53				
Cutoff: 5%	Threshold	28.96	1	7×10^{-8}
	Linear	24.13	1	9×10^{-7}
Continuous	Polynomial with splines	45.51	3	7×10^{-8}

Conversely, the functional relation between TLI and hazard of metastasis appeared to be monotonic and linearly increasing, with a steeper increase for TLI values around 3% [9].

4.2 Hormone Receptors

The recent update of the American Society of Clinical Oncology guidelines on the use of tissue tumor markers in the management of breast cancer patients recommended only the measurement of ER and PgR on all primary tumors, to be successively repeated on metastatic lesions only when the results of such a determination could induce a change in patient management [1]. ER and PgR have been studied in clinical breast cancer for more than 25 years, initially as indicators of endocrine responsiveness, then as prognostic factors for early recurrence. During the last two decades, hundreds of papers have been published on these two related, although different, clinically relevant aspects. Whereas the role of ER and PgR as predictors of response to treatment has been consistently recognized, their prognostic relevance is still debated. In fact, although findings independently reported by several laboratories support a modest prognostic significance of receptor status, the short-term association between ER-positivity and lower recurrence rate is counterbalanced at longer times by a higher recurrence rate for the same receptor subset.

On a case series of 1800 patients with node-negative resectable breast cancer, treated with radical or conservative surgery plus radiotherapy until relapse, we investigated and described the interrelations between ER and PgR, together with other prognostically relevant features including patient age, tumor size, and the risk of relapse considering continuous and time-dependent effects. Restricted cubic spline regression was used to analyze the relation between the logarithm of the hazard ratio (HR) and each covariate [12]. On the basis of prior knowledge, a 4-knot spline and a 3-knot spline were adopted for age and tumor size, respectively, whereas for ER and PgR only linear terms were considered. In the final multivariate model (Table 3), ER, PgR, age and tumor size were significantly related to prognosis, and a time-dependent effect for ER and tumor size was identified. In particular, for ER the pattern of dependence of log(HR) with time was linear, whereas a complex time pattern was observed for tumor size.

The time-dependent relationship between the HR and prognostic variables was evaluated by comparing plots in which the HR was related to covariate values at 36 months, as the time representative of an early event, and at 72 months, as the follow-up time most commonly reported in translational studies. For ER, no prognostic effect of receptor content was observed at 36 months of follow-up, whereas at 72 months the HR was positively related to ER content. In contrast, the HR did not show a time-dependent relation with PgR content since, considering the value of 1 fmol/cytosolic protein as a reference, a decrease in the HR with increasing receptor concentration was always observed.

Table 3. Multivariate analysis of 10-year relapse-free survival in 1800 node-negative breast cancers.

	Wald chi square	Degrees of freedom	*P* value
ER	8.87	2	0.0118
Fixed (linear term of the variable)	0.78	1	0.376
Time-dependent (interaction between variable and time linear terms)	6.30	1	0.012
PgR *Fixed* (linear term of the variable)	6.27	1	0.0123
Age *Fixed*	25.66	3	0.0001
Linear term of the variable	9.30	1	0.0023
Nonlinear terms of the 4-knot restricted cubic spline	4.81	2	0.090
Tumor size	33.80	8	0.000044
Fixed	20.51	2	0.000035
Linear term of the variable	1.27	1	0.26
Nonlinear terms of the 3-knot restricted cubic spline	0.88	1	0.35
Time-dependent	14.29	6	0.027
Interaction between linear and non-linear terms of the variable with the linear term of time	6.14	2	0.0465
Interaction between linear and nonlinear terms of the variable with the nonlinear terms of time (restricted cubic spline with 4 knots)	9.87	4	0.043

As regards patient age, for which the median age of the case series (57 years) was considered as a reference category, the relation with HR was nonlinear, since the HR of about 2 for patients younger than 30 years decreased progressively to 1 for those aged 45 years, remained stable for women aged between 45 and 60 years, and thereafter progressively dropped below 1. For tumor size, the pattern of dependence of log(HR) with time was nonlinear. By considering 0.5 cm (i.e., the smallest tumor size on which steroid receptor determination was performed in our laboratory) as a reference value, at 36 months the HR appeared to be directly related to tumor size up to 2.5 cm in diameter, whereas at a longer follow-up the impact of tumor size on prognosis decreased. In conclusion, ER content, which did not provide any prognostic information within the first years of follow-up, was thereafter positively associated with relapse, whereas high PgR concentrations were negatively related to risk of relapse, and such a finding was consistent over the entire follow-up period.

The switch of ER predictive value on prognosis 3 years following initial breast cancer diagnosis is supported by the findings observed by the San Antonio group on about 2900 women [25], including cases submitted to adjuvant treatment. It could be explained by a faster non-estrogen-related growth rate of subclinical metastases from ER-poor tumors and by a preventive effect of estrogens in the development of metastases for an initial period following the removal of primary ER-rich tumors. Present findings suggest a pivotal role of ER in the mechanism by which quiescent tumor cells switch towards a metastatic behavior, with a possible link between estrogen-related mechanisms and acquisition of angiogenic properties.

In a series of about 1800 patients with node-negative, resectable breast cancer (that partially overlapped the previously reported series) who had received local-regional treatment from 1977 to 1992 at the Institute, steroid receptors were the only investigated biological variable that provided prognostic information on the risk of contralateral tumors [26]. For these women, for whom, besides information on age, tumor site and size, and histologic type, TLI evaluation was also available, the risk of a contralateral cancer increased linearly with increasing PgR content. For the presence of an interaction between PgR and histology, such a finding was mainly evident in infiltrating ductal carcinoma or in tumors with an associated extensive intraductal component, whereas a low hazard was observed as a function of PgR concentration in infiltrating lobular carcinoma and in other histotypes. In addition, due to an interaction with patient age,

ER appeared to play a protective role in young patients, whereas the opposite was true in older women.

4.3 Integration of Biological and Clinicopathologic Information

In the aforementioned case series of 1800 patients with node-negative breast cancer, we analyzed the role of cell proliferation and steroid hormone receptors, in association with pathologic tumor size and patient age, in predicting new disease manifestations [10]. Hormone receptors failed to predict the 8-year incidence of local-regional recurrence, but they were significant indicators of distant metastasis. Conversely, cell proliferation predicted local-regional and distant metastases. In multivariate analysis, only TLI retained its independent prognostic relevance regardless of patient age, tumor size, ER, PgR, and type of surgical approach (radical or conservative). We then combined clinicopathologic and biological information to define subgroups of patients at different risk of developing new disease manifestations. For the best identification of risk groups, the same variables included in the Cox multivariate models (i.e., TLI, ER, PgR, patient age and tumor size) were considered in the recursive partitioning and amalgamation analysis [16], which represents a formal method for optimal categorization of continuous variables such as TLI and hormone receptor concentrations and is briefly summarized in Section 2.4. For local-regional relapse (Figure 1), the entire series of cases contributed to the final tree, and the first significant split was by TLI, with the best cut-point of 3%. The subset of slowly proliferating tumors had no other significant split.

Conversely, patients with rapidly proliferating tumors had a further split by age, and a better prognosis was observed for patients older than 55 years than for those aged 55 years or younger. Tumor size and hormone receptors were not selected in this procedure. Patients with slowly proliferating tumors or with rapidly proliferating tumors but older than 55 years, with similar HRs, were combined, and the final model provided two distinct prognostic subgroups, with a cumulative incidence of local-regional recurrence significantly lower in patients at any age with slowly proliferating tumors and in older patients with rapidly proliferating tumors (accounting for 64% of the cases) than in younger patients with rapidly proliferating tumors (accounting for 36% of the cases) ($P<0.0001$).

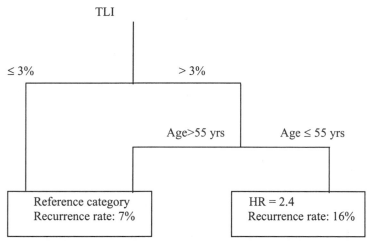

Figure 1. Identification of patients at different risk of locoregional relapse in a series of 1800 women with node-negative resectable breast cancer using a regression tree derived by recursive partitioning and amalgamation analysis.

For distant metastasis, 1684 cases (for which information on pathologic tumor size was available) were considered in the final tree (Figure 2). The first split was by tumor size, and within tumors smaller than or equal to 2 cm in diameter, the next split was again by size, equal to or less than 1 cm, or greater than 1 cm. Within 1- to 2-cm tumors, the next split was by TLI. On the opposite side of the tree, the most important prognostic factor within tumors larger than 2 cm was patient age. Patients aged 45 or younger or 56 to 65 years of age had a worse prognosis than the other age subgroups. Subsets with similar outcome were combined, and three distinct prognostic groups were identified. The cumulative incidence of 8-year distant metastasis was low for patients with tumors smaller than 1 cm or 1 to 2 cm in diameter, but slowly proliferating (34% of the cases); high for patients younger than 45 years or 56 to 65 years old and with tumors larger than 2 cm (18% of the cases); and intermediate for the other patients, accounting for 48% of the cases.

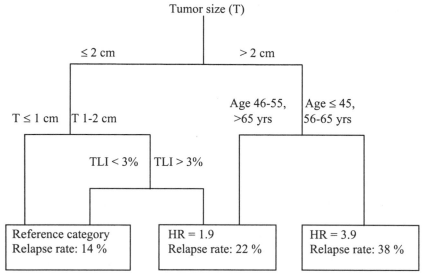

Figure 2. Identification of patients at different risk of distant metastasis in a series of 1684 women with node-negative resectable breast cancer using a regression tree derived by recursive partitioning and amalgamation analysis.

It is noteworthy that such an approach provided superimposable results when TLI was used as a continuous or dichotomous variable [10]. Such a finding was consistent with data reported in Table 2 for another case series of patients with node-negative tumors, for whom the probability to develop distant metastasis was investigated as a function of TLI.

5   Biomarkers and Prediction of Treatment Response

The interest of investigators involved in translational studies in breast cancer has been progressively directed to identify biomarkers for predicting sensitivity or resistance to specific treatments and able to provide worthwhile information to aid in choosing treatment options in patient subsets defined by other factors (i.e., number of involved axillary lymph nodes, presence of ER, etc.). In general, prognostic factors do not always provide predictive information (for example, lymph node status is the most powerful prognostic factor but there is no evidence that it has a predictive role), whereas all known predictive factors also appear to be related to prognosis (for example, ER and

PgR, cell proliferation and HER2 [HER2/*neu*, c-erbB-2]). Investigations on predictive factors are relatively recent, and available information has been generally derived from the retrospective determination of biomarkers in case series not always included in randomized controlled clinical studies. Only recently has the determination of biological markers been foreseen in the clinical treatment protocol and prospectively planned. In addition, the putative predictive role of biomarkers on response to specific treatments could be correctly analyzed only in a few reports owing to the limited availability of subsets of patients (with biologically characterized tumors) randomized to receive the systemic treatment under investigation or placebo.

5.1 Chemotherapy

The evidence of a relation between tumor proliferative activity and response to chemotherapy, derived from studies on experimental models of animal and human tumors, recently appeared to be confirmed also in clinical tumors. However, results in favor of a direct association between proliferation and benefit of systemic cytotoxic treatment have been generally obtained in studies on advanced tumors [27] and only rarely derived from adjuvant settings [21].

We recently tested the hypothesis that tumor proliferative activity could influence the clinical outcome of patients with resectable breast cancer subjected to postsurgical adjuvant chemotherapy in which the same drugs have been administered at the same dose intensity but with a different scheduling. Patients were randomized to receive alternating or sequential treatment with doxorubicin or CMF as part of their participation in a prospective trial [7], in which the determination of cell proliferation was prospectively foreseen in planning the clinical study and was performed on tumor specimens at the time of surgery. In the overall series, a complex relation between TLI, considered as a continuous variable, and relapse-free survival or distant metastasis-free survival was observed, whereas a linear relation was observed with overall survival (Table 4). The cubic spline approach showed that the most suitable model to describe the functional relationships between TLI and relapse or distant metastasis was a spline with four knots and the linearity constraints on the tails. The equation describing the spline function has three terms [12], and the corresponding regression coefficients are indicated as "A," "B," and "C," whereas for overall survival TLI is considered in its original continuous scale (linear term).

Table 4. Univariate analysis of 12-year clinical outcome as a function of continuous TLI values in patients with node-positive breast cancer treated with adjuvant chemotherapy.

	Relapse-free survival			Distant metastasis-free survival			Overall survival		
	β (s.e.)	P*	P**	β (s.e.)	P*	P**	β (s.e.)	P*	P**
Original values[1]							0.064 (0.019)	0.001	0.002
Coefficient spline[2]									
A	−0.184 (0.102)	0.072	0.009	−0.231 (0.129)	0.073	0.001			
B	0.008 (0.003)	0.012		0.010 (0.004)	0.006				
C	−0.026 (0.010)	0.012		−0.036 (0.013)	0.004				

[1] Coefficients of the linear term of the variable.
[2] Coefficients of the linear and nonlinear terms of the 4-knot restricted cubic spline of the variable.
* Referred to Wald chi square.
** Referred to the likelihood ratio test.

Besides TLI, treatment regimen (sequential or alternating), number of positive axillary lymph nodes, TLI and, marginally, tumor size but not ER individually were significantly associated with relapse-free survival in univariate analysis (Table 5). All the considered variables were significantly associated with overall survival, except the number of positive lymph nodes, whereas only treatment regimen and tumor size were significantly related to distant metastasis-free survival. When a Cox multiple regression analysis was applied to the data, only TLI and treatment regimen were retained as common predictors for all the three unfavorable events, whereas the number of positive nodes or tumor size and ER status were independent predictors of relapse-free and overall survival, respectively. Since TLI and treatment regimens were the only variables maintaining an independent role on all the unfavorable events in multivariate analysis, we analyzed relapse-free survival as a function of TLI within each treatment regimen (Figure 3). The best clinical outcome was observed for patients submitted to sequential treatment, in agreement with the results from the clinical study [7].

Table 5. Univariate analysis of 12-year clinical outcome as a function of biological and clinico-pathologic variables in patients with node-positive breast cancer treated with adjuvant chemotherapy.

	Relapse-free survival		Distant metastasis-free survival		Overall survival	
	HR (95%CI)	P	HR (95%CI)	P	HR (95%CI)	P
Tumor size >2 vs ≤ 2cm	1.3 (1.0-1.8)	0.058	1.5 (1.0-2.1)	0.031	1.7 (1.2-2.3)	0.002
Positive nodes >10 vs 4-10	1.4 (1.1-1.9)	0.014	1.3 (0.9-1.8)	0.21	1.3 (1.0-1.8)	0.086
ER (fmol/mg prot.) >10 vs ≤10	1.1 (0.8-1.6)	0.43	1.1 (0.7-1.7)	0.60	1.7 (1.2-2.3)	0.004
Therapy CMF/A vs A→CMF	1.5 (1.1-2.0)	0.008	1.5 (1.1-2.2)	0.02	1.4 (1.0-1.9)	0.033

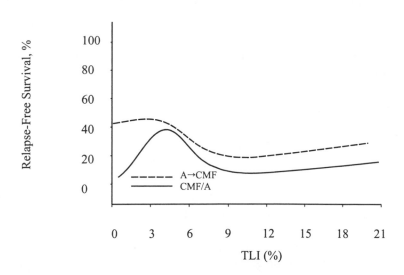

Figure 3. Relapse-free survival curves in breast cancer patients treated with sequential (A→CMF) or alternating (CMF/A) doxorubicin and CMF regimens.

By considering TLI as a continuous variable, we could identify a cell kinetic subset which seems to specifically benefit from the relapse-free survival advantage observed on the overall series after sequential rather than alternating administration of doxorubicin and CMF. In fact, in the subset given the sequential regimen, the probability of 12-year relapse-free survival was around 45% for patients whose tumor had a TLI of up to 5%. For higher TLI values, the probability to remain relapse-free dropped to 25-30% and remained constant regardless of increasing TLI values. Conversely, in the subset given the alternating regimen, the probability of relapse-free survival was very low for patients with slowly proliferating tumors with respect to that observed for patients treated in the sequential regimen and reached a maximum at a TLI of about 5%, then decreased to 10% for a TLI equal to or higher than 9%.

The possible benefit of sequential treatment for slowly proliferating tumors could be explained in the light of preclinical data. In fact, anthracyclines induce cell accumulation in the G_2 phase of the cell cycle, in experimentally growing tumor cell lines as well as in clinical breast cancers treated with neoadjuvant chemotherapy. Such a cell cycle perturbation could be less relevant in the alternating regimen than in the sequential treatment for the significantly high-dose intensity of doxorubicin in the latter and could result in a partial synchronization and subsequent presentation of a large number of cells sensitive to S-phase-specific drugs, such as methotrexate and 5-fluorouracil in the CMF regimen.

5.2   Hormonal Therapy

Steroid hormone receptors represent the strongest predictors of response to endocrine treatment. The information they provide to identify those patients who fail to benefit from different forms of hormonal therapy is still peculiar and clinically relevant, after more than 25 years from their introduction [1], [28]. In recent years, the quantitative evaluation of steroid receptors by the ligand-binding assay has been paralleled by the semiquantitative determination of the fraction of cells expressing hormone receptors that are immunohistochemically detectable by using specific, recently developed reagents [29], [30], and their predictive values on response to endocrine treatments are similar when single cut-points are used to define steroid-positive and negative tumors. However, the initial finding by Heuson et al. [31] of a direct quantitative relation between likelihood to respond to hormonal treatment and estrogen receptor content evaluated by the ligand-binding assay has not been systematically validated. Only recently have the consideration of steroid receptor concentration on a continuous scale, instead of dichotomous status, and the use of flexible statistical models allowed us to confirm previous findings [31], to compare results from independent studies carried out by different groups, and to improve the predictivity of the ligand-binding assay.

In a series of 83 elderly breast cancer patients who underwent radical surgery between 1982 and 1986 and received in 64% of the cases 20 mg daily of tamoxifen for 1 year, the logarithm of the relative hazard for relapse decreased linearly with the increase in log(ER) or log(PgR) [32]. Such a finding indicates an improved clinical outcome with an increase in steroid receptor content and is in keeping with the initial evidence of Heuson [31] and with successive results from other groups [33]. Superimposable results, in terms of an inverse relationship between hazard of relapse and log(ER) or log(PgR), were reported at a 4-year follow-up by Gion *et al.* [34] in a comparable series of 81 postmenopausal women submitted to surgery followed by a 4-year adjuvant treatment with Tamoxifen, thus supporting the possibility of a direct inter-laboratory comparison of assay and clinical results. Overall, the quantitative relation between clinical outcome following Tamoxifen treatment and ER content was further validated in a series of postmenopausal patients with node-positive tumors who underwent surgery at the INT in 1981 [35]. In particular, in 73 patients who received anti-estrogen therapy, besides patient age and number of involved axillary lymph nodes (Table 6), ER, but not PgR, was significantly associated with clinical outcome, with a decrease in the hazard of relapse with increasing ER content up to about 90 fmol/mg cytosol protein. Such a specific relation between steroid receptor content and clinical outcome was only observed following hormonal treatment. In fact, a similar analysis carried out on the subset of 124 patients receiving in the same period adjuvant CMF failed to evidence any relationship between steroid receptor content and course of the disease, in keeping with the outcome of a number of translational studies [28].

Table 6. Univariate analysis of 10-year relapse-free survival in node-positive breast cancer patients treated with adjuvant Tamoxifen or CMF.

	Chi square[1]	Degrees of freedom	P value
Tamoxifen-treated patients			
LogER (3-knot restricted cubic spline with linear term of the variable)	6.910	2	0.032
LogPgR (Linear term of the variable)	1.111	1	0.292
Age (4-knot restricted cubic spline with linear term of the variable)	7.076	2	0.029
pN (Linear term of the variable)	5.321	1	0.021
CMF-treated patients			
LogER (3-knot restricted cubic spline without linear term of the variable)	2.496	1	0.114
LogPgR (3-knot restricted cubic spline with linear term of the variable)	2.298	2	0.317
Age (Linear term of the variable)	2.409	1	0.121
pN (Linear term of the variable)	23.002	1	0.0001

[1] By the likelihood ratio test

A multivariate analysis carried out in the tamoxifen-treated group showed that, in the final model, only the prognostic contribution of ER and axillary lymph node involvement was retained (Table 7) and that the number of metastatic nodes, as measured by Harrell's c statistics, appeared to strongly contribute to the predictive ability of the model.

Table 7. Multivariate analysis of 10-year relapse-free survival in node-positive breast cancer patients treated with adjuvant Tamoxifen.

	Chi square[1]	Degrees of freedom	P value	Harrell's c
Full model	13.792	3	0.0032	0.723
LogER (3-knot restricted cubic spline with linear term of the variable)	8.293	2	0.0158	0.704[2]
pN (Linear term of the variable)	6.848	1	0.0089	0.582[2]

[1] By the likelihood ratio test
[2] Obtained by subtracting the specific variable

The estimated relapse-free survival curves, obtained from the final Cox multivariate regression model and plotted according to four values of ER content (namely 0, 5, 15, and 90 fmol/mg cytosolic protein), adjusted for lymph node involvement [35] showed the worst prognosis for patients whose tumors exhibited an ER concentration equal to 0 fmol/mg cytosolic protein and a marked reduction in the expected relapse rates for a small increase in ER level, even for a concentration falling below the cut-point value of 10 fmol/mg cytosolic protein, conventionally used for clinical purposes (5 fmol/mg protein vs 0 fmol/mg protein, HR=0.31 [0.15-0.68]; 15 fmol/mg protein vs 5 fmol/mg protein, HR=0.53 [0.36-0.69]; 90 fmol/mg protein vs 15 fmol/mg protein, HR=0.63 [0.44-0.90]). Such findings provide support by formal statistics for the early observation of Heuson *et al.* [31].

Additionally, it is noteworthy that threshold values of ER concentration were used after fitting flexible models in the initial phase of the analysis and following the assessment that the simpler model did not imply a net loss of prognostic information.

6   Discussion and Conclusions

In the near future, we are expecting a substantial improvement in the assessment of the clinical usefulness of determining biofunctional markers in breast cancer. In fact, the simultaneous availability of long-term results of randomized treatment protocols in which the determination of biological variables has been prospectively foreseen, of guidelines for designing, conducting, analyzing and reporting biomarker studies, and of flexible statistical modeling techniques in survival analysis will allow us to thoroughly investigate the functional relationship between risk of unfavorable events or of treatment failure and functional aspects of tumor cells and to assess the clinical impact of such information by discriminating between statistical significance and clinical usefulness. In particular, the latter aspect will be the object of future investigations, since we still lack formal categorization of the prognostic advantage and treatment benefit as a function of biological markers, except for the criteria recently proposed by Hayes *et al.* [19], which need to be validated.

It is consequently preferable to retain and evaluate all the clinically relevant information provided by biological markers, and for such an aim quantitative variables should be analyzed in a continuous scale. Such an approach, besides reducing the subjectiveness in defining cut-points, allows us to investigate the functional relation between biological variables and clinical events and is useful to select statistical models with the best predictive ability by a correct modeling of the continuous prognostic relation. Flexible regression techniques represent appropriate statistical tools to reliably assess the nature of the relation between marker and hazard of relapse or death and consequently provide information on the modulation of patient outcome as a function of marker value, thus allowing modeling of nonlinear prognostic relationships. To aid acquisition and interpretation of the information by clinicians, it is therefore appropriate to group patients according to the risk of developing an unfavorable event in an advanced phase of the evaluation process, after generation of the statistical model, rather than in the first part of the study, when defining the measurement modalities of the variable.

Acknowledgments

We grateful to Drs. Patrizia Boracchi, Elia Biganzoli and Paolo Verderio for statistical support and Prof. Ettore Marubini for stimulating discussion. Supported in part by grants from the Italian Health Ministry and Consiglio Nazionale delle Ricerche (CNR).

References

[1] Tumor Marker Expert Panel Members (1996), "Clinical practice guidelines for the use of tumor markers in breast and colorectal cancer," *J. Clin. Oncol.*, 14, pp. 2843-2877.

[2] Gasparini, G. (guest editor), "Prognostic variables in node-negative and node-positive breast cancer – Part I & II," *Breast Cancer Res. Treat.*, 51 & 52 (special issues).

[3] Altman, D.D. and Lyman, H.H. (1998), "Methodological challenges in the evaluation of prognostic factors in breast cancer," *Breast Cancer Res. Treat.*, 52, pp. 289-303.

[4] Hayes, D.F., Bast, R., Desch, C.E., Fritsche, H., Kemeny, N.E., Jessup, J., Locker, G.Y., Macdonald, J., Mennel, R.G., Norton, L., Ravdin, P., Taube, S., and Winn, R. (1996), "A tumor marker

utility grading system (TMUGS): a framework to evaluate clinical utility of tumor markers," *J. Natl. Cancer Inst.*, 88, pp. 1456-1466.

[5] Gion, M., Boracchi, P., Biganzoli, E., and Daidone, M.G. (1999), "A guide for reviewing submitted manuscripts (and indications for the design of translational research studies on biomarkers)," *Int. J. Biol. Markers*, 14, pp. 123-133.

[6] Biganzoli, E., Boracchi, P., Daidone, M.G., Gion, M., and Marubini, E. (1998), "Flexible modeling in survival analysis. Structuring biological complexity from the information provided by tumor markers," *Int. J. Biol. Markers*, 13, pp. 107-123.

[7] Bonadonna, G., Zambetti, M., and Valagussa, P. (1995), "Sequential or alternating doxorubicin and CMF regimens in breast cancer with more than three positive nodes," *JAMA*, 273, pp. 542-547.

[8] Silvestrini, R. (1991), "Feasibility and reproducibility of the ^{3}H-thymidine labelling index in breast cancer," *Cell Prolif.*, 21, pp. 437-445.

[9] Silvestrini, R., Daidone, M.G., Benini, E., Faranda, A., Tomasic, G., Boracchi, P., Salvadori, B., and Veronesi, U. (1996), "Validation of p53 accumulation as a predictor of distant metastasis at 10 years of follow-up in 1400 node-negative breast cancer," *Clin. Cancer Res.*, 2, pp. 2007-2013.

[10] Silvestrini, R., Daidone, M.G., Luisi, A., Boracchi, P., Mezzetti, M., Di Fronzo, G., Andreola, S., Salvadori, B., and Veronesi, U. (1995), "Biologic and clinicopathologic factors as indicators of specific relapse types in node-negative breast cancer," *J. Clin. Oncol.*, 13, pp. 697-704.

[11] Piffanelli, A., Pelizzola, D., Giovannini, G., Catozzi, L., Faggioli, L., and Giganti, M. (1989), "Characterization of laboratory working standard for quality control of immunometric and radiometric estrogen receptor assays. Clinical evaluation on breast cancer biopsies. Italian Committee for Hormone Receptor Assays Standardization," *Tumori*, 75, pp. 550-556.

[12] Durrleman, S. and Simon, R. (1989), "Flexible regression models with cubic splines," *Stat. Med.,* 8, pp. 551-561.

[13] Harrell, F.E. Jr, Lee, K.L., and Mark, D.B. (1996), "Tutorial in biostatistics multivariable prognostic models, issues in developing models, evaluating assumptions and adequacy, and measuring and reducing errors," *Stat Med.,* 15, pp. 361-387.

[14] Akaike, H. (1973), "Information theory and an extension of the maximum likelihood principle," in Patrov, B.N. and Csaki, F. (Eds.), *Proceedings of the Second International Symposium in Information Theory*, Akademia Kiado, Budapest.

[15] Heinzl, H. and Kaider, A. (1997), "Gaining more flexibility in Cox proportional hazards regression models with cubic spline functions," *Computer Methods & Programs in Biomedicine*, 54, pp. 201-208.

[16] Ciampi, A. and Thiffault, J. (1988), "Recursive partitioning and amalgamation (RECPAM) for censored survival data. Criteria for tree selection," *Stat. Software Newsletter*, 14, pp. 78-81.

[17] Altman, D.G., Lausen, B., Sauerbrei, W., and Schumacher, M. (1994), "Dangers of using 'optimal' cutpoints in the evaluation of prognostic factors," *J. Natl. Cancer Inst.*, 86, pp. 829-835.

[18] Henderson, I.C. and Patek, A.J. (1998), "The relationship between prognostic and predictive factors in the management of breast cancer," *Breast Cancer Res. Treat.*, 52, pp. 261-288.

[19] Hayes, D.F., Trock, B., and Harris, A.L. (1998), "Assessing the clinical impact of prognostic factors: when is 'statistically significant' clinically useful?" *Breast Cancer Res. Treat.*, 52, pp. 305-319.

[20] Silvestrini, R., Daidone, M.G., and Costa, A. (1995), "Determination of the proliferative fraction in human tumors," in Studzinski, G.P. (Ed.), *Cell growth and Apoptosis. A pratical approach*, IRL Oxford University Press, Oxford, pp. 59-77.

[21] Amadori, D. and Silvestrini, R. (1998), "Prognostic and predictive value of thymidine labelling index in breast cancer," *Breast Cancer Res. Treat*, 51, pp. 267-281.

[22] Wenger, C.R. and Clark, G.M. (1998), "S-phase fraction and breast cancer – a decade of experience," *Br. Cancer Res. Treat.*, 51, pp. 255-265.

[23] Silvestrini, R., Daidone, M.G., Luisi, A., and Salvadori, B. (1997), "Cell proliferation in 3800 node-negative breast cancers: Consistency over time of biological and clinical information provided by ^{3}H-thymidine labelling index," *Int J. Cancer (Pred. Oncol.)*, 74, pp. 122-127.

[24] Harris, C.C. and Hollstein, M. (1993), "Clinical implications of the p53 tumor suppressor gene," *N. Engl. J. Med.*, 329, pp. 1318-1327.

[25] Hilsenbeck, S.G., Ravdin, P.M., de Moor, C.A., Chamness, G.C., Osborne C.K., and Clark, G.M. (1998), "Time-dependence of hazard ratios for prognostic factors in primary breast cancer," *Breast Cancer Res. Treat.*, 52, pp. 227-237.

[26] Mariani, L., Coradini, D., Biganzoli, E., Boracchi. P., Marubini, E., Pilotti, S., Salvadori, B., Silvestrini, R., Veronesi, U., Zucali, R., and Rilke, F. (1997), "Prognostic factors for metachronous contralateral breast cancer: a comparison of the Cox regression model and its artificial neural network extension," *Breast Cancer Res. Treat.*, 44, pp. 167-178.

[27] Silvestrini, R. (1994), "Cell kinetics: prognostic and therapeutic implications in human tumors," *Cell Prolif.*, 27, pp. 579-596.

[28] Osborne, C.K. (1998), "Steroid hormone receptors in breast cancer management," *Breast Cancer Res. Treat.*, 51, pp. 227-238.

[29] Barnes, D.M., Harris, W.H., Smith, P., Millis, R.R., and Rubens, R.D. (1996), "Immunohistochemical determination of oestrogen receptor: comparison of different methods of assessment of staining and correlation with clinical outcome of breast cancer patients," *Br. J. Cancer,* 74, pp. 1445-1451.

[30] Harvey, J.M., Clark, G.M., Osborne, C.K., and Allred, D.C. (1999), "Estrogen receptor status by immunohistochemistry is superior to the ligand-binding assay for predicting response to adjuvant endocrine therapy in breast cancer," *J. Clin. Oncol.*, 17, pp. 1474-1481.

[31] Heuson, J.C., Longeval, E., Mattheiem, W.H., Deboel, M.C., Sylvester, R.J., and Leclercq, G. (1977), "Significance of quantitative assessment of estrogen receptors for endocrine therapy in advanced breast cancer," *Cancer*, 39, pp. 1971-1977.

[32] Coradini, D., Biganzoli, E., Boracchi, P., Bombardieri, E., Seregni, E., De Palo, G., Martelli, G., and Di Fronzo, G. (1998), "Effect of steroid receptors, pS2 and cathepsin D on the outcome of elderly breast cancer patients: an exploratory investigation," *Int. J. Cancer,* 79, pp. 305-311.

[33] Bezwoda, W.R., Esser, J.D., Dansey, R., Kessel, I., and Lange, M. (1991), "The value of estrogen and progesterone receptor determinations in advanced breast cancer. Estrogen receptor level but not progesterone receptor level correlates with response to tamoxifen," *Cancer*, 68, pp. 867-872.

[34] Dittadi, R., Biganzoli, E., Boracchi, P., Salbe, C., Mione, R., Gatti, C., and Gion, M. (1998), "Impact of steroid receptors, pS2 and cathepsin D on the outcome of N+ postmenopausal breast cancer patients treated with tamoxifen," *Int. J. Biol. Markers*, 13, pp. 30-41.

[35] Coradini, D., Oriana, S., Biganzoli, E., Marubini, E., Boracchi, P., Bresciani, G., Di Fronzo, G., and Daidone, M.G. (1999), "Relationship between steroid receptors (as continuous variables) and response to adjuvant treatments in postmenopausal women with node-positive breast cancer," *Int. J. Biol. Markers,* 14, pp. 60-67.

Chapter 6

Computer-Aided Breast Cancer Diagnosis

H.-P. Chan, **N. Petrick**, and **B. Sahiner**

At present, mammography is the only proven method that can detect minimal breast cancers. The most common indicators of breast cancer on mammograms are masses and microcalcifications. Computer-aided diagnosis (CAD) can provide a second opinion to radiologists in the interpretation of mammograms. The promise of CAD in improving breast cancer diagnosis has driven many investigators to develop soft-computing techniques for the analysis of mammograms. In this chapter, we will review computer vision techniques used for the detection and characterization of mammographic lesions. We will concentrate on some of the methods that we have developed in these areas. The effects of CAD on radiologists' diagnostic accuracy will also be discussed.

1   Introduction

Breast cancer is one of the leading causes of death in women between 40 to 55 years of age. In the United States, the mortality for breast cancer in women is the second highest of all cancer deaths, and it was estimated to account for 16% of all cancer deaths in 1998 [1]. Studies have indicated that early detection and treatment improve the chances of survival for breast cancer patients. At present, mammography is the only proven method that can detect minimal breast cancers [2], [3]. However, 10-30% of the breast cancers that are visible on mammograms in retrospective studies are not detected due to various technical or human factors [4]-[7]. The specificity of mammography for differentiating lesions to be malignant and benign is also very low. In the United States, the positive predictive value of mammography ranges from about 15 to 30% [8], [9].

Various methods are being developed to improve the sensitivity and specificity of breast cancer detection [10]. Double reading can reduce the miss rate of radiographic reading [11], [12]. However, double-reading by radiologists is costly. Computer-aided diagnosis (CAD) is considered to be one of the promising approaches that may improve the efficacy of mammography [13]. Properly designed CAD algorithms can automatically detect suspicious lesions on a mammogram and alert the radiologist to these regions. They can also extract image features from regions of interest (ROIs) and estimate the likelihood of malignancy for a given lesion, thereby providing the radiologist with additional information for making diagnostic decisions. It has been shown that CAD can improve radiologists' detection accuracy significantly [14], [15]. Computer classifiers also improve radiologists' ability in differentiating malignant and benign masses or microcalcifications [16], [17]. CAD is thus a viable cost-effective alternative to double reading by radiologists.

A number of research groups have been developing algorithms for the detection and characterization of microcalcifications and masses. Although the specific methods used in different stages of the processes vary, the approaches generally include several major steps: image enhancement, signal segmentation, feature extraction, and feature classification. In this chapter, we will review some of the image analysis methods used for detection and characterization of mammographic lesions, and concentrate on some of the methods that we have used as examples to demonstrate the applications of image processing techniques for CAD in mammography.

2   Computerized Detection of Microcalcifications

One of the important indicators of the presence of breast cancers is clustered microcalcifications [18]. Clustered microcalcifications can be seen on mammograms in 30 to 50% of breast cancers [19]-[22]. It is difficult to detect subtle microcalcifications because of the noisy mammographic background. A number of investigators have been developing computerized methods for detection of microcalcifications. Chan *et al.* [14], [23]-[25] devised a difference-image technique to detect microcalcifications on digitized mammograms. Fam *et al.* [26] and Davies *et al.* [27] detected microcalcifications using conventional image processing techniques. Qian *et al.* [28] devised a tree-structure filter and wavelet transform for enhancement of microcalcifications to facilitate detection. Other groups extracted morphological features such as contrast, size, shape, and edge gradient of microcalcifications and classified them with various feature classifiers [29]-[37]. Wu *et al.* [38] scanned for suspected microcalcifications with the difference-image technique [23], then further classified true and false detections by an artificial neural network based on features extracted from their power spectra. Similarly, Zhang *et al.* [39] used a shift-invariant neural network to reduce false-positive microcalcifications. Zheng *et al.* [40] used a difference-of-Gaussian band-pass filter to enhance the micro-calcifications and used multilayer feature analysis to identify true and false microcalcifications. The detection algorithms from these research groups generally show very promising results.

2.1 Methods

Computerized microcalcification detection programs generally include similar major steps. First, the image is processed to enhance the signal-to-noise ratio (SNR) of the microcalcifications. Second, the potential signals are segmented from the image background and features of the signals are extracted. A classifier is trained or some rule-based methods are designed to classify true signals from false signals. Finally, the remaining signals are grouped into clusters based on some clustering criteria. Signals that do not pass the clustering criteria may be treated as false signals or scattered calcifications. Specific techniques used in our detection programs are described below.

Chan *et al.* [14], [23]-[25], [41] first demonstrated that a difference-image technique can effectively detect microcalcifications on digitized mammograms. In the difference-image technique, a signal-enhance-ment filter is used to enhance the microcalcifications and a signal-suppression filter is used to remove or suppress the microcalcifications and smooth the noise. Subtracting the two filtered images results in an

SNR-enhanced image in which the low-frequency structured background is removed and the high-frequency noise is suppressed. When both the signal-enhancement filter and the signal-suppression filter are linear as used in this study, the difference-image technique is equivalent to band-pass filtering. Nonlinear filters can also be used for signal enhancement or signal suppression. For example, a median filter of an appropriate kernel size can effectively remove microcalcifications and noise from the mammogram and thus serve as a signal-suppression filter [23]. Variations of the difference-image technique, such as wavelet filtering [28] and difference-of-Gaussian filters [39], have been used by most investigators in the initial step of their microcalcification detection programs. The degree of SNR enhancement depends on the filter parameters used. The filter parameters have to be optimized based on the resolution and noise characteristics of the population of mammograms to which the automated detection algorithm is to be applied.

In the segmentation step, the program determines the gray level histogram of the preprocessed image within the breast region. A gray level thresholding technique is used to locate potential signal sites above a global threshold. The threshold is changed iteratively until the number of sites obtained falls within the chosen input maximum and minimum numbers. At each potential site, a locally adaptive gray level thresholding technique in combination with region growing is performed to determine the number of connected pixels above a local threshold, which is calculated as the product of the local root-mean-square (RMS) noise and an input SNR threshold. The signal characteristics to be used in the false-positive reduction step, such as the size, maximum contrast, SNR, and its location, are obtained in this step.

In the false-positive reduction step, the previous computer program performs three tests to distinguish signals from noise or artifacts. A lower bound is imposed on the size to exclude signals below a certain size which are likely to be noise and an upper bound is set to exclude signals greater than a certain size which are likely to be large benign calcifications. A contrast upper bound is also set to exclude potential signals that have a contrast higher than an input number of standard deviations above the average contrast of all potential signals found with local thresholding. This criterion excludes the very high-contrast signals that are likely to be artifacts and large benign calcifications.

After the number of potential signal sites in the image is reduced by the rule-based methods, a convolution neural network (CNN) [25] that has been trained to recognize true microcalcifications is applied to the remaining signals to further reduce false-positives. The CNN is described in greater detail below. A regional clustering procedure is then used to identify clustered microcalcifications. A signal is kept if the number of signals found within a neighborhood of a chosen input diameter around that signal is greater than an input minimum number. The remaining signals which are not found to be in the neighborhood of any potential clusters will be considered isolated noise points or calcifications and excluded. This clustering criterion is useful for reducing false positives because true microcalcifications of clinical interest always appear in clusters on mammograms [18]-[22]. The specific parameters used in each step depend on the spatial and gray level resolution of the digitized mammograms. Examples of the parameters can be found in our previous publications [25], [41].

2.1.1 Convolution Neural Network Classifier

The artificial neural network (ANN) used in microcalcification recognition is a convolution type neural network [42]. The CNN can be considered a simplified version of the neocognitron [43] designed to simulate the human visual system. The general architecture of the CNN used in this study is shown in Figure 1. It consists of an input layer, one to several hidden layers, and an output layer. The input layer of the CNN contains $K \times K$ input nodes, each of the input nodes is a sensor for an input pixel value in a $K \times K$-pixel region of interest (ROI) containing the normal or abnormal pattern to be recognized. The value of N depends on the size of the signal of interest and the resolution of the digital system for image acquisition. In the hidden layers, the nodes are organized in groups and the groups between adjacent layers are interconnected by weights which are organized in kernels. Learning is constrained such that the kernel of weights connecting the kth group in the $(L-1)^{th}$ layer to the nth group in the Lth layer is invariant with nodes in the same groups. Forward signal propagation is thus similar to a spatially invariant convolution operation; the signals from the nodes in the lower layer are convolved with the weight kernel and the resultant value of the convolution is collected into the corresponding node in the upper layer. This value is further processed by the node through an activation function and produces an output signal which will, in turn, be forward-propagated to the subsequent layer in a similar manner. The convolution kernel incorporates the neighborhood information in the input image pattern and transfers the information to the receiving layers, thus providing the pattern recognition capability of the CNN. The activation function between two layers is a sigmoidal function, and the signal at the Lth layer is obtained from the signal at the $(L-1)^{th}$ layer. In the output layer, there are n_{out} individual output nodes. Each output node is fully connected to all nodes in each group of the preceding hidden layer.

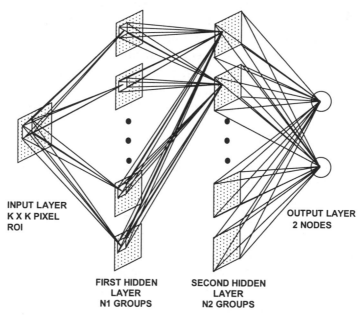

Figure 1. Architecture of the CNN used for differentiating true microcalcifications and false signals. The input to the CNN is an ROI containing an individual signal. The output is a probability indicating the likelihood that the input region contains a true microcalcification.

The error backpropagation learning rule is used for supervised training of the CNN. The error function is minimized by backpropagation training using the conventional steepest descent delta rule. Training may be terminated at a selected level of total error, which is the sum of the error for an individual case over all cases in the training set, a selected level of classification accuracy (A_z) as defined below, or a preset number of iterations. For the detection of microcalcifications, we used the total error as the termination criterion. The total error allowed at termination was chosen so that the classification accuracy could reach a maximum level.

2.1.2 Convolution Neural Network Training – an Example

For our microcalcification detection program, the CNN was trained to distinguish true and false signals that are segmented by adaptive gray level thresholding and have subsequently passed the size and contrast tests. For a given input SNR threshold, the program will identify a number of potential signals. A low SNR threshold corresponds to a lax criterion with a large number of false-positive (FP) signals. A high SNR threshold corresponds to a stringent criterion with a small number of FP signals and a loss in true-positive (TP) signals. We chose one of the SNR thresholds that yielded a moderate number of FPs and a sufficiently large number of TPs for segmenting the training ROIs. Because the number of FPs were still a few times more than the number of TPs, a subset of FPs with approximately the same number as the TPs were randomly chosen for the training set. It should be noted that the chosen SNR threshold level was not critical as long as the numbers of FP and TP were sufficiently large to provide the variety of ROI patterns for training the CNN. The signals obtained by using a high SNR threshold were generally a subset of those obtained by using a low SNR threshold. A chosen ROI input to the CNN was obtained from the SNR-enhanced image as a K×K-pixel region centered at the potential site. The gray level values of the pixels in the ROI were thus independent of the SNR threshold at which it was chosen, and all ROIs had the same average background pixel value. All weights in the CNN were initialized to be between -0.5 to $+0.5$ using a random number generator with a different seed in each training run and normalized by the number of weights in the exponential factor of the sigmoidal activation function.

The shape of the microcalcifications in the breast parenchyma could be considered randomly oriented if we considered all possible locations of the microcalcifications in the breast and all mammographic views. To increase the variability of the training group, eight input ROIs to the CNN were generated from each ROI by rotating the ROI and its mirror image to 0°, 90°, 180°, and 270°. Each training cycle thus included training of the complete set of training ROIs with the eight orientations.

This rotation method effectively increases the training sample size by a factor of 8. The input order of the training ROIs was randomized with a different random number sequence in each run. A test ROI would be rotated in the eight orientations and the average output value of the eight rotated ROIs would be taken to be the output value of that test ROI. During training, the desired output of an ROI with micro-calcification was set to 1 and that of an ROI without microcalcification was set to 0.

In our study, the input mammograms were digitized at 0.1 mm × 0.1 mm pixel size and 12 bit gray levels with a laser scanner. For training the CNN, we arbitrarily divided the mammogram samples into two subgroups. When the ROIs obtained from one subgroup were used for training, the trained CNN would be applied to the second subgroup for testing and vice versa. For each subgroup, over one hundred micro-calcifications (positives) and over five hundred false-positive signals (negatives) were extracted from the mammograms in the preceding segmentation steps. When the subgroup served as a training set, about one-fifth of the negatives, (approximately equal to the number of positives) were randomly selected as training samples. When the subgroup served as a test set, all extracted signals were used as test samples. With the rotation method, over 800 positive and over 900 negative ROIs were generated in each training set.

One of the commonly used method for evaluation of classification accuracy in computer-aided diagnosis is receiver operating charac-teristic (ROC) analysis [44]. ROC analysis uses the output values from the classifier as the decision variable. An ROC curve represents the relationship between the true-positive fraction (TPF) and the false-positive fraction (FPF) as the decision threshold varies. A computer program was first developed by Dorfman et al. [45] and later modified by Metz et al. [46] to fit an ROC curve to the TPF and FPF data based on maximum likelihood estimation. The ROC curve fitting assumes binormal distributions of the decision variable for the normal and abnormal cases. However, the assumption can still be satisfied if the distributions can be transformed to normal distributions by a monotonic function.

The classification accuracy of positive and negative ROIs depends on the CNN configurations that include the number of layers and the number of nodes in each layer. Figure 2 shows the ROC curves of a CNN that had two hidden layers, each with 12 node groups. Every three node groups in the second hidden layer were selectively connected to the same 8 node groups in the first hidden layer, and the weight kernel sizes were 5×5 and 3×3. Since the data set was divided into two subgroups, a weight set trained with one group was used to test the classification accuracy for the other group and vice versa so that two ROC curves for testing the CNN were obtained. The A_Z values of the curves were 0.91 and 0.90, which corresponded to the best performance obtained with the different CNN configurations that we evaluated.

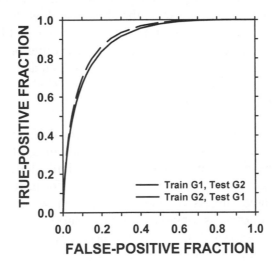

Figure 2. Performance of the CNN in classification of the true and false microcalcifications in the test groups. The areas under the ROC curves, A_z, are 0.90 and 0.91, respectively.

2.2   Analysis of Detection Accuracy

2.2.1   FROC Analysis

After passing the size and contrast criteria, being screened by the trained CNN, and passing the regional clustering criterion, the detected individual microcalcifications and clusters would be compared with the "truth" file of the input image. The number of TP and FP micro-calcifications and the number of TP and FP clusters were scored. The scoring method varies among researchers. In this study, the detected signal was scored as a TP microcalcification if it was within 0.5 mm from a true microcalcification in the "truth" file. A detected cluster was scored as a TP if its centroid coordinate was within a cluster radius (5 mm) from the centroid of a true cluster and at least two of its member microcalcifications were scored as TP. Once a true micro-calcification or cluster was matched to a detected microcalcification or cluster, it would be eliminated from further matching. Any detected microcalcifications or clusters that did not match to a true micro-calcification or cluster were scored as FPs. The trade-off between the TP and FP detection rates by the computer program was evaluated by the free-response receiver operating characteristic (FROC) analysis [47] by varying the input SNR threshold. A low SNR threshold corresponded to a lax criterion with a large number of FP clusters. A high SNR threshold corresponded to a stringent criterion with a small number of FP clusters and a loss in TP clusters. The detection accuracy of the computer program with and without the CNN classifier could then be assessed by comparison of the FROC curves.

Examples of FROC curves for our microcalcification detection program are shown in Figure 3. The performance of the program depends on the degree of subtlety of the microcalcifcations. Three FROC curves are shown to demonstrate the performance of the same program for three subsets of mammograms on which a radiologist classified the cluster as obvious, average subtle, and very subtle, respectively. As expected, the detection accuracy or the FROC curve for obvious clusters is much higher than that for very subtle clusters. The performance of various microcalcification detection programs published in the literature therefore varies over a wide range. While some differences in their performance may be caused by the different image processing techniques used, they are also strongly influenced by the different degrees of difficulty of the input data sets.

2.2.2 Performance of Computer Detection Program in Unknown Cases

It is important to evaluate the performance of any detection or classification program on clinical cases that have not been used for training or validation. Our trained computer detection program was applied to a set of clinical mammograms randomly selected from patient files that had undergone biopsy in the University of Michigan Hospital to evaluate its performance on unknown cases. The data set consisted of 260 mammograms from 49 patients. Of the 260 mammograms, 197 were pre-operative films, i.e., the exam that the radiologists decided to send the microcalcifications for biopsy, and 63 were prior films from previous exams. There were 220 microcalcification clusters on 172 images; 143 were benign and 77 were malignant as proven by biopsy or follow up. The data set was digitized with a laser scanner that had a slightly wider optical density (nominal 0-4 O.D.) range than the one (nominal 0-3.5 O.D.) used for digitization of the training set. The detection program was not trained with images from the new digitizer. The performance of the detection program at a false-positive detection rate of 0.8 FP/image is summarized in Table 1.

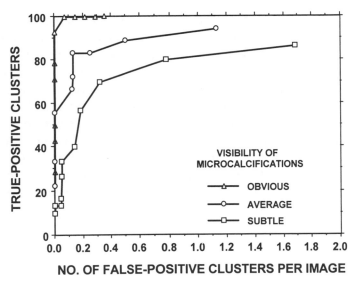

Figure 3. Free response receiver operating characteristic (FROC) curves in one of our data sets when a CNN was used for distinguishing false and true microcalcifications [25]. The visibility of the microcalcifications was classified into obvious, average, and subtle by an experienced mammographer. For obvious cases, the true-positive (TP) rate is 100% at a false-positive (FP) rate of 0.1 cluster per image. For average cases, the TP rate is about 93% at an FP rate of 1 cluster per image. For subtle cases, the TP rate was 87% at an FP rate of 1.5 clusters per image.

Table 1. Performance of our computerized microcalcification programs in 260 unknown cases.

Micro-calcifications	All years (by film)	Pre-operative films (by film)	Prior films (by film)	Pre-operative films (by case)	Prior films (by case)
All	80%	81%	71%	86%	73%
Malignant	81%	85%	58%	89%	57%
Benign	79%	80%	77%	84%	80%

2.3   Effects of Computer-Aided Detection on Radiologists' Performance

In the early stage of computer-aided diagnosis research, we performed an observer ROC study to evaluate the effects of CAD on radiologists' performance in the detection of microcalcifications [14]. In the ROC study, a set of 60 mammograms were used as case samples. Half of the mammograms were normal, and the other half contained very subtle microcalcifications. The detection accuracy of our computer program at the time of the study was 87% at 4 FPs/image for this data set. A simulated detection accuracy of 87% at 0.5 FP/image was also included in the ROC experiment to evaluate the influence of false-positive detection on radiologists' reading. Seven attending radiologists and eight radiology residents participated as observers. They read the set of 60 images under three different conditions; one without CAD, the second with CAD where the computer accuracy was 87% at 4 FPs/image, and the third condition with CAD where the computer accuracy was 87% at 0.5 FP/image. The reading for each observer was divided into three sessions and the reading order of the radiologists using the three conditions was counter-balanced so that no one condition would be used more often in the first reading than the others by the observers. The details of our observer experiment have been described previously [14]. The important issues involved in the design of ROC experiments can be found in the literature [48]. The ROC curves obtained from the observer experiment are shown in Figure 4. It was found that the area under the ROC curve, A_Z, was improved significantly ($p<0.001$) when the radiologists read the mammograms with the computer aid, either at 0.5 FP/image or at 4 FPs/image, compared to that when they read the mammograms without the computer aid. Although the A_Z of the CAD reading with 0.5 FP/image was slightly higher than that with 4 FPs/image, the difference did not achieve statistical significance. This ROC study is the first experiment that demonstrates CAD has the potential to improve breast cancer detection and establishes the significance of CAD research in mammography.

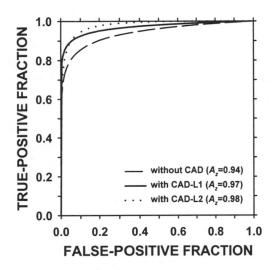

Figure 4. Comparison of the average ROC curves for detection of micro-calcifications with and without CAD. L1 is the computer performance level of 87% sensitivity at 4 FPs per image and L2 is the simulated computer performance level of 87% sensitivity at 0.5 FP per image. The average ROC curves were obtained by averaging the slope and intercept parameters of the individual ROC curves from the 15 observers. The improvement in the detection accuracy, A_z, was statistically significant at $p<0.001$ for both CAD conditions.

3 Computerized Classification of Microcalcifications

There are two major approaches to the development of CAD schemes for classification of mammographic abnormalities. One approach uses computer vision techniques to extract image features from the digitized mammograms and classify the lesions based on the computer-extracted features. The computer-extracted features can include morphological features that are commonly used by radiologists for diagnosis, as well as texture features that may not be readily perceived by human eyes. The computerized analysis may therefore increase the utilization of mammographic image information and improve the accuracy of differentiating malignant and benign lesions. The other approach uses radiologists' ratings of mammographic features or to encode the radiologists' readings with numerical values and classify the lesions based on these radiologist-extracted features. This approach assists radiologist by requiring them to systematically extract image features and by optimally merging the features with a statistical classifier to reach a diagnostic decision. Additional risk factors based on patient demographic information and medical or family histories may also be included as input in either approach.

A number of investigators have developed feature extraction and classification methods for characterization of mammographic micro-calcifications. Ackerman *et al.* [49] developed four measures of malignancy and classified lesions recorded on 120 digitized xeroradio-graphs by three decision methods. Wee *et al.* [49] analyzed 51 micro-calcification clusters on specimen radiographs using the average gray level, contrast, and horizontal length of the microcalcifications and obtained 84% correct classification. Fox *et al.* [50] used cluster features in their classifier and obtained 67% correct classification in a data set of 100 clusters from specimen radiographs. Chan *et al.* [51]-[58] developed morphological and texture features and evaluated various feature classifiers for differentiation of malignant and benign micro-calcifications. Shen *et al.* [59] used three shape features, compactness, moments, and Fourier descriptors to classify 143 individual micro-calcifications with a nearest neighbor classifier and obtained 100% classification accuracy. Wu *et al.* [60] classified 80 pathologic specimens radiographs with a convolution neural network and obtained an A_z of 0.90. Jiang *et al.* [61] trained a neural network classifier to analyze eight features extracted from microcalcification clusters and obtained an A_z of 0.92 in a data set of 53 patients. Thiele *et al.* [62] extracted texture and fractal features from the tissue region surrounding a microcalcification cluster for classification and achieved a sensitivity of 89% at a specificity of 83% for 54 clusters. Dhawan *et al.* [63] used features derived from first-order and second-order gray-level histogram statistics and obtained an A_z of 0.81 with a neural network classifier for a data set of 191 clusters.

Computerized classification of mammographic lesions using radiolo-gist-extracted features has also been reported by a number of investigators. Ackerman *et al.* [64] estimated the probability of malignancy of mammographic lesions by analyzing 36 radiologist-extracted characteristics with an automatic clustering algorithm and obtained a specificity of 45% at a sensitivity of 100% in a data set of 102 cases. Gale *et al.* [65] analyzed 12 radiologist-extracted features of mammographic lesions with a computer algorithm and obtained a specificity of 88% at a sensitivity of 79% in a data base of 500 patients. Getty *et al.* [66] developed a computer classifier to enhance the differentiation of malignant and benign lesions by a radiologist during interpretation of xeromammograms. Using a similar approach, D'Orsi *et al.* [67] evaluated a computer aid and obtained an improvement of about 0.05 in sensitivity or specificity in mammographic reading. Wu *et al.* [68] trained a neural network to merge 14 radiologist-extracted features for classification of mammographic lesions and obtained an A_z of 0.89. Baker *et al.* [69] trained a neural network based on the lexicon of the Breast Imaging Recording and Data System (BI-RADS) of the American College of Radiology and found that the neural network could improve the positive predictive value from 35% to 61% in 206 lesions. Lo *et al.* [70] used a similar approach to predict breast cancer invasion and obtained an A_z of 0.91 for 96 lesions. Although the results of these studies varied over a wide range and the performances of the computer algorithms are expected to depend strongly on data set, they indicate the potential of using CAD techniques to improve the diagnostic accuracy of differentiating malignant and benign lesions.

In this section, we will concentrate on computer-aided classification of mammographic microcalcifications using computer-extracted features. The classifier design generally involves three major steps: feature extraction, feature selection, and feature classification. We will review some of the techniques that we used for this classification task in order to illustrate classifier design methods for CAD applications.

3.1   Methods

In our early studies, we found that texture features extracted from spatial gray level dependence (SGLD) matrices at multiple distances were useful for differentiating malignant and benign masses on mammograms. This may be attributed to the texture changes in the breast tissue due to a developing malignancy. The usefulness of SGLD texture measures in differentiating malignant and benign breast tissues was further demonstrated by analysis of mammographic microcalcifications [55], [56], [71]. In an early study, we developed morphological features to describe the size, shape, and contrast of the individual microcalcifications and their variation within a cluster. These features were used to classify the microcalcifications and moderate results were obtained [51], [53]. More recently, we explored the feasibility of combining texture and morphological features for classification of microcalcifications [58]. The classification accuracy in the combined feature space was compared with those obtained in the texture feature space or in the morphological feature space alone. We found that the use of a genetic algorithm [72]-[74] to select a feature subset from the large-dimensional feature spaces could achieve higher classification accuracy than those obtained from features selected with stepwise linear discriminant analysis (LDA) [75]. The techniques used in the design of the classifier are described in the following.

3.1.1   Feature Extraction

<u>Morphological feature space</u>

For the extraction of morphological features, the locations of the individual microcalcifications have to be known. The microcalcifications may be identified manually or automatically by a computer detection program. In the latter approach, some true microcalcifications may be missed and the extracted true signals will be mixed with a fraction of false signals because no detection programs can achieve 100% sensitivity or specificity. For the discussion below, the microcalcifications were manually identified as those visible on the film mammograms with a magnifier.

An automated signal extraction program was developed to segment the microcalcifications from a mammogram based on the coordinate of each individual microcalcification. In a local region of N × N pixels at each signal site, the low frequency structured background is estimated and subtracted from the local region. A region growing technique using a locally adaptive SNR threshold was used to segment the connected pixels around the manually identified signal location which have SNR values greater than the selected threshold from the breast tissue background. The size and shape of the microcalcifications extracted from the image depend on the selected SNR threshold. A high threshold will result in extracting only the peak pixels of the microcalcification which may not represent its shape perceived on the mammogram. A low threshold will cause the microcalcification region to grow into the surrounding background pixels. Since there is no objective standard as to what the actual shape of a microcalcification is on a mammogram, the proper threshold to extract the signals was determined by visually comparing the microcalcifications in the original image and the thresholded image of the microcalcifications superimposed on a background of constant pixel values. After an experienced radiologist compared a subset of randomly selected microcalcification clusters extracted at different thresholds, an appropriate SNR threshold was chosen for all cases. An example of a malignant cluster and the microcalcifications extracted at an SNR threshold of 2.0 is shown in Figure 5.

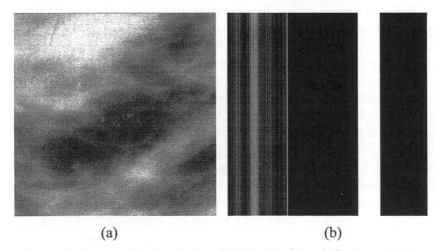

(a)   (b)

Figure 5. An example of a cluster of malignant microcalcifications: (a) the cluster with mammographic background, (b) the cluster after segmentation. Morphological features are extracted from the segmented microcalcifications.

We designed morphological features based on radiologists' experience in evaluation of microcalcifications. The presence of linear micro-calcifications and varying size and shape of the microcalcifications in a cluster are important features that indicate malignancy. We therefore designed five feature descriptors to quantify the morphology of the individual microcalcifications extracted from the mammograms. These included the size, the mean density, and three shape descriptors: the eccentricity of an effective ellipse fitted to the shape of the microcalcification, the ratio of the major to minor axis of the effective ellipse, and the ratio of the second moments. From the morphological features of the individual microcalcifications, the variations of the size, contrast, and shape of the microcalcifications in a cluster were derived. These cluster features included the maximum, the average, the standard deviation, and the coefficient of variation of each of the five individual features (size, mean density, moment ratio, axis ratio, and eccentricity) within a cluster. Another feature describing the number of micro-calcifications in a cluster was also added, resulting in a 21-dimensional morphological feature space.

Texture feature space

Texture features were extracted from a region of interest (ROI) that contained the cluster of microcalcifications [71]. For a given ROI, background correction was first performed to reduce the low frequency gray level variation due to the density of the overlapping breast tissue and the x-ray exposure conditions. The background level at each pixel along the edge of the ROI was first estimated by gray-level averaging in a rectangular region surrounding the pixel. The background level of a pixel inside the ROI was estimated by interpolation using the back-ground pixel values on the edges. A more detailed description of this background correction method can be found in the literature [76], [77]. The estimated background image was subtracted from the original ROI to obtain a background-corrected image. Texture features were derived from the SGLD matrices of the background-corrected ROI. The SGLD matrix element, $p_{\theta,d}(i,j)$, is the joint probability of the occurrence of gray levels i and j for pixel pairs which are separated by a distance d and at a direction θ [78]. We analyzed the texture features in four directions: $\theta = 0°$, $45°$, $90°$, and $135°$ at each pixel pair distance d. The pixel pair distance was varied from 4 to 40 pixels in increments of 4 pixels. Therefore, a total of 40 SGLD matrices were derived from each ROI. The SGLD matrix also depended on the bin width (or gray level interval) used in accumulating the histogram. A bin width of 4 gray levels was chosen for constructing SGLD matrices from the 12 bit image.

From each of the SGLD matrices, we derived thirteen texture measures including correlation, entropy, energy (angular second moment), inertia, inverse difference moment, sum average, sum entropy, sum variance, difference average, difference entropy, difference variance, information measure of correlation 1, and information measure of correlation 2. The formulation of these texture measures can be found in the literature [71], [78]. We did not observe a significant dependence of the discriminatory power of the texture features on the direction of the pixel pairs for mammographic textures [76]. However, since the actual distance between the pixel pairs in the diagonal direction was a factor of $\sqrt{2}$ greater than that in the axial direction, the feature values in the axial directions (0° and 90°) and in the diagonal directions (45° and 135°) were averaged separately for each texture feature derived from the SGLD matrix at a given pixel pair distance. The average texture features at the ten pixel pair distances and two directions formed a 260-dimensional texture feature space.

3.1.2   Feature Selection

Feature selection is one of the most important steps in classifier design because the presence of ineffective features often degrades the performance of a classifier on test samples. This is partly caused by the "curse of dimensionality" problem that the classifier is inadequately trained in a large-dimension feature space when only a finite number of training samples is available [79]-[83]. We compared two feature selection methods to extract useful features from the morphological, texture, and the combined feature spaces. One is a genetic algorithm approach, and the other is the commonly used stepwise linear discriminant analysis method. The following example shows the application of these two methods in classifier design.

Genetic algorithm for feature selection

The genetic algorithm (GA) methodology was first introduced by Holland in the early 1970s [73], [84]. A GA solves an optimization problem based on the principles of natural selection. In natural selection, a population evolves by finding beneficial adaptations to a complex environment. The characteristics of a population are carried onto the next generation by its chromosomes. New characteristics are introduced into a chromosome by crossover and mutation. The probability of survival or reproduction of an individual depends more or less on its fitness to the environment. The population therefore evolves toward better-fit individuals.

The application of GA to feature selection has been described in the literature [85], [86]. We have demonstrated previously that a GA could select effective features for classification of masses and normal breast tissue from a very large-dimensional feature space [87]. The GA was adapted to the problem for classification of malignant and benign microcalcifications. A brief outline is given as follows. Each feature in a given feature space is treated as a gene and is encoded by a binary digit (bit) in a chromosome. The number of genes (bits) on a chromosome is equal to the dimensionality (k) of the feature space, but only the features that are encoded as "1" are actually present in the subset of selected features. A chromosome therefore represents a possible solution to the feature selection problem.

The implementation of GA for feature selection is illustrated in the block diagram shown in Figure 6. To allow for diversity, a large number, n, of chromosomes, X_1, ..., X_n, is chosen as the population. The number of chromosomes is kept constant in each generation. At the initiation of the GA, each bit on a chromosome is initialized randomly with a small but equal probability, P_{init}, to be "1." The selected feature subset on a chromosome is used as the input feature variables to a classifier, which was chosen to be the Fischer's linear discriminant in this study.

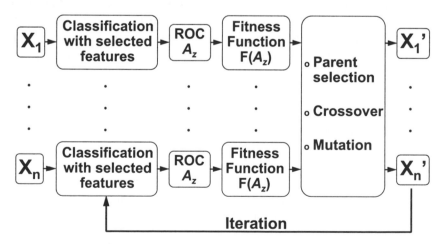

Figure 6. A schematic diagram of the genetic algorithm designed for feature selection used in this study. X_1, ..., X_n represents the set of parent chromosomes and X_1', ..., X_n' represents the set of offspring chromosomes.

The available samples in the data set are randomly partitioned into a training set and a test set. The training set is used to formulate a linear discriminant function with each of the selected feature subsets. The effectiveness of each of the linear discriminants for classification is evaluated with the test set. The classification accuracy is determined as the area, A_z, under the ROC curve. To reduce biases in the classifiers due to case selection, training and testing are performed a large number of times, each with a different random partitioning of the data set. In this study, the data set was partitioned 80 times and the 80 test A_z values were averaged and used for determination of the fitness of the chromosome.

The fitness function for the ith chromosome, $F(i)$, is formulated as

$$F(i) = \left[\frac{f(i) - f_{min}}{f_{max} - f_{min}} \right]^2 , \quad i = 1, \cdots, n \tag{1}$$

where $f(i) = \overline{A_z(i)} - \alpha\, N(i)$, $\overline{A_z(i)}$ is the average test A_z for the ith chromosome over the 80 random partitions of the data set, f_{min} and f_{max} are the minimum and maximum $f(i)$ among the n chromosomes, $N(i)$ is the number of features in the ith chromosome, and α is a penalty factor, whose magnitude is less than $1/k$, to suppress chromosomes with a large number of selected features. The value of the fitness function $F(i)$ ranges from 0 to 1. The probability of the ith chromosome being selected as a parent, $P_s(i)$, is proportional to its fitness function:

$$P_s(i) = \frac{F(i)}{\sum\limits_{i=1}^{n} F(i)} , \quad i = 1, ..., n \tag{2}$$

A random sampling based on the probabilities, $P_s(i)$, will allow chromosomes with higher fitness value to be selected more frequently.

For every pair of selected parent chromosomes, X_i and X_j, a random decision is made to determine if crossover should take place. A uniform random number in $(0,1]$ is generated. If the random number is greater than P_c, the probability of crossover, then no crossover will occur; otherwise, a random crossover site is selected on the pair of chromosomes. Each chromosome is split into two strings at this site and one of the strings will be exchanged with the corresponding string from the other chromosome. Crossover results in two new chromosomes of the same length.

After crossover, another chance of introducing new features is obtained by mutation. Mutation is applied to each gene on every chromosome. For each bit, a uniform random number in (0,1] is generated. If the random number is greater than P_m, the probability of mutation, then no mutation will occur; otherwise, the bit is complemented. The processes of parent selection, crossover, and mutation result in a new generation of n chromosomes, X_1', ..., X_n', which will again be evaluated with the 80 training and test set partitions as described above. The chromosomes are allowed to evolve over a preselected number of generations. The best feature subset is chosen to be the chromosome that provides the highest average A_z during the evolution process.

For our task of microcalcification characterization, 500 chromosomes were used in the population. Each chromosome had 281 gene locations, corresponding to the 281 extracted features. P_{init} was chosen to be 0.01 so that each chromosome started with 2 to 3 features on the average. We varied P_c from 0.7 to 0.9, P_m from 0.001 to 0.005, and α from 0 to 0.001. These ranges of parameters were chosen based on our previous experience with other feature selection problems using GA [87].

Stepwise linear discriminant analysis

The stepwise linear discriminant analysis (LDA) is a commonly used method for selection of useful feature variables from a large feature space. Detailed descriptions of this method can be found in the literature [88]. The procedure is briefly outlined below. The stepwise LDA uses a forward selection and backward removal strategy. When a feature is entered into or removed from the model, its effect on the separation of the two classes can be analyzed by several criteria. We use the Wilks' lambda criterion which minimizes the ratio of the within-group sum of squares to the total sum of squares of the two class distributions; the significance of the change in the Wilks' lambda is estimated by F-statistics. In the forward selection step, the features are entered one at a time. The feature variable that causes the most significant change in the Wilks' lambda will be included in the feature set if its F value is greater than the F-to-enter (F_{in}) threshold. In the feature removal step, the features already in the model are eliminated one at a time. The feature variable that causes the least significant change in the Wilks' lambda will be excluded from the feature set if its F value is below the F-to-remove (F_{out}) threshold. The stepwise procedure terminates when the F values for all features not in the model are smaller than the F_{in} threshold and the F values for all features in the model are greater than the F_{out} threshold. The number of selected features will decrease if either the F_{in} threshold or the F_{out} threshold is increased. Therefore, the number of features to be selected can be adjusted by varying the F_{in} and F_{out} values.

3.1.3   Feature Classification

After the best subset of features is selected, the features are used as predictor variables in a feature classifier. One of the commonly used classifiers is the Fischer's linear discriminant, which is the optimal classifier if the class distributions are multivariate normal with equal covariance matrices [79]. Even if these conditions are not satisfied, as in most classification tasks, the LDA may still be a preferred choice in terms of generalizability when the number of available training samples is limited [82], [83].

The data set for this study consisted of 145 clusters of microcalcifications from mammograms of 78 patients. Eighty-two of the clusters were benign and 63 were malignant, as proven by biopsy. The selected mammograms were digitized with a laser scanner (Lumisys DIS-1000) at a pixel size of 0.035 mm × 0.035 mm and 12-bit gray levels. In our study, the linear discriminant analysis [89] procedure in the SPSS software package [88] was used to classify the microcalcification clusters. A cross-validation resampling scheme was used for training and testing the classifier. The data set of 145 samples was randomly partitioned into a training set and a test set by an approximately 3:1 ratio. The partitioning was constrained so that ROIs from the same patient were always grouped into the same set. The training set was used to determine the coefficients (or weights) of the feature variables in the linear discriminant function. The performance of the trained classifier was evaluated with the test set. In order to reduce the effect of case selection, the random partitioning was performed 50 times. The results were then averaged over the 50 partitions.

The classification accuracy of the LDA was evaluated by ROC methodology. The output discriminant score from the LDA classifier was used as the decision variable in the ROC analysis. The LABROC program [46] was used to estimate the ROC curve of the classifier. The area under the ROC curve and the standard deviation of the A_z were provided by the LABROC program for each partition of training and test sets. The average performance of the classifier was estimated as the average of the 50 test A_z values from the 50 random partitions.

3.2   Analysis of Classification Accuracy

3.2.1   Comparison of Feature Selection Methods

Table 2 compares the training and test A_z values from the best feature set in each feature space for the GA and the stepwise LDA methods. The GA was run for 75 generations in each feature space and the feature set that provided the best classification performance was chosen as the best set. The corresponding GA parameters were used to run the GA again for 500 generations. The A_z values obtained with the best GA selected feature sets are listed together with those obtained with the best stepwise LDA selected feature sets. The two feature selection methods provided feature sets that had similar test A_z values in the morphological and texture feature spaces. In the combined feature space, there was a slight improvement in the test A_z value obtained with the GA selected features. The differences in the paired A_z values from the 50 partitions demonstrated a consistent trend (40 out of 50 partitions) that the A_z values from the GA selected features were higher than those obtained by the stepwise LDA. This trend was also observed in our previous study in which mass and normal tissue were classified [87].

For the linear discriminant classifier, the stepwise LDA procedure can select near-optimal features for the classification task. We have shown that the GA could select a feature set comparable to or slightly better than that selected by the stepwise LDA. The number of generations that the GA had to evolve to reach the best selection increased with the dimensionality of the feature space as expected. However, even in a 281-dimensional feature space, it only took 169 generations to find a better feature set than that selected by stepwise LDA. Further search up to 500 generations did not find other feature combinations with better performance. Although the difference in A_z did not achieve statistical significance, probably due to the large standard deviation in A_z when the number of case samples in the ROC analysis was small, the improvements in A_z in this and our previous studies [87] indicate that the GA is a useful feature selection method for classifier design. One of the advantages of GA-based feature selection is that it can search for near-optimal feature sets for any types of linear or non-linear classifiers, whereas the stepwise LDA procedure is tailored to linear discriminant classifiers. Furthermore, the fitness function in the GA can be designed such that features with specific characteristics are favored. One of the applications in this direction is to select features to design a classifier with high sensitivity and high specificity for classification of malignant and benign lesions [90]. Although the GA requires much longer computation time than the stepwise LDA to search for the best feature set, the flexibility of the GA makes it an increasingly popular alternative for solving machine learning and optimization problems. Since feature selection is performed only during training of a classifier, the speed of a trained classifier for processing test cases is not affected by the choice of the feature selection method. Therefore, the longer computation time of GA is not a problem in practice if the GA can provide a better feature set for a given classification task.

Table 2.   Classification accuracy of linear discriminant classifiers in the different feature spaces using feature sets selected by the GA and the stepwise LDA procedure. (a) Training, (b) Test.

(a)

Feature Selection	Training A_z		
	Morphological	Texture	Combined
GA (75 generations)	0.84 ± 0.04	0.88 ± 0.03	0.94 ± 0.02
GA (500 generations)	0.84 ± 0.04	0.88 ± 0.03	0.96 ± 0.02
Stepwise LDA	0.83 ± 0.04	0.91 ± 0.03	0.96 ± 0.02

(b)

Feature Selection	Test A_z		
	Morphological	Texture	Combined
GA (75 generations)	0.79 ± 0.07	0.85 ± 0.07	0.89 ± 0.05
GA (500 generations)	0.79 ± 0.07	0.85 ± 0.07	0.90 ± 0.05
Stepwise LDA	0.79 ± 0.07	0.85 ± 0.06	0.87 ± 0.06

3.2.2   Computer-Aided Classification of Microcalcifications

Using the best feature set and a leave-one-case-out resampling scheme, we could obtain the discriminant scores of the case samples in the entire data set when they were used as test samples. This allowed us to generate ROC curves to evaluate the relative performances of the classifiers in the different feature spaces at various decision thresholds. The ROC curves for the test samples using the feature sets selected by the GA were plotted in Figure 7. The classification accuracy in the combined feature space was significantly higher than those in the morphological (p = 0.002) or the texture feature space (p = 0.04) alone. The ROC curve using the feature set selected by the stepwise procedure in the combined feature space was also plotted for comparison. These results demonstrate that both the morphological features of the microcalcifications and the texture features in the surrounding tissue contained important information for characterization of the microcalcifications.

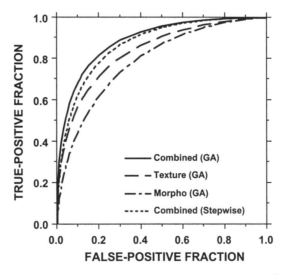

Figure 7. Comparison of ROC curves of the LDA classifier performance using the best GA selected feature sets in the three feature spaces. In addition, the ROC curve obtained from the best feature set selected by the stepwise LDA procedure in the combined feature space is shown. The classification was performed with a leave-one-case-out resampling scheme.

The distribution of the discriminant scores for the test samples using the feature set selected by the GA in the combined feature space is shown in Figure 8a. If a decision threshold is chosen at 0.3, 29 of the 82 (35% specificity) benign samples can be correctly classified without missing any malignant clusters (100% sensitivity). If the average discriminant score from all views of the same cluster was used for classification (Figure 8b), the accuracy improved to 50% specificity at 100% sensitivity. This indicates the potential of using CAD to reduce unnecessary biopsies, thereby improving the positive predictive value of mammography. Although these results were obtained with a relatively small data set, they demonstrate the potential of using CAD techniques to analyze mammograms and to assist radiologists in making diagnostic decisions. Further studies will have to be conducted to evaluate the generalizability of the approach in large data sets.

In our recent observer ROC study [16], we evaluated the effects of CAD on radiologists' accuracy in characterization of malignant and benign masses. The relative malignancy rating of the masses estimated by the computer classifier was provided to the radiologists during the reading with CAD. We found that the radiologists' ability to classify malignant and benign masses was improved significantly. Jiang *et al.* [17] also conducted an observer ROC study to evaluate the effects of CAD on radiologists' classification of microcalcifications. They estimated the likelihood of malignancy of the microcalcification clusters within the sample population used in their study and provided this information to the radiologists in a CAD reading. They compared radiologists' accuracy in characterization of microcalcifications and biopsy recommendation without the computer aid to those with aid. It was found that the radiologists' accuracy was improved significantly. These observer performance studies demonstrate the potential that CAD may reduce the number of unnecessary biopsies. However, since the prevalence of malignant breast lesions in the general population is very different from that in the laboratory samples, a large scale clinical trial will be needed to investigate if these potential benefits of CAD can be realized in a clinical environment.

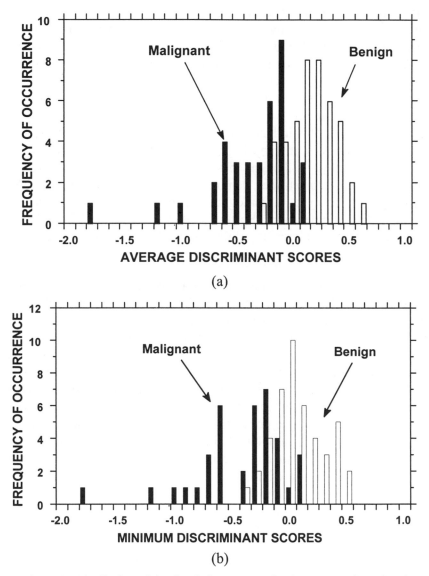

Figure 8. Distribution of the discriminant scores for the test samples using the best GA selected feature set in the combined texture and morphological feature space: (a) classification by cluster using the average scores, (b) classification by cluster using the minimum scores.

4   Computerized Detection of Masses

The fundamental step in many CAD methods is the segmentation of target signals in the input image. For mammograms manifesting masses this corresponds to the detection of suspicious mass regions. The detection of breast masses in mammograms is difficult because masses can be simulated or obscured by normal breast parenchyma [91]. In this section, we will review some of the computer techniques proposed for automatically detecting breast masses.

Many researchers have been interested in computerized analysis of mammograms and a number of groups have developed algorithms for automated detection of breast masses. The detection of spiculated masses has been of particular importance because of their high likelihood of malignancy. Therefore, researchers have proposed methods tuned to the detection of spiculated masses [15], [92]-[96]. Kegelmeyer used the Analysis of Local Oriented Edges (ALOE) feature to identify stellate lesions where the ALOE feature was derived from the local edge orientation histogram. Laws texture energy measures were also included as features to reduce false alarm detections. Karssemeijer's method employed statistical analysis to develop a multiscale map of pixel orientations. Two operators sensitive to radial patterns of straight lines were constructed from the pixel orientation map. The operators were then used by a classifier to detect stellate patterns in the mammogram. Kobatake *et al.* also detected the existence of spicules but their method used line skeletons and a modified Hough transform to detect radiating line structures. Finally, Ng *et al.* used a spine-oriented approach to detect the microstructure of mass spicules.

Not all malignant masses are spiculated so the detection of non-spiculated masses is also very important. This has led researchers to tackle the more general problem of identifying all suspicious masses in a mammogram (spiculated and non-spiculated) [97]-[111]. These general detection schemes can be divided into single- and multiple-image techniques. Many of the single-image techniques use some type of preprocessing filter, based on morphological and/or gray-scale information, to identify or enhance suspicious regions, although pixel-based approaches have also been used. Laine *et al.* proposed a contrast enhancement method based on multiscale wavelet analysis applied to a mammogram [97], [98]. Kallergi *et al.* employed adaptive thresholding and a modified Markov random field model to segment regions in an image. This was followed by a fuzzy binary-decision tree classifier to classify the regions as suspicious or normal [99]. A fuzzy region growing method for mass detection was proposed by Guliato *et al.* [100]. An alternative method proposed by Zheng *et al.* used Gaussian band-pass filtering to detect suspicious regions and rule-based multilayer topographic feature analysis to classify the regions [101]. Petrick *et al.* used adaptive enhancement, region growing and feature classification to detect suspicious mass region in a mammogram [109].

Giger *et al.* developed mass detection methods based on multiple images. Their technique, bilateral subtraction, subtracted corresponding left and right mammogram after the two images were aligned. Morphological and texture features were then extracted from the detected regions to decrease the number of false positive detections [103], [104]. This technique was also applied to current and previous mammograms from the same patient. Methods for comparing current with previous mammograms have been proposed by other authors as well. Brzakovic *et al.* registered the current and previous mammograms using a principal axis method. The mammograms were then partitioned using hierarchical region growing and compared using region statistics [105]. Another proposed method by Sanjay-Gopal *et al.* [112] used a regional registration technique. Mammograms were aligned based on maximizing mutual information between the breast regions on the two films. Polar coordinate systems, based on the nipple and breast centroid locations, were established for both films. The center of the lesion on the current image was then transformed to the previous image. A fan-shaped region, based on this centroid, was defined and searched to obtain a final estimate of the mass location in the previous film.

In the remainder of this section, we will use our segmentation approach as an example of an automated technique for detection of masses. We will also present detection results on an independent data set to demonstrate its performance on unknown clinical mammograms.

4.1 Methods

Our mass detection algorithm uses a detection/classification approach. The advantage of this general approach is that it has the ability to identify masses not having a typical mammographic appearance because the segmentation is not based on any specific mass properties.

Our mass detection scheme uses adaptive enhancement, local object-based growing and feature classification. The block diagram for the scheme is shown in Figure 9. This segmentation method utilizes the density-weighted contrast enhancement (DWCE) filter as a preprocessing step. The DWCE filter adaptively enhances the contrast between the breast structures and the background. Object-based growing is then applied to each of the identified structures. The growing technique uses gray-scale information to improve the initial object borders and to reduce merging between adjacent and/or overlapping structures. Each object is then classified as a breast mass or a normal structure based on extracted morphological and texture features. In order to overcome the problems associated with the large number of initial structures, we have split the feature classification into two stages. The first-stage classifier, based on morphological features, is used to provide an initial reduction in regions whose shapes are significantly different from breast masses. The first-stage classifier has been found to improve the performance of the second-stage texture classifier that acts as a final arbiter between true masses and normal structures.

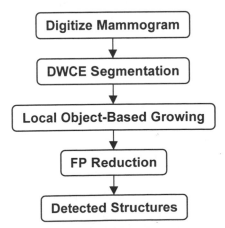

Figure 9. The block diagram for the mass detection scheme.

4.1.1 Density-Weight Contrast Enhancement Segmentation

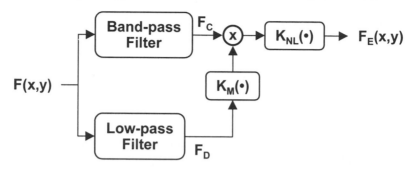

Figure 10. The block diagram for the DWCE filter.

We have developed a global segmentation technique which uses DWCE filtering with Laplacian-Gaussian (LG) edge detection for segmentation of low contrast objects in digital mammograms. The DWCE algorithm is used to enhance objects in the original image so that a simple edge detector can define the object boundaries. The DWCE technique employs an adaptive filter to enhance the local contrast thus accentuating mammographic structures in the breast [107]. This adaptive filter is an expansion of the adaptive contrast and mean filter of Peli and Lim [113]. As the name implies, the amount of enhancement is based on the density within the image with the filter being applied to the image on a pixel-by-pixel basis. The block diagram for the enhancement filter is shown in Figure 10. The original image first undergoes filtering to obtain $F_C(x,y)$ and $F_D(x,y)$, the contrast and density, respectively. The contrast is then modified by a multiplication factor derived from the density

$$F_{K_M}(x,y) = K_M(F_D(x,y)) \cdot F_C(x,y) \tag{3}$$

and finally undergoes a nonlinear scaling to produce the final "enhanced" pixel value

$$F_E(x,y) = K_{NL}(F_{K_M}(x,y)). \tag{4}$$

Graphs of the particular multiplication and nonlinear scaling functions used in this application, $K_M(\cdot)$ and $K_{NL}(\cdot)$, can be found in the literature [107]. The goal of the filter design was to suppress very low contrast values, to emphasize low to medium contrast values and to slightly de-emphasize high contrast values. The effect of suppressing the extremely low contrast values is to reduce bridging between adjacent breast structures. Pixels with low to medium contrast values are enhanced so that more subtle structures can be detected. Finally, the slight de-emphasis of the high contrast structures is included to provide a more uniform intensity distribution for detected structures. Figures 11a and 11b shows an original mammogram at 800 μm resolution and the corresponding DWCE filtered image.

After contrast enhancement, Laplacian-Gaussian edge detection [114], [115] is applied and all enclosed objects are filled to produce a set of detected structures for the image. Figure 11c shows the final objects segmented by Laplacian-Gaussian edge detection.

The DWCE stage has been found to be effective in detecting most breast structures including a significant portion of breast masses. However, the DWCE borders usually fall well inside the true borders of an object and a significant number of adjacent structures are merged together. This occurs most frequently when the adjacent breast structures have some tissue overlap.

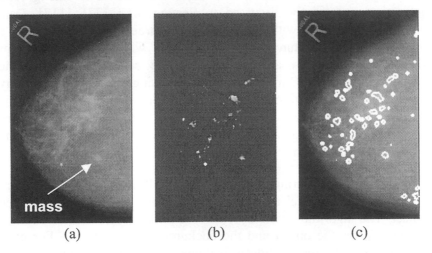

(a)   (b)   (c)

Figure 11. Example of (a) a digitized mammogram (800 μm resolution), (b) the enhanced image obtained by filtering, and (c) the DWCE segmented structures.

4.1.2 Local Growing

Local object-based growing is applied following DWCE segmentation to a set of seed objects. The seed objects are identified by finding all local maxima in the original gray-scale image occurring inside the DWCE structures. Local maxima are defined using the ultimate erosion technique described by Russ [116]. In simple terms, a pixel is a local maximum if and only if its value is at least as large as all nearest neighbor pixel values. All maxima are then grown into seed objects by applying Gaussian smoothing ($\sigma = 0.4$ mm). The maxima are then expanded to include all connected pixels within a radius of 4 mm such that

$$0.99 G_i^{\max} \leq F_G(x, y) \leq 1.01 G_i^{\max} \tag{5}$$

where $F_G(x,y)$ is a smoothed gray-scale value for pixel (x,y) and $G_i^{\max}$ is the ith maximum.

We use a pixel-by-pixel K-means clustering algorithm applied to square 2.5 mm × 2.5 mm background corrected ROIs centered on each seed object to refine the initial object borders. The background correction was briefly discussed in Section 3.1.1 [77], [117]. Data points for each pixel within a region are regarded as components of a multidimensional feature vector, and pixels with feature vectors of similar characteristics are assigned to the same class using the clustering algorithm. Our data set contains a single data point (the gray level) and a median filtered value ($w = 1.0$ mm) for each pixel. The original and filtered values are combined to form a feature vector for each pixel in the image and then these feature vectors are used in the clustering algorithm to separate the object from the background.

The goal of the clustering algorithm [87], [118] is to assign the feature vector F_i of each pixel as either belonging to the background or the object. The algorithm starts by choosing initial cluster center vectors, C_o and C_b for the object and the background, respectively. For each feature vector F_i, the Euclidean distance $d_o(i)$ between F_i and C_o, and the Euclidean distance $d_b(i)$ between F_i and C_b are computed. If the ratio $d_b(i)/d_o(i)$ is larger than a pre-determined threshold R, then the vector is temporarily assigned to the group of object pixels; otherwise, it is temporarily assigned to the group of background pixels. Using the new pixel assignments, a new object cluster center vector is computed as the mean of the vectors temporarily assigned to the group of object pixels, and a new background cluster center vector is computed as the mean of the vectors temporarily assigned to the group of background pixels. This completed one iteration of the clustering algorithm. The iterations are continued until the new and old cluster center vectors are the same, which meant that the class assignment for each pixel is stationary.

After clustering a region may contain several disconnected objects. To obtain a single structure for each region, we select the largest connected object among all detected objects in the region. Figure 12 shows examples of the extracted regions and the results before and after clustering is applied.

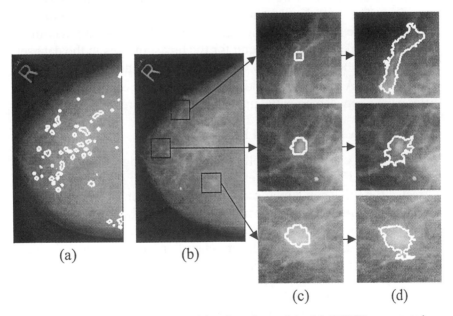

Figure 12. Example of local object-based growing: (a) DWCE segmented objects (800 µm resolution), (b) original mammogram with 3 of the 37 selected 2.5 mm × 2.5 mm regions of interest, (c) the corresponding DWCE segmented objects placed on the corresponding regions and (d) the final grown objects after clustering and filling (200 µm resolution).

4.1.3   Morphological Feature-Based FP Reduction

Eleven morphological features are used in the initial differentiation of the detected structures [108], [109]. Ten of these features are based solely on the binary object defined by the segmentation with five of these based on the normalized radial length (NRL). NRL is defined as the Euclidean distance from an object's centroid to each of its edge pixels and normalized relative to the maximum radial length for the object [119]. The morphological features are: number of perimeter pixels; area; perimeter-to-area ratio; circularity; rectangularity; contrast; and NRL mean, standard deviation, entropy, area ratio, and zero crossing count. The definition for each feature can be found in the literature [109].

The morphological features are used as input variables to a simple threshold classifier followed by a linear discriminant analysis (LDA) classifier. The simple threshold classifier sets a maximum and minimum value for each morphological feature based on the maximum and minimum feature values found for the breast masses in the data set. LDA classification was applied to all objects remaining after threshold classification. A single threshold is then applied to each LDA score to differentiate between potential masses and normal breast structures.

4.1.4   Texture Feature-Based FP Reduction

Texture-based classification follows the morphological FP reduction [108], [109], [120], [121]. A set of multiresolution texture features is extracted for ROIs containing each detected object in the mammogram. Stepwise feature selection is then used to choose the most appropriate set of features for linear classification. The selected features are subsequently used by the linear classifier to produce a single discriminant score for each detected object.

Regions of interest (ROIs) containing each object remaining after morphological FP reduction are extracted from 100 μm resolution mammograms. The ROIs have a fixed size of 256×256 pixels and the center of each ROI corresponds to the centroid location of a detected object. The only exception is when the object is located near the border of the breast and a complete 256×256 pixel ROI cannot be defined. In this case, the ROI is shifted until the appropriate edge coincided with the border of the original mammogram.

Global and local multiresolution texture features, based on the spatial gray level dependence (SGLD) are used in texture analysis [132]. The SGLD and the thirteen texture features are the same measures described in Section 3.1.1. The wavelet transform with a four-coefficient Daubechies kernel is used to decompose individual ROIs into different scales. For global texture features, four different wavelet scales, 14 different inter-pixel distances and 2 different angles are used to produce 28 SGLD matrices. This resulted in 364 global multi-resolution texture feature for each ROI. To further describe the information specific to the mass and its surrounding normal tissue, a set of local texture features are calculated for each ROI [108], [121], 122]. Five rectangular subregions are segmented from each ROI; an object subregion with the detected object in the center and four peripheral regions at the corners. Eight SGLD matrices (4 inter-pixel distances and 2 angles) and a total of 208 local features are calculated from the object subregion and the periphery. They included 104 features in the object region and an additional 104 features defined as the difference between the feature values in the object and the periphery.

In order to improve the generalization of the texture classification, stepwise feature selection is used to select a subset of features from the pool of 572 global and local features. Feature selection is performed using texture features derived from the ROIs obtained from all 253 images. Details on the application of stepwise feature selection can be found in the literature [76], [120] and in Section 3.1.2. LDA classification is applied using the selected texture features for each remaining structure. Finally a single discriminating threshold is used to differentiate between true masses and false positives. In this implementation, all scores in an individual image are scaled before thresholding so that the minimum score in the image is zero and the maximum score is one. This scaling minimizes the non-uniformity seen between mass structures in different images. It also results in at least one structure being detected in each image.

4.2   Analysis of Detection Accuracy

Breast mass detection schemes are commonly evaluated by free-response receiver operating characteristic (FROC) analysis [123]. FROC curves show the tradeoff between TP detections and the number of FPs per image. They can be used to assess overall performance, and they provide a means for comparing different detection schemes.

4.2.1 Database of Digitized Mammograms

The clinical mammograms used in this study were selected from the files of patients who had undergone biopsy at the University of Michigan Hospital. The mammograms were acquired with American College of Radiology accredited mammography systems and. were digitized with a LUMISYS laser film scanner with a pixel size of 100 μm and 12 bit gray level resolution.

The criterion used by the radiologists for selecting mammographic cases was simply that a biopsy-proven mass existed on the mammo-gram. The data set consisted of 253 mammograms from 102 patients, and it included 128 malignant and 125 benign masses. Sixty-three of the malignant and six of the benign masses were judged to be spiculated by a radiologist experienced in mammography. The size of each mass and its visibility were estimated by the radiologist where the mass size was a measure of the largest axis of the mass and visibility ranged from 1 (obvious) to 5 (subtle). The size of the masses ranged from 5 mm to 29 mm (mean size = 12.5 mm), and their mean visibility was 2.1. Figures 13 and 14 show the histograms of mass size and mass visibility for the data set. These two distributions are useful for characterizing the difficulty and diversity of the cases contained in the data set.

4.2.2 Definition of a True Positive

An important consideration when evaluating any detection schemes is the definition of a TP. In our evaluation, the location and extent of all the biopsy-proven masses were marked on the original films. The radiologist then identified both the centroid of the lesion and the smallest bounding box containing the entire lesion using an interactive image manipulation tool on a workstation. We base our definition of a TP on the percentage of an identified structure's bounding box that overlaps with the bounding box of the true mass. In this study, at least 25% of the identified structure's bounding box had to overlap with the mass bounding box to be considered a TP detection. All detected objects that did not meet this criterion were considered as FPs.

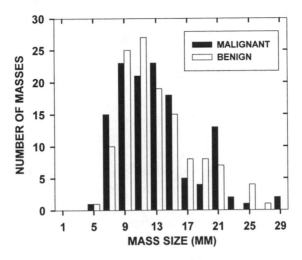

Figure 13. Histogram of mass sizes for the 253 masses in the data set.

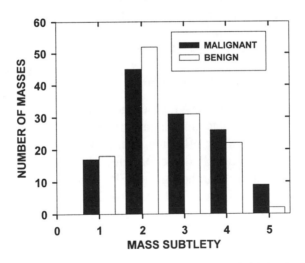

Figure 14. Histogram of mass subtlety (1:obvious to 5:subtle) for the 253 masses.

4.2.3   Training and Testing

In this study, training is complicated by the fact that it must be performed in morphological FP reduction with a fixed threshold and then again during texture FP reduction. Ideally, we would like to use a leave-one-case-out training/test resampling scheme for the entire process. However, a modified version was used because of the extremely long time it takes to perform both reduction stages independently on all test partitions. The most time consuming task in FP reduction was that of feature selection in the texture-based classification step.

For the morphological classification step, the 253 mammograms were partitioned into 102 independent groups, each of which contained all mammograms from one patient. The image groups were used for training and test in a leave-one-case-out fashion. Morphological classification within each individual group was performed with a classifier trained using the remaining groups (no overlap in images between training and test). This allowed an approximate 100:1 training-to-test ratio for morphological classification. By rotating the test group through all image sets, each mammogram served as a test case once. Thresholds for the simple threshold and LDA classifiers were set after training. Texture classification was performed in a similar fashion. The only variation was that the feature selection, based on all the detected structures, was performed only once, and the test scores were recombined into a single test set before FROC analysis was performed.

4.2.4 Performance of Mass Detection

The purpose of the initial DWCE segmentation stage was to have a sensitive method for detecting breast masses. We have found the DWCE segmentation to be effective in this task. Table 3 summarizes the number of TP and FP detections found following the DWCE, region growing and morphological FP reduction stages of the segmentation algorithm. In this study, DWCE segmentation identified 248 of the 253 masses (98%) in the images. Masses missed at this initial stage could be attributed to several factors. First, a dense pectoral muscle visible on some mammograms overwhelmed all lower-density structures. The dense pectoral muscle caused the lower level of the DWCE intensity range to be set so that lower intensity structures were missed. Second, the contrast difference between the mass and its surrounding background tissue was relatively small even though the mass was not particularly small or subtle. Finally, many mammograms contain significant amounts of dense breast tissue. It was observed that DWCE segmentation had problems detecting masses that were located near much denser normal structures. The dense structures were detected but the masses were missed. Other than these noted problems, the

DWCE was very effective as a first stage in mass segmentation. It identified the breast structures while eliminating the lower contrast background.

The DWCE segmentation usually underestimated the actual borders of most structures. It also had a tendency to merge the mass with neighboring structures when there was some tissue overlap with the breast mass. This limited the effectiveness of the morphological FP reduction step and limited the localization of the mass during texture-based classification. Clustering-based growing reduced the effects of object merging and significantly increased the size of the initial DWCE objects so that they better characterized the breast structures. Clustering usually provided a good approximation to the true object borders and the objects it produced had a low probability of merging with neighboring structures. The clustering-based growing performed adequately in our detection task and led to an improvement in both morphological and texture-based FP reduction.

Table 3. The true positive detection fraction (TPF), the number of FPs per image and the reduction percentage for the initial detection stages.

Stage	TPF	FPs/Image (Initial Stages)	Reduction
DWCE	98%	47.2	-
Local Growing	98%	44.1	0%
Morph. FP Reduction	98%	28.1	35%

The morphological classification reduced the number of FPs per image from 44.1 to 28.1 as shown in Table 3. The morphological reduction tended to eliminate objects that were either much larger or much smaller than the average object size but had trouble differentiating between TPs and FPs of similar sizes. Therefore, a texture classifier that better differentiates between these similar shaped objects was used in the subsequent step.

The LDA classifier combined with SGLD texture features has proven to be effective in differentiating between similar shaped objects. The training and test FROC performance curves following final texture classification are shown in Figure 15 for the combined set of 253 films. A summary of the performances shown in Figure 15 is given in Table 4. In this evaluation, the test value was calculated from the accumulated test cases of all subgroups, and its training value was the average performance obtained with the different training group combinations. The texture classification was able to reduce the number of FPs per image from an initial value of 28.1 to approximately 10.8 with only a small loss in TPs (95% detection compared with 98%) on the combined data set. Additional reductions in the number of FPs can be achieved with lower TP detection thresholds. For example, at a 90% TP fraction, the FPs decreased to 5.9 per image and to 1.4 per image at an 80% TP detection fraction.

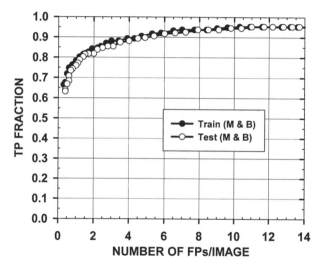

Figure 15. The training and test FROC curve obtained following LDA classification using the selected texture feature. The results are based on the combined set of 253 films containing both malignant and benign masses.

We also examined the performance of subsets of malignant and benign cases. These subsets contained 128 and 125 films, respectively. The test FROC curves are plotted in Figure 16 and a summary of the performances is also given in Table 4. The malignant mass detection curve is much higher than the benign mass detection curve over the full range of sensitivities. The malignant cases had 1.0 FPs per image compared with 2.7 FPs per image for the benign cases at an 80% TP detection fraction. This result indicates that the texture classification was more sensitive to malignant masses than benign appearing masses. It indicates that the algorithm can be implemented with a more stringent operating point to reduce FP detection if benign masses are not of particular concern.

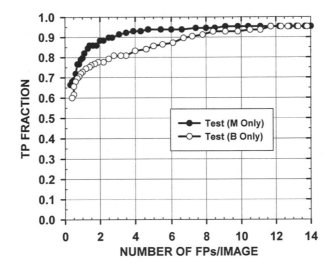

Figure 16.   The individual test FROC curve obtained following LDA classification for subsets of malignant and benign cases. The malignant and benign subsets contain 128 and 125 films, respectively.

Table 4.   Summary of the FROC results depicted in Figures 15 and 16. Training results are given for the combined set of 253 films containing both malignant (M) and benign (B) cases. Test results are given for the combined set as well as for the individual subsets of malignant (128 films) and benign (125 films) cases.

TPF	FPs/Image			
	Train (M,B)	Test (M,B)	Test (M Only)	Test (B Only)
95%	9.8	10.8	8.9	11.6
90%	4.5	5.9	2.8	7.0
80%	1.2	1.4	1.0	2.7

4.2.5   Performance of Computer Detection Program with Unknown Cases

The FROC curve describes the entire range of detection sensitivity as a function of FP rate. In a clinical situation, the decision thresholds in the detection program have to be fixed so that the computer operates at a desired level of sensitivity and an acceptable FP rate. We selected the decision thresholds for all classifiers in our detection algorithm based on the training and validation results described above. - We tested the performance of the detection program with the chosen thresholds - on a set of unknown cases in a preliminary preclinical study. The data set consisted of 233 mammograms (119 malignant and 114 benign) where each image contained a single biopsy proven mass. In a similar fashion to the microcalcification evaluation (Section 2.2.1), the data set was digitized with a laser scanner that had a wider optical density range than the one used to digitize the training set. The detection program produced approximately 2.2 FPs per image with a TP detection rate of 73% for the combined data set, and 82% and 64% for the individual malignant and benign subsets, respectively.

In this section, we have reviewed some of the different computer algorithms proposed for automatically detecting breast mass on digital mammograms including our current detection scheme. Our method employs DWCE segmentation, local object-based growing using a clustering algorithm, and morphological and texture based FP reduction. The DWCE was effective in segmenting breast structures on the mammograms. The local growing stage was found to improve the borders of the initial DWCE structures and reduced merging between adjacent and/or overlapping structures. This improved the morphological information extracted from the detected breast masses and thus the differentiation between masses and normal tissues. The next step in the development is to evaluate the mass detection on a larger set of independent mammograms. Further work is also needed to improve the local segmentation and especially to improve the features that differentiate breast masses and normal structures.

5 Computerized Characterization of Breast Masses

Masses are important indicators of malignancy on mammograms. However, only a small percentage of masses found on mammograms are malignant. Many benign conditions, such as cysts and fibroadenomas are detected as breast masses. Some of these benign masses may look suspicious enough for the radiologist to recommend biopsy so that the pathology of the mass can be determined. In three recent studies, it was found that only between 20 to 30% mammographically suspicious nonpalpable breast masses that underwent biopsy were malignant [124]-[126]. This means that a large percentage of mass biopsies are performed for benign lesions. In order to reduce costs and patient discomfort, it is important to reduce the number of benign biopsies without reducing the sensitivity of detecting malignant masses. A computerized program that assists the radiologists in the classification of mammographic masses can contribute to this purpose.

In recent years, considerable research effort has been devoted to the development of computerized methods for characterization of breast masses on mammograms. As discussed in Section 3, these approaches can be grouped into two main categories: those that combine mammographic features extracted by a radiologist into a malignancy rating, and those that automatically extract features from ROIs, and characterize the masses based on the computer-extracted features. In this section, we review methods that use computer-extracted features for characterization of mammographic masses.

Similar to characterization of mammographic microcalcifications, different algorithms developed for characterization of masses have similar major steps. These include preprocessing, mass segmentation, extraction of shape and texture features, and classifier design. Kilday *et al.* [119] extracted mass shapes using interactive gray-level thresholding, and classified them into cancer, cyst, and fibroadenoma categories using morphological features and patient age with a linear classifier. Pohlman *et al.* [127] segmented masses using an adaptive region growing algorithm, whose parameters were interactively adjusted. After mass segmentation, features related to tumor shape and boundary roughness were automatically extracted and used for the classification of the lesions. They found that their tumor boundary roughness feature provided slightly inferior classification accuracy compared to two experienced radiologists who specialized in mammography. Rangayyan *et al.* [128] used a measure of the diffusion of a mass into the surrounding mammogram termed edge acutance, as well as a number of shape factors, including Fourier descriptors, moments, and compactness, to classify masses. They found the edge acutance measure to be superior to any feature extracted from the mass shape. Using the acutance measure alone, they were able to correctly classify 93% of masses in a database of 54 cases. Viton *et al.* characterized the degree of spiculation and the presence of fuzzy areas in the region surrounding a mass by means of polar and pseudopolar representations of this region. Huo *et al.* [129] extracted features related to margin and the density of the masses for classification. Their results indicated that a spiculation measure based on the radial gradients provided the best classification accuracy. They designed and tested a two-stage hybrid classifier consisting of a rule-based stage and an artificial neural network stage on a data set of 95 cases. The hybrid classifier had a similar accuracy to that of an experienced mammographer, and a significantly higher accuracy than that of a radiologist with less mammographic experience. Sahiner *et al.* and Chan *et al.* used texture features extracted from transformed images for characterization of breast masses [130], and investigated the effect of their CAD method on radiologists' rating of breast masses [16]. They showed that their CAD method can significantly improve radiologists' malignancy rating, and thereby potentially help reduce unnecessary biopsies.

In clinical practice, when a suspicious mass is detected on a mammogram, radiologists often use another imaging modality to further evaluate the mass before recommending biopsy. Ultrasound and magnetic resonance imaging (MRI) are two commonly used modalities as an adjunct to mammography. Furthermore, some mammographically occult palpable breast masses can only be evaluated using these modalities. Recently, several researchers investigated the use of these modalities for characterization of breast masses.

For breast mass characterization based on dynamic contrast enhanced MR images, Sahiner *et al.* [131] used image texture in ROIs on dynamic subtraction images containing the masses. Sinha *et al.* [132] used texture, the contrast uptake curve, and boundary features for the same purpose. Gilhuijs *et al.* [133] investigated the use of margin descriptors and radial gradient analysis as a function of space and time. Although the results of these and other studies seem promising, the small sample size used in almost all investigations on computerized characterization of breast MR images makes it difficult to generalize the results.

Clinically, breast ultrasound is used much more extensively than MR due to its low cost. However, breast ultrasound is mainly used for differentiation of solid masses and cysts at present because of the difficulty in distinguishing benign and malignant solid masses by visual criteria. If computerized method can be developed to assist radiologists in characterization of solid masses on ultrasound images, it will improve the efficacy of ultrasonic breast imaging. Garra *et al.* [134] studied the use of texture on breast sonograms for characterization of malignant and benign lesions. They were able to identify more than 75% of benign lesions in their data set without missing any malignancies. Giger *et al.* [135] used radial gradients, as well as texture and shape features based on hand-extracted mass shapes for the same purpose. On a data set of 40 biopsy-proven lesions, their classifier achieved an A_z value of 0.87. Sahiner *et al.* [136], [137] extracted shape and texture features from automatically segmented masses on three-dimensional sonograms. On a data set of 51 biopsied lesions, they obtained an A_z value of 0.92. These promising results indicate the potential usefulness of CAD in this area.

In the rest of this section, we will review some of the techniques that we developed in our laboratory for characterization of breast masses on mammograms.

5.1 Methods

Computerized characterization of breast masses can be either a part of an integrated CAD system that first detects potential masses, or a stand-alone technique that analyzes a lesion identified by the radiologist. In our current work, we use radiologist-identified lesion location and extract an ROI that contains the mass to be characterized. Our data set thus does not include false-positives, i.e., suspicious non-mass breast structures that are falsely identified by a computer algorithm. Before any processing, each ROI in our data set was corrected for low-frequency background gray level variation using the background correction technique discussed in Section 3.1.1.

In the clinical evaluation of a mammographic mass, its shape and margin characteristics are very important [138]. Therefore, accurate delineation of mass boundaries is an important step in computerized mass characterization. We have developed a two-stage segmentation method for this purpose [139]. The goal of the first stage segmentation is to find the general outline of the mass shape. This stage is based on a clustering algorithm followed by morphological filtering. The goal of the second stage is to detect possible spiculations and to include them as a part of the mass shape for morphological feature extraction. This stage is based on an active contour model followed by spiculation detection. The block diagram for our mass segmentation algorithm is shown in Figure 17, and the individual steps of the segmentation algorithm are explained below.

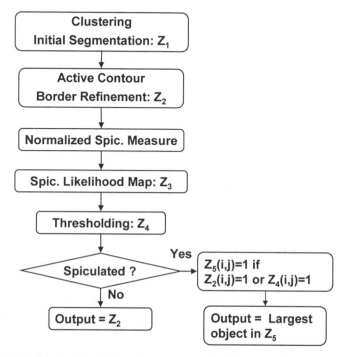

Figure 17. The block diagram for the mass segmentation algorithm. All images Z_k, for $k \neq 3$, are binary images, with a nonzero value indicating an object pixel.

5.1.1 First Stage Segmentation

The mass segmentation method employed in this study started with the initial detection of a mass shape within an ROI using a pixel-by-pixel K-means clustering algorithm, which was discussed in Section 4.1.2. The clustering algorithm requires a feature vector for each pixel location. In the current application, we used three filtered images along with the original image to form the feature vectors. The first filtered image was obtained by median filtering. The second and third filtered images were edge-enhanced images at different spatial resolutions. The use of the filtered pixel values made it possible to incorporate neighborhood information into the classification of each pixel.

Figures 18(a)-(f) show the result of the first stage segmentation for a spiculated mass and a nonspiculated mass.

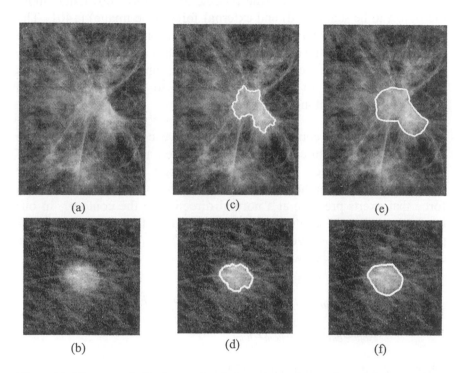

Figure 18   The mass ROI, the result of clustering segmentation, and the result of active contour segmentation for a spiculated mass (a, c and e) and a nonspiculated mass (b, d and f).

5.1.2   Second Stage Segmentation

The goal of the second stage segmentation was to obtain more accurate border delineation, and to include possible spiculations into the mass shape, so that morphological features extracted from these shapes could be effective in distinguishing malignant and benign masses. In order to reach this goal, we used an active contour model followed by a spiculation detection and segmentation method based on the image gradient directions.

Active contour model

An active contour is a deformable continuous curve, whose shape is controlled by internal forces (the model, or *a priori* knowledge about the object to be segmented) and external forces (the image) [140]. The internal forces impose a smoothness constraint on the contour, and the external forces push the contour towards salient image features, such as edges. To solve a segmentation problem, an initial boundary is iteratively deformed so that the energy due to internal and external forces is minimized along the contour.

The internal energy components in our active contour model are the continuity and curvature of the contour, as well as the homogeneity of the segmented object. The external energy components are the negative of the smoothed image gradient magnitude, and a balloon force that exerts pressure at a normal direction to the contour. In our implementation, the contour was represented by the vertices of an *N*-point polygon whose vertices were $v(i)=(x(i),y(i))$, $i=1,...,N$. The energy to be minimized was defined as

$$E = \sum_{i=1}^{N} w_{curv}E_{curv}(i) + w_{cont}E_{cont}(i) + w_{grad}E_{grad}(i) \\ + w_{bal}E_{bal}(i) + w_{hom}E_{hom} \tag{6}$$

where each energy term has a weight, w.

To minimize the contour energy, we used a greedy algorithm that was first proposed by Williams and Shah [141]. In this algorithm, the contour was iteratively optimized, starting with the initial contour provided by the output of the first stage segmentation. At each iteration, a neighborhood of each vertex was examined, and the vertex was moved to the location that minimizes the contour energy. The algorithm stopped when there was no movement of the vertices, or when all the vertices of the contour were at locations visited at a previous iteration. Figures. 18(c)-(f) show the initial and final contours of the model for a spiculated mass and for a nonspiculated mass. A binary image, denoted by Z_2 in the schematic shown in Figure 17, is produced by filling the interior of the resulting contour, such that any pixel within the object has a pixel value of 1, and any background pixel has a pixel value of 0.

Spiculation detection and segmentation

In our experience, the active contour model was not suitable for the segmentation of spiculations. The curvature term in the model prevents the contour from having sharp turns unless w_{curv} is very small. However, a small value for w_{curv} is not practical, because it results in mass shapes that are too irregular all around the contour. For this reason, we designed an additional stage for detection of spiculations.

Spiculations on mammograms appear as linear structures with a positive image contrast, and they usually lie in a radial direction to the mass. As a result of their linearity, the gradient directions at image pixels on or close to the spiculation are more or less in the same orientation. In order to investigate whether a pixel (i_c, j_c) on the mass contour lies on the path of a spiculation, one can make use of this property as follows: In a search region S of the image, compute the statistics of the angular difference θ between the image gradient direction at image pixel (i,j), and the direction of the vector joining pixels (i_c, j_c), and (i,j) (Figure 19). If a spiculation extends from the pixel (i_c, j_c), then θ will be close to $\pi/2$ whenever the image pixel (i,j) is on the spiculation. Therefore, the distribution of θ (as the image pixel (i,j) sweeps the search region S) will have a peak around $\pi/2$. If there is no spiculation, and if the gray levels in S are randomly distributed, then this distribution will be uniform. Karssemeijer *et. al.* have made use of this idea for detecting spiculated lesions on mammograms [93], but not for the detection of the actual spiculations. In our method, we combined this idea with the fact that spiculations generally lie in a radial direction to the mass. Therefore, the region S can be limited so that other gradients, such as those resulting from the mass contour itself, can be excluded from the computation of the distribution.

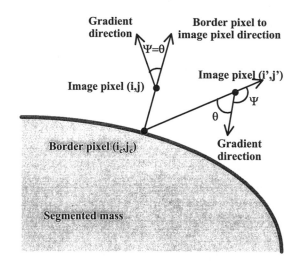

Figure 19. The definition of the angular difference θ.

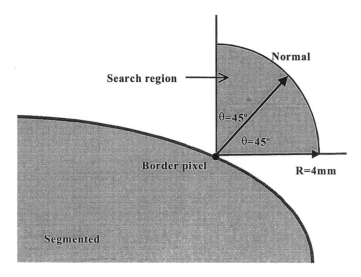

Figure 20. The definition of the search region for a given border pixel.

For a pixel (i_c, j_c) on the mass boundary, the search region S is defined as the set of all pixels that i) lie outside the mass; ii) have a positive contrast; iii) are at a distance less than 4 mm to (i_c, j_c); and iv) are within $\pm \pi/4$ of the normal to the mass contour at (i_c, j_c) (Figure 20). The number of pixels in S is denoted as N_s.

Let (i,j) be a point in S, and let $\mathbf{g}(i,j)$ denote the image gradient vector at (i,j). Let $\Psi(i,j)$ denote the angle between the vector $(i-i_c, j-j_c)$ and the vector $\mathbf{g}(i,j)$. Define $0 \le \theta(i, j) \le \pi/2$ such that (see Figure 19)

$$\theta(i, j) = \begin{cases} \Psi(i, j) & \text{if } 0 \le \Psi(i, j) < \pi/2 \\ \pi - \Psi(i, j) & \text{if } \pi/2 \le \Psi(i, j) < \pi \end{cases}. \qquad (7)$$

If the search region S contains a spiculation radiating from (i_c, j_c), then there will be a large number of pixels (i,j) for which $\theta(i,j)$ will be close to $\pi/2$. In order to measure this statistic, we defined a spiculation measure $x(i_c, j_c)$ for each pixel (i_c, j_c) on the mass border such that

$$x(i_c, j_c) = \frac{1}{N_s} \sum_{(i,j) \in S} \theta(i, j) \qquad (8)$$

One possible way of detecting whether a mass is spiculated is to compute the profile of the spiculation measure $x(i_c, j_c)$ for all points (i_c, j_c) on the mass contour. This is illustrated by using the masses shown in Figure 18 (one spiculated and one nonspiculated) as an example. Figure 21 plots $x(i_c, j_c)$ as (i_c, j_c) moves sequentially along the mass contour for these masses. The locations of some of the local maxima in Figure 21 are also shown in Figure 22. It is observed that the maxima in Figure 21 correspond to locations where a linear structure extends from the mass. Note that there is a linear structure overlapping with the nonspiculated mass, which is reflected in the plot. These plots illustrate that large values of $x(i_c, j_c)$ may be an indication for spiculations. However, thresholding these plots does not segment the individual spiculations. For the segmentation task, we compute $x(i_c, j_c)$ for a sequence of 30 contours. The first contour in the sequence is that provided by the active contour model. The following contours in the sequence are obtained by expanding the previous contour by one pixel at a time, so that x is computed in a 30-pixel-wide (3mm) band around the mass. The resulting image in the 30-pixel-wide band around the mass is named the spiculation likelihood map, and is denoted by Z_3 in Figure 17. Figure 23 shows the spiculation likelihood map for the masses used in this example.

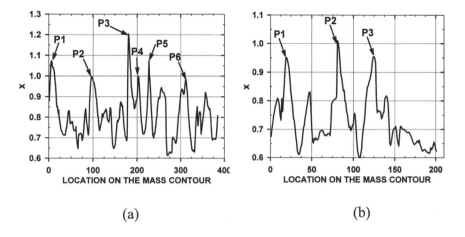

(a)   (b)

Figure 21. The profile of the normalized spiculation measure $x(i_c,j_c)$ for (a) a spiculated mass, and (b) a nonspiculated mass.

The spiculation likelihood map Z_3 is used for both detecting whether a mass is spiculated, and for segmenting the spiculations. To detect whether a mass is spiculated, a binary image Z_4 is produced by thresholding Z_3, at a threshold T, so that

$$Z_4(i,j) = \begin{cases} 1 & \text{if } Z_3(i,j) \geq T \\ 0 & \text{otherwise} \end{cases} \tag{9}$$

After initial experimentation, the value of T was chosen to be 0.85. This threshold was kept constant in the segmentation algorithm for all images used in the study. After thresholding, all connected objects in Z_4 are detected. The number of objects is used as an estimate of the number of possible spiculations. The ratio of the total area of the objects in Z_4 to the mass area is used as an indication of the relative size of the spiculations. The product of the two features above (number of objects and the size ratio) is used as a spiculation detection statistic to classify the mass as spiculated or nonspiculated. The choice of the threshold for this classification is discussed in Section 5.1.4. If the mass is classified as spiculated, then the algorithm will combine the binary image that represents the mass outline detected by the active contour model (Z_2) and the binary image that represents the result of thresholding (Z_4) to segment the spiculations (Figure 17). An intermediate image Z_5, which contains the union of the objects in the images Z_2 and Z_4, is found by applying a pixelwise "or" operation to Z_2 and Z_4. To eliminate objects that are not connected to the general outline of the mass, the largest object in Z_5 (which invariably contains the object segmented by the active contour model) is chosen as the final output of the segmentation process. If the mass is classified as nonspiculated, then the output of the segmentation is Z_2. Figure 24 shows the result of spiculation detection and segmentation for the masses used in this example.

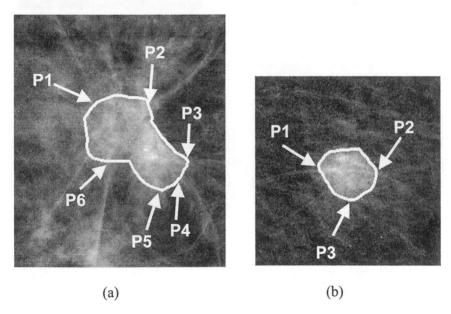

(a)　　　　　　　　　　　　　(b)

Figure 22. The locations of some of the peaks in the normalized spiculation measure profiles shown in Figures 21(a) and 21(b).

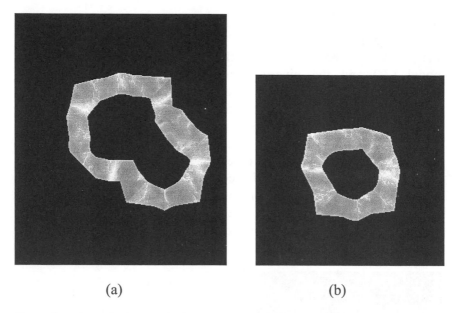

(a)   (b)

Figure 23. The spiculation likelihood map for (a) a spiculated mass, and (b) a nonspiculated mass.

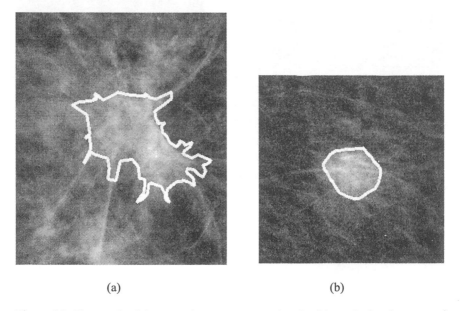

(a)   (b)

Figure 24. The result of the second stage segmentation for (a) a spiculated mass, and (b) a nonspiculated mass.

5.1.3 Feature Extraction

We used texture features extracted from a band of pixels surrounding the mass, and morphological features extracted from the shape of the segmented mass, for classifying the mass as malignant or benign.

Texture features

The texture of the region surrounding the mass can yield important features for its classification. Since possible spiculations and the gradient of the opacity caused by the mass are approximately radially oriented, the texture of the region surrounding a mass is expected to have a radial dependence. However, most texture extraction methods are designed for texture orientations in a uniform direction (horizontal, vertical, or at a certain angle between these two directions). To be able to extract meaningful texture features from the region surrounding a mass, we have designed a rubber band straightening transform (RBST) that maps a band of pixels surrounding the mass onto the Cartesian plane (a rectangular region) [130], [142], [143]. In the transformed image, the border of the mass is expected to appear approximately as a horizontal edge, and spiculations are expected to appear approximately as vertical lines (Figure 25).

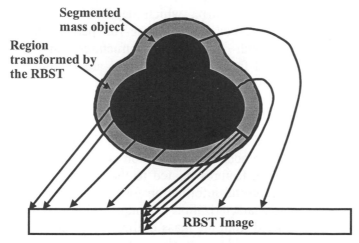

Figure 25. An illustration of the RBST. The pixels along the object boundary are mapped to the first row of the RBST image. Pixels along a normal to the object boundary are mapped to a column of the RBST image.

The mass outline produced by the first stage segmentation discussed above is used for defining the RBST image. The mass object produced by this stage is usually slightly smaller than that which can be visually determined on the mammogram. Thus a thin border region along the mass margin is included in the RBST image. Important texture and gradient information at the mass margin is therefore included in the analysis of the region surrounding the mass. A 40-pixel-wide region, corresponding to a 4-mm band is used to determine the RBST image.

The texture features extracted from the RBST images include SGLD [78] and run-length statistics (RLS) [144] features. SGLD features have been discussed in Section 3. A brief description of RLS features is as follows. RLS features are extracted from the RLS matrix, which describes the run-length statistics for each gray-level value in the image. The element in row r, column c of the RLS matrix is the number of times that the gray level r in the images possesses a run length of c in a given direction. The RLS matrices in our application are obtained from the vertical and horizontal gradient magnitudes of the RBST images. From each RLS matrix, five texture measures, namely, short runs emphasis, long runs emphasis, gray-level nonuniformity, run-length nonuniformity and run percentage, are extracted in the horizontal and vertical directions. These features describe the distribution of the RLS matrix, which depends on the run-length statistics of the images. For example, the run percentage feature is small for images with long linear structures, and gray-level nonuniformity is small for images where runs are equally distributed throughout the gray levels.

Morphological features

Malignant masses tend to have more irregular or ill-defined contours than benign masses. In addition, spiculation is a strong indication for malignancy. Therefore, features related to the segmented mass shape are expected to yield useful information for characterization of breast masses. In our mass characterization technique, thirteen morphological features were extracted from the mass outline produced by the second stage segmentation. In addition to the eleven morphological features summarized in Section 4.1.3, we extracted a convexity feature and a Fourier descriptor feature, which describe the irregularity of the segmented mass contour. Both of these features are independent of object size, rotation, and translation.

The convexity feature is defined as the ratio of the area of the segmented object to the area of the smallest convex shape that contains the object. If the object is convex, as is the case with many benign masses, then this feature will attain its maximum value of unity. If the object shape is highly non-convex, as is the case with many spiculated or malignant masses, then the value of this feature will be small.

The Fourier descriptor feature is based on the Fourier transform of the object boundary sequence. To compute the Fourier transform of the object boundary sequence, the x and y coordinates of each border pixel i are represented as a complex number, $z(i) = x(i) + jy(i)$, $0 < i < N$. A summary of the Fourier descriptor measure described in [59], which emphasizes low-frequency components, is extracted from the Fourier transform of the object boundary sequence.

5.1.4   Classifier Design

Stepwise linear discriminant analysis, discussed in Section 3.1.2, is used for feature classification. To train and test the classifier with the available case samples, we partitioned the data set into ten random partitions with the constraint that all mammograms from the same patient were grouped into the same partition. Nine of the partitions were used for classifier training, and the remaining partition was used for test. The test partition was rotated in round robin order, so that all partitions served as test partition once and only once. For each test partition, the classification accuracy was evaluated as the area A_z under the ROC curve. A mean A_z value for the data set was obtained by averaging these ten A_z values.

Classifier training consisted of three stages. The first stage was related to mass segmentation. As discussed in Section 5.1.2, the decision to classify a mass as spiculated or nonspiculated was based on thresholding the spiculation detection statistics obtained from the spiculation likelihood map. The value of this threshold was determined from the training set, such that the sum of correct decision percentages for the spiculated and nonspiculated masses was maximized for the training set. The second stage of the training involved feature selection. The features were selected using the change in Wilks' lambda for the training set as the selection criterion. Finally, the coefficients of the linear classifier were also determined based on the training set. By making these three decisions independent of the test set, we aimed at improving the generalizability of our classification results to independent data sets.

5.2   Analysis of Classification Accuracy

A data set of 249 mammograms from 102 patients was used to design and test the classification technique. The data set contained 127 malignant masses (63 spiculated) and 122 benign masses (6 spiculated). The likelihood of malignancy of the mass on each mammogram was rated by an experienced radiologist on a scale of 1 to 10. As shown in Figure 26, the data set contained masses with varying degrees of difficulty for characterization.

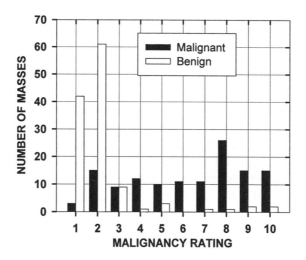

Figure 26. The distribution of the malignancy rating of the masses in our data set, by an experienced radiologist. 1: Very likely benign; 10: Very likely malignant.

Figure 27 shows the distribution of the spiculation detection statistics used for the classification of a mass as spiculated or nonspiculated. It is observed that by using the correct threshold, more than 30% (60/180) of nonspiculated masses can be correctly identified without misidentifying any spiculated masses.

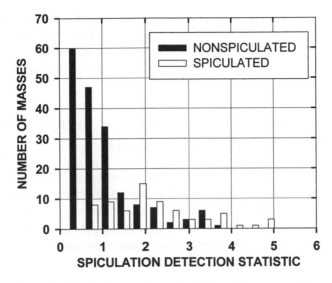

Figure 27. The distribution of the spiculation detection statistics for the spiculated and the nonspiculated masses.

Table 5. The test A_z values for each partition using linear discriminant analysis with morphological, texture, and combined feature spaces.

Partition number	Morphological feature space	Texture feature space	Combined feature space
1	0.90±0.06	0.92±0.06	0.92±0.07
2	0.92±0.06	0.98±0.03	1.000000
3	0.83±0.10	0.93±0.06	0.94±0.05
4	0.80±0.08	0.83±0.08	0.86±0.08
5	0.94±0.05	0.80±0.16	0.92±0.07
6	0.82±0.08	0.66±0.12	0.85±0.08
7	1.000000	1.000000	0.96±0.04
8	0.77±0.10	0.71±0.10	0.71±0.11
9	0.64±0.11	0.73±0.10	0.74±0.10
10	0.93±0.05	0.91±0.06	0.98±0.03
Average	0.85	0.85	0.89

We investigated the classification of the masses as malignant or benign using the morphological feature space alone, the texture feature space alone, and the combined morphological and texture feature spaces. The resulting test A_z values for each of the ten partitions are shown in Table 5. It is observed that combining the morphological and texture spaces improves the classification accuracy. The average test A_z value for the ten partitions in this study was 0.85 for both texture and morphological features used alone. Using the combined feature space, the average test A_z value for the ten partitions was 0.89. The average number of selected features was 2, 10, and 14 for the morphological, texture, and combined feature spaces.

5.3 Radiologists' Performance for Breast Mass Characterization Using CAD

To evaluate the effects of CAD on radiologists' classification of malignant and benign masses, we conducted an observer performance experiment in which six radiologists experienced in mammographic interpretation assessed ROIs containing biopsy-proven masses with and without CAD. The results of the experiment were analyzed using ROC methodology [16].

At the time the observer experiment was conducted, the computer classifier was based on texture features extracted from RBST images alone. In order to select a single feature set, feature selection was based on the entire data set that contained 253 mammograms. A leave-one-case-out method was used to design a classifier and to obtain the test score for each case. Figure 28 shows the distribution of the classifier test scores for malignant and benign masses. For radiologist reading with CAD, these scores were converted to a relative malignancy rating by linearly scaling them to a range of 1-10 and rounding to the nearest integer.

A subset of fifteen mammograms was used as a training set to familiarize the radiologists with the computer algorithm, and the remaining 238 mammograms (117 benign, 121 malignant) were used for the evaluation of the effects of CAD. The observers were asked to rate the likelihood of malignancy of the masses on a 10-point scale with and without CAD in two experiments. In the first experiment, the radiologists rated the likelihood of malignancy of each single-view mass, with and without CAD. In the second experiment, from the 238 single-view mammograms, 76 matched pairs (37 benign, 39 malignant) of craniocaudal and mediolateral oblique or lateral views were found. For the reading session without CAD, the radiologists provided a single rating for the mass after reviewing both views. For the reading session with CAD, the computer provided different relative malignancy ratings for each view. It was up to the observer to decide how to merge the two-view information with their own evaluation and provided a single confidence rating. The reading order of the observers in each experiment was carefully balanced to avoid any learning effects [48].

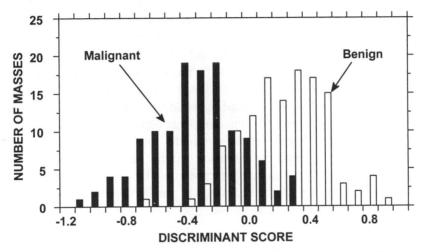

Figure 28. The distribution of the test scores of the computer classifier for malignant and benign masses.

The A_z values for the six radiologists for the reading conditions with and without CAD are listed in Table 6. The average A_z value for a reading condition was obtained by averaging the slope and intercept parameters of the six individual ROC curves, deriving the average ROC curve from the average parameters, and computing the A_z value of the resulting ROC curve. The A_z value of the computer classifier for the 238 cases used in single view reading, and the 76 matched pairs, were 0.92 and 0.96, respectively. To compute the computer classifier's A_z value for the matched pairs, the computer scores for the two views were averaged.

Table 6. Areas under the ROC curve with and without CAD for six radiologists.

Radiologist No.	A_z (Single View)		A_z (Two View)	
	Without CAD	With CAD	Without CAD	With CAD
1	0.84±0.03	0.87±0.02	0.90±0.03	0.93±0.03
2	0.92±0.02	0.96±0.01	0.95±0.02	0.97±0.02
3	0.86±0.02	0.91±0.02	0.92±0.03	0.93±0.03

4	0.79±0.03	0.87±0.02	0.88±0.04	0.95±0.03
5	0.86±0.02	0.92±0.02	0.93±0.03	0.97±0.02
6	0.89±0.02	0.87±0.02	0.89±0.04	0.93±0.03
Average	0.87	0.91	0.92	0.96

From Table 6, it can be observed that for single view interpretation, reading with CAD improved the accuracy of five of the radiologists. The improvement was statistically significant (p = 0.022 using the Student paired t-test). For two view interpretation, all radiologists showed improvement with CAD, and the improvement was again statistically significant (p = 0.007). In the first reading condition, one radiologist's (No. 2) accuracy with CAD was higher than that of the computer alone; in the second reading condition, two radiologists (Nos. 2 and 5) performed better than the computer alone when the were aided by the computer. These results indicate that the second opinion provided by the computer classifier might have strengthened the radiologists' confidence in the interpretation of some difficult cases, but had less influence on the radiologists' decision when the computer made mistakes or when the radiologists were confident about their decision.

6   Classifier Design

In the preceding sections, we discussed some computer vision techniques used for detection and classification of mammographic lesions. The results of our studies indicate that the techniques used are effective for these applications. Further, our observer performance ROC studies showed that CAD is a promising approach to improving breast cancer diagnosis. Similar CAD algorithms have been developed by other research groups. However, the sample sizes used in all studies published so far were small, relative to the spectrum of shapes, sizes, or other characteristic features of the masses or microcalcifications in the patient population. The generalizability of the test results obtained in the laboratory experiments to the patient population is yet to be proven.

It has been shown that the performance of a classifier for unknown cases depends on the sample size used for training [79]. When a finite design (training) sample size is used, the performance is pessimistically biased in comparison to that obtained from an infinitely large design sample. In order to design a classifier with a performance generalizable to the population at large, one has to use a sufficient number of case samples that are representative of the population. However, the availability of case samples is often limited in medical imaging research.

A number of investigators have studied the finite-sample-size problem [79], [80], [82], [145]-[150]. Recently, we conducted a computer simulation study [83] to investigate the dependence of the mean performance, in terms of A_z, on design sample size for a linear discriminant and two non-linear classifiers, the quadratic discriminant and the backpropagation neural network (ANN). The performances of the classifiers were compared for four types of class distributions that have specific properties: multivariate normal distributions with equal covariance matrices and unequal means, unequal covariance matrices and unequal means, and unequal covariance matrices and equal means, and a feature space where the two classes were uniformly distributed in disjoint checkerboard regions. For all three classifiers, we found that the classifier performance $A_z(tr)$, obtained by resubstitution (applying the classifier to the training set), is biased optimistically while the $A_z(ts)$, obtained by testing with an independent test set, is biased pessimistically, relative to the A_z in the limit of infinite sample size. The magnitude of the biases increases as the design sample size decreases and as the dimensionality of the feature space increases. In the cases where a given classifier has no discriminatory power for a given class distribution, the training $A_z(tr)$ at small sample sizes can reach very high values whereas the test $A_z(ts)$ remains almost constant at 0.5, independent of the design sample size. These findings emphasize the importance of evaluating the classifier performance using random samples from the general population that are independent of both the training samples and the "test" samples used for validation during development of the algorithms.

When a finite design sample set is available, the bias on the performance of the trained classifier depends on the class distribution and the type of classifiers chosen. With the equal-covariance-matrix class distributions, the linear discriminant is the optimal classifier [79]. The biases are low and the computation is efficient. With the unequal-covariance-matrices and equal-mean class distributions, the linear discriminant has no discriminatory power. In this type of class distribution, the back-propagation neural network is inferior to the quadratic classifier when the design sample size is large. The ANN needs a relatively large number of hidden nodes and a large number of training epochs in order to reach the optimal performance. Its hold-out (test) performance and the computation efficiency are both inferior to those of the quadratic classifier. However, for the unequal-covariance-matrices and unequal-mean case and a small design sample size, the linear classifier or an ANN with very few hidden nodes, e.g., n=2, can actually achieve better hold-out performance than the more complex ANNs or the optimal quadratic classifiers. An example comparing the training and hold-out performances of the three classifiers in a 9-dimensional feature space with unequal-covariance matrices and unequal means is shown in Figure 29. Our study [83] indicates that the bias on classifier performance increases with increasing complexity (loosely related to the number of parameters to be estimated) of the classifier. For an input feature space with a dimensionality of k, the linear classifier contains $(k+1)$ independent parameters and the quadratic classifier contains $(k+1)(k+2)/2$ independent parameters in their formulations. The number of weights to be estimated for the ANN depends on the number of hidden nodes, n, as $n(k+1)+(n+1)$. The number of weights in an ANN can therefore easily exceed that of a quadratic classifier, although the estimation of the mean and covariance matrices for the linear and quadratic discriminants may contribute additional "complexity" to the classifier design. Thus, when the available sample size is small, a simple classifier will provide better generalization than a more complex classifier. A complex ANN or a quadratic classifier trained with an insufficient number of design samples generalizes poorly, even if it is the optimal classifier for the class distributions. It is therefore important to select an appropriate classifier by taking into consideration the design sample size.

As demonstrated in our studies, one of the important steps in a classifier design problem is the selection of the best subset of features from the many features that can be extracted from the images. We have shown that the bias on the classifier performance depends strongly on the dimensionality of the feature space [83], [151]. Since feature selection is usually performed on the available design samples, the feature selection step will introduce additional biases to the classifier performance. We have investigated the dependence of classifier performance on design sample size when both the feature selection and classifier training are performed with the available case samples [151]. The study reveals that both positive and negative biases on the hold-out performance can occur in this more complex situation. Details of the study will be published [152].

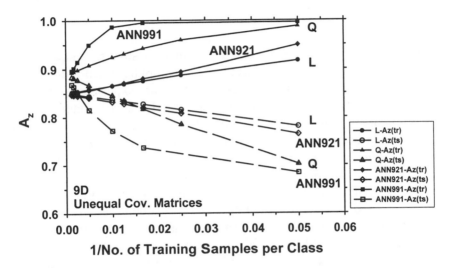

Figure 29. Comparison of the performance curves of the linear, quadratic, ANN(9-2-1), and ANN(9-9-1) classifiers in the 9-D feature space for class distributions with unequal covariance matrices and unequal means. Legends: L = linear; Q = quadratic, ANN = neural network, solid lines = $A_z(tr)$, dashed lines = $A_z(ts)$.

A further problem in classifier design is that the true population distributions of the classes in the feature space are generally unknown. It was suggested that the quantile-quantile (Q-Q) plot and the chi-square plot may be used for investigating the normality of univariate and multivariate sample distributions, respectively [153]. However, it is still unknown under what criteria the chi-square plot will indicate that it is optimal to use a classifier designed under the normality assumption. For any measure of goodness-of-fit, when the sample size is small, only the most aberrant deviations from the normal distribution can be identified as a lack of fit from these plots [153]. Therefore, there is often no a priori knowledge to select an "optimal" classifier or to predict whether the observed performance is caused by the sample size, the choice of an unnecessary complex classifier, or by an actual poor separation of the classes in the feature space. If one observes poor generalization of a trained classifier in a truly independent test set, it will be important to take into consideration all these factors and redesign the classifier.

7   Summary

In this chapter, we have discussed computer vision techniques and classifier design methods used in computer-aided diagnosis applications. The discussion focused on our experiences in the development of CAD algorithms for breast cancer diagnosis in mammography. Numerous variations of the techniques used in each step of the process can be found in the literature. We do not attempt to compare the various methods or performances of the different approaches. Our goal is to demonstrate the feasibility of using computer vision methods to assist radiologists in breast cancer diagnosis, and discuss some of the issues encountered in classifier design. Although the current results from many research groups indicate that CAD will be useful for improving the accuracy of breast cancer diagnosis, the performance of many computer programs has not reached clinically acceptable level where the false-positive rate is expected to be very low. Further investigation will be needed to develop more effective techniques in improving the sensitivity as well as the specificity before CAD will be widely accepted in clinical practice. The effects of CAD on radiologists' performance, and the most effective methods to present information to the radiologists during mammographic interpretation also need to be further studied. Methods that can correlate information from multiple images and multiple modalities or that can merge image information with patient demographic and other clinical information will be important areas to explore for CAD applications.

Acknowledgments

This work is supported by USPHS Grant CA 48129 and by U.S. Army Medical Research and Materiel Command Grant DAMD 17-96-1-6254. Berkman Sahiner is also supported by a Career Development Award by the U.S. Army Medical Research and Materiel Command (DAMD 17-

96-1-6012). Nicholas Petrick is also supported by a grant from The Whitaker Foundation. The content of this publication does not necessarily reflect the position of the government and no official endorsement of any equipment and product of any companies mentioned in the publication should be inferred.

References

[1]   Landis, S.H., Murray, T., Bolden, S., and Wingo, P.A. (1998), "Cancer statistics, 1998," *CA Cancer J Clin*, vol. 48, pp. 6-29.

[2]   Byrne, C., Smart, C.R., Cherk, C., and Hartmann, W.H. (1994), "Survival advantage differences by age: evaluation of the extended follow-up of the Breast Cancer Detection Demonstration Project," *Cancer*, vol. 74, pp. 301-310.

[3]   Feig, S.A. and Hendrick, R.E. (1993), "Risk, benefit, and controversies in mammographic screening," in Haus, A.G. and Yaffe, M.J. (Eds.), *Syllabus: a Categorical Course in Physics Technical Aspects of Breast Imaging*, Oak Brook, IL: Radiological Society of North America, Inc., pp. 119-135.

[4]   Martin, J.E., Moskowitz, M., and Milbrath, J.R. (1979), "Breast cancer missed by mammography," *AJR*, vol. 132, pp. 737-739.

[5]   Wallis, M.G., Walsh, M.T., and Lee, J.R. (1991), "A review of false negative mammography in a symptomatic population," *Clinical Radiology*, vol. 44, pp. 13-15.

[6]   Bird, R.E., Wallace, T.W., and Yankaskas, B.C. (1992), "Analysis of cancers missed at screening mammography," *Radiology*, vol. 184, pp. 613-617.

[7]   Harvey, J.A., Fajardo, L.L., and Innis, C.A. (1993), "Previous mammograms in patients with impalpable breast carcinomas: Retrospective vs blinded interpretation," *AJR*, vol. 161, pp. 1167-1172.

[8]   Adler, D.D. and Helvie, M.A. (1992), "Mammographic biopsy recommendations," *Current Opinion in Radiology*, vol. 4, pp. 123-129.

[9]   Kopans, D.B. (1991), "The positive predictive value of mammography," *AJR*, vol. 158, pp. 521-526.

[10] Sabel, M. and Aichinger, H. (1996), "Recent developments in breast imaging," *Phys. Med. Biol.*, vol. 41, pp. 315-368.

[11] Thurfjell, E.L., Lernevall, K.A., and Taube, A.A.S. (1994), "Benefit of independent double reading in a population-based mammography screening program," *Radiology*, vol. 191, pp. 241-244.

[12] Anderson, E.D.C., Muir, B.B., Walsh, J.S., and Kirkpatrick, A.E. (1994), "The efficacy of double reding mammograms in breast screening.," *Clin Radiol*, vol. 49, pp. 248-251.

[13] Shtern, F., Stelling, C., Goldberg, B., and Hawkins, R. (1995), "Novel technologies in breast imaging: National Cancer Institute perspective," presented at Society of Breast Imaging, Orlando, Florida.

[14] Chan, H.P., Doi, K., Vyborny, C.J., Schmidt, R.A., Metz, C.E., Lam, K.L., Ogura, T., Wu, Y., and MacMahon, H. (1990), "Improvement in radiologists' detection of clustered microcalcifications on mammograms. The potential of computer-aided diagnosis," *Invest Radiol*, vol. 25, pp. 1102-1110.

[15] Kegelmeyer, W.P., Pruneda, J.M., Bourland, P.D., Hillis, A., Riggs, M.W., and Nipper, M.L. (1994), "Computer-aided mammographic screening for spiculated lesions," *Radiology*, vol. 191, pp. 331-337.

[16] Chan, H.-P., Sahiner, B., Helvie, M.A., Petrick, N., Roubidoux, M.A., Wilson, T.E., Adler, D.D., Paramagul, C., Newman, J.S., and Gopal, S.S. (1999), "Improvement of radiologists' characterization of mammographic masses by computer-aided diagnosis: an ROC study," *Radiology*, vol. 212, pp. 817-827.

[17] Jiang, Y., Nishikawa, R.M., Schmidt, R.A., Metz, C.E., Giger, M.L., and Doi, K. (1999), "Improving breast cancer diagnosis with computer-aided diagnosis," *Acad Radiol*, vol. 6, pp. 22-33.

85), *Teaching Atlas of*

2 breast carcinomas," *AJR*,

kemeti, K. (1978), "Isolated breast: radiologic-pathologic 335-341.

A.J. (1976), "The detection he breast: A radiological and . 49, pp. 12-26.

graphic features of 300 ers," *AJR*, vol. 146, pp. 661-

yborny, C.J., MacMahon, H., ature analysis and computer-hy. 1. Automated detection of hy," *Med Phys*, vol. 14, pp.

J., Lam, K.L., and Schmidt, ction of microcalcifications in preliminary clinical study,"

., Lam, K.L., and Helvie, M.A. on of mammographic micro-n with an artificial neural network," *Med Phys*, vol. 22, pp. 1555-1567.

[26] Fam, B.W., Olson, S.L., Winter, P.F., and Scholz, F.J. (1988), "Algorithm for the detection of fine clustered calcifications on film mammograms," *Radiology*, vol. 169, pp. 333-337.

[27] Davies, D.H. and Dance, D.R. (1990), "Automatic computer detection of clustered calcifications in digital mammograms," *Phys Med Biol*, vol. 35, pp. 1111-1118.

[28] Qian, W., Clarke, L.P., Kallergi, M., Li, H.D., Velthuizen, R., Clark, R.A., and Silbiger, M.L. (1993), "Tree-structured nonlinear filter and wavelet transform for microcalcification segmentation in mammography," *Proc SPIE*, vol. 1905, pp. 509-520.

[29] Mascio, L.N., Hernandez, J.M., and Logan, C.M. (1993), "Automated analysis for microcalcifications in high resolution digitial mammograms," *Proc SPIE*, vol. 1898, pp. 472-479.

[30] Nishikawa, R.M., Giger, M.L., Doi, K., Vyborny, C.J., Schmidt, R.A., Metz, C.E., Wu, Y., Yin, F.F., Jiang, Y., Huo, Z., Lu, P., Zhang, W., Ema, T., Bick, U., Papaioannou, J., and Nagel, R.H. (1993), "Computer-aided detection and diagnosis of masses and clustered microcalcifications from digitial mammograms," *Proc SPIE*, vol. 1905, pp. 422-431.

[31] Brzakovic, D., Brzakovic, P., and Neskovic, M. (1993), "Approach to automated screening of mammograms," *Proc SPIE*, vol. 1905, pp. 690-701.

[32] Astley, S., Hutt, I., Adamson, S., Miller, P., Rose, P., Boggis, C., Taylor, C., Valentine, T., Davies, J., and Armstrong, J. (1993), "Automation in mammography: computer vision and human perception," *Proc SPIE*, vol. 1905, pp. 716-730.

[33] Bankman, I.N., Christens-Barry, W.A., Kim, D.W., Weinberg, I.N., Gatewood, O.B., and Brody, W.R. (1993), "Automated recognition of microcalcification clusters in mammograms," *Proc SPIE*, vol. 1905, pp. 731-739.

[34] Karssemeijer, N. (1993), "Recognition of clustered microcalcifications using a random field model," *Proc SPIE*, vol. 1905, pp. 776-786.

[35] Shen, L., Rangayyan, R.M., and Desautels, J.E.L. (1993), "Automatic detection and classification system for calcifications in mammograms," *Proc SPIE*, vol. 1905, pp. 799-805.

[36] Dhawan, A.P., Chitre, Y.S., and Moskowitz, M. (1993), "Artificial-neural-network-based classification of mammographic microcalcifications using image structure features," *Proc SPIE*, vol. 1905, pp. 820-831.

[37] Woods, K.S., Solka, J.L., Priebe, C.E., Doss, C.C., Bowyer, K.W., and Clarke, L.P. (1993), "Comparative evaluation of pattern recognition techniques for detection of microcalcifications," *Proc SPIE*, vol. 1905, pp. 841-852.

[38] Wu, Y., Doi, K., Giger, M.L., and Nishikawa, R.M. (1992), "Computerized detection of clustered microcalcifications in digital mammograms: applications of artificial neural network," *Med Phys*, vol. 19, pp. 555-560.

[39] Zhang, W., Doi, K., Giger, M.L., Wu, Y., Nishikawa, R.M., and Schmidt, R.A. (1994), "Computerized detection of clustered microcalcifications in digital mammograms using a shift-invariant artificial neural network," *Med Phys*, vol. 21, pp. 517-524.

[40] Zheng, B., Chang, Y.S., Staiger, M., Good, W., and Gur, D. (1995), "Computer-aided detection of clustered microcalcifications in digitized mammograms," *Academic Radiology*, vol. 2, pp. 655-662.

[41] Chan, H.P., Niklason, L.T., Ikeda, D.M., Lam, K.L., and Adler, D.D. (1994), "Digitization requirements in mammography: effects on computer-aided detection of microcalcifications," *Med Phys*, vol. 21, pp. 1203-1211.

[42] Lo, S.-C.B., Freedman, M.T., Lin, J., and Mun, S.K. (1993), "Automtic lung nodule detection using profile matching and back-propagation neural network techniques," *J Digital Imaging*, vol. 6, pp. 48-54.

[43] Fukushima, K., Miyake, S., and Ito, T. (1983), "Neocognitron: a neural network model for a mechanism of visual pattern recognition," *IEEE Trans Systems Man Cybernetics*, vol. SME-13, pp. 826-834.

[44] Swets, J.A. and Pickett, R.M. (1982), *Evaluation Of Diagnostic System: Methods From Signal Detection Theory*. New York: Academic Press.

[45] Dorfman, D. and Alf Jr, E. (1969), "Maximum likelihood estimation of parameters of signal detection theory and determination of confidence intervals-rating method data.," *J Math Psych*, vol. 6, pp. 487-496.

[46] Metz, C.E., Shen, J.H., and Herman, B.A. (1990), "New methods for estimating a binormal ROC curve from continuously-distributed test results," presented at *Annual Meeting of the American Statistical Association*, Anaheim, CA.

[47] Bunch, P.C., Hamilton, J.F., Sanderson, G.K., and Simmons, A.H. (1977), "A free response approach to the measurement and characterization of radiographic observer performance," *Proc SPIE*, vol. 127, pp. 124-135.

[48] Metz, C.E. (1989), "Some practical issues of experimental design and data analysis in radiological ROC studies," *Invest Radiol*, vol. 24, pp. 234-245.

[49] Wee, W.G., Moskowitz, M., Chang, N.-C., Ting, Y.-C., and Pemmeraju, S. (1975), "Evaluation of mammographic calcifications using a computer program.," *Radiology*, vol. 116, pp. 717-720.

[50] Fox, S.H., Pujare, U.M., Wee, W.G., Moskowitz, M., and Hutter, R.V.P. (1980), "A computer analysis of mammographic micro-calcifications: global approach.," presented at *Proceedings of the IEEE 5th International Conference on Pattern Recognition*.

[51] Chan, H.P., Niklason, L.T., Ikeda, D.M., and Adler, D.D. (1992), "Computer-aided diagnosis in mammography: detection and

characterization of microcalcifications," *Med Phys*, vol. 19, pp. 831.

[52] Chan, H.P., Wei , D., Niklason, L.T., Helvie, M.A., Lam, K.L., Goodsitt, M.M., and Adler, D.D. (1994), "Computer-aided classification of malignant/benign microcalcifications in mammography," *Med Phys*, vol. 21, pp. 875.

[53] Chan, H.P., Wei, D., Lam, K.L., Lo, S.-C.B., Sahiner, B., Helvie, M.A., and Adler, D.D. (1995), "Computerized detection and classification of microcalcifications on mammograms," *Proc. SPIE*, vol. 2434, pp. 612-620.

[54] Chan, H.P., Sahiner, B., Lam, K.L., Wei, D., Helvie, M.A., and Adler, D.D. (1995), "Classification of malignant and benign microcalcifications on mammograms using an artificial neural network," *Proc. of World Congress on Neural Networks*, vol. II, pp. 889-892.

[55] Chan, H.P., Wei, D., Lam, K.L., Sahiner, B., Helvie, M.A., Adler, D.D., and Goodsitt, M.M. (1995), "Classification of malignant and benign microcalcifications by texture analysis," *Med Phys*, vol. 22, pp. 938.

[56] Chan, H.P., Sahiner, B., Wei, D., Helvie, M.A., Adler, D.D., and Lam, K.L. (1995), "Computer-aided diagnosis in mammography: effect of feature classifier on characterization of microcalcifications," *Radiology*, vol. 197(P), pp. 425.

[57] Chan, H.-P., Sahiner, B., Petrick, N., Helvie, M.A., Lam, K.L., Adler, D.D., and Goodsitt, M.M. (1997), "Computerized classification of malignant and benign microcalcifications on mammograms: texture analysis using an artificial neural network," *Phys. Med. Biol.*, vol. 42, pp. 549-567.

[58] Chan, H.P., Sahiner, B., Lam, K.L., Petrick, N., Helvie, M.A., Goodsitt, M.M., and Adler, D.D. (1998), "Computerized analysis of mammographic microcalcifications in morphological and texture feature space," *Med. Phys.*, vol. 25, pp. 2007-2019.

[59] Shen, L., Rangayyan, R.M., and Desautels, J.E.L. (1994), "Application of shape analysis to mammographic calcifications," *IEEE Trans Med Imaging*, vol. 13, pp. 263-274.

[60] Wu, Y., Freedman, M.T., Hasegawa, A., Zuurbier, R.A., Lo, S.C.B., and Mun, S.K. (1995), "Classification of microcalcifications in radiographs of pathologic specimens for the diagnosis of breast cancer," *Academic Radiology*, vol. 2, pp. 199-204.

[61] Jiang, Y., Nishikawa, R.M., Wolverton, D.E., Metz, C.E., Giger, M.L., Schmidt, R.A., Vyborny, C.J., and Doi, K. (1996), "Malignant and benign clustered microcalcifications: automated feature analysis and classification," *Radiology*, vol. 198, pp. 671-678.

[62] Thiele, D.L., Kimme-Smith, C., Johnson, T.D., McCombs, M., and Bassett, L.W. (1996), "Using tissue texture surrounding calcification clusters to predict benign vs malignant outcomes," *Med. Phys.*, vol. 23, pp. 549-555.

[63] Dhawan, A.P., Chitre, Y., KaiserBonasso, C., and Moskowitz, M. (1996), "Analysis of mammographic microcalcifications using gray-level image structure features," *IEEE Trans Med Imag*, vol. 15, pp. 246-259.

[64] Ackerman, L.V., Mucciardi, A.N., Gose, E.E., and Alcorn, F.S. (1973), "Classification of benign and malignant breast tumors on the basis of 36 radiographic properties," *Cancer*, vol. 31, pp. 342.

[65] Gale, A.G., Roebuck, E.J., Riley, P., and Worthington, B.S. (1987), "Computer aids to mammographic diagnosis," *Br J Radiol*, vol. 60, pp. 887-891.

[66] Getty, D.J., Pickett, R.M., D'Orsi, C.J., and Swets, J.A. (1988), "Enhanced interpretation of diagnostic images," *Invest Radiol*, vol. 23, pp. 240-252.

[67] D'Orsi, C.J., Getty, D.J., Swets, J.A., Pickett, R.M., Seltzer, S.E., and McNeil, B.J. (1992), "Reading and decision aids for

improved accuracy and standardization of mammographic diagnosis," *Radiology*, vol. 184, pp. 619-622.

[68] Wu, Y., Giger, M.L., Doi, K., Vyborny, C.J., Schmidt, R.A., and Metz, C.E. (1993), "Artificial neural networks in mammography: application to decision making in the diagnosis of breast cancer," *Radiology*, vol. 187, pp. 81-87.

[69] Baker, J.A., Kornguth, P.J., Lo, J.Y., Williford, M.E., and Floyd, C.E. (1995), "Breast cancer: prediction with artificial neural network based on BI-RADS standardized lexicon," *Radiology*, vol. 196, pp. 817-822.

[70] Lo, J.Y., Baker, J.A., Kornguth, P.J., Iglehart, J.D., and Floyd, C.E. (1997), "Predicting breast cancer invasion with artificial neural networks on the basis of mammographic features," *Radiology*, vol. 203, pp. 159-163.

[71] Chan, H.P., Sahiner, B., Petrick, N., Helvie, M.A., Leung, K.L., Adler, D.D., and Goodsitt, M.M. (1997), "Computerized classification of malignant and benign microcalcifications on mammograms: texture analysis using an artificial neural network," *Phys. Med. Biol.*, vol. 42, pp. 549-567.

[72] Holland, J. (1992), "Genetic algorithms," *Scientific America*, pp. 66-72.

[73] Goldberg, D.E. (1989), *Genetic algorithms in search, optimization, and machine learning.* New York: Addison-Wesley.

[74] Sahiner, B., Chan, H.P., Petrick, N., Wei, D., Helvie, M.A., Adler, D.D., and Goodsitt, M.M. (1996), "Image feature selection by a genetic algorithm: application to classification of mass and normal breast tissue," *Med. Phys.*, vol. 23, pp. 1671-1684.

[75] SPSS (1993), *SPSS for Windows Release 6 Professional Statistics.* Chicago, IL: SPSS Inc.

[76] Chan, H.P., Wei, D., Helvie, M.A., Sahiner, B., Adler, D.D., Goodsitt, M.M., and Petrick, N. (1995), "Computer-aided

classification of mammographic masses and normal tissue: linear discriminant analysis in texture feature space," *Phys. Med. Biol.*, vol. 40, pp. 857-876.

[77] Sahiner, B., Chan, H.P., Petrick, N., Wei, D., Helvie, M.A., Adler, D.D., and Goodsitt, M.M. (1996), "Classification of mass and normal breast tissue: a convolution neural network classifier with spatial domain and texture images," *IEEE Trans. Medical Imaging*, vol. 15, pp. 598-610.

[78] Haralick, R.M., Shanmugam, K., and Dinstein, I. (1973), "Texture features for image classification," *IEEE Trans Systems Man Cybernetics*, vol. SMC-3, pp. 610-621.

[79] Fukunaga, K. (1990), *Introduction to Statistical Pattern Recognition*, 2nd ed., New York: Academic Press.

[80] Chan, H.P., Sahiner, B., Wagner, R.F., Petrick, N., and Mossoba, J. (1997), "Effects of sample size on classifier design: quadratic and neural network classifiers," *Proc. SPIE*, vol. 3034, pp. 1102-1113.

[81] Chan, H.P., Sahiner, B., Wagner, R.F., and Petrick, N. (1997), "Classifier design for computer-aided diagnosis in mammography: effects of finite sample size," *Med. Phys.*, vol. 24, pp. 1034-1035.

[82] Wagner, R.F., Chan, H.P., Sahiner, B., Petrick, N., and Mossoba, J.T. (1997), "Finite-sample effects and resampling plans: applications to linear classifiers in computer-aided diagnosis," *Proc. SPIE*, vol. 3034, pp. 467-477.

[83] Chan, H.P., Sahiner, B., Wagner, R.F., and Petrick, N. (1999), "Classifier design for computer-aided diagnosis: effects of finite sample size on the mean performance of classical and neural network classifiers," *Med. Phys.*, vol. 26, pp. 2654-2668.

[84] Holland, J.H. (1975), *Adaptation in Natural and Artificial Systems*. Ann Arbor, MI: University of Michigan Press.

[85] Ferri, F.J., Pudil, P., Hatef, M., and Kittler, J. (1994), "Comparative study of techniques for large-scale feature selection," *Pattern Recognition in Practice*, vol. IV, pp. 403-413.

[86] Siedlecki, W. and Sklansky, J. (1989), "A note on genetic algorithm for large-scale feature selection," *Pattern Recognition Letters*, vol. 10, pp. 335-347.

[87] Sahiner, B., Chan, H.P., Petrick, N., Wei, D., Helvie, M.A., Adler, D.D., and Goodsitt, M.M. (1996), "Image feature selection by a genetic algorithm: application to classification of mass and normal breast tissue on mammograms," *Med Phys*, vol. 23, pp. 1671-1684.

[88] Norusis, M.J. (1993), *SPSS for Windows Release 6 Professional Statistics*. Chicago, IL: SPSS Inc.

[89] Lachenbruch, P.A. (1975), *Discriminant Analysis*. New York: Hafner Press.

[90] Sahiner, B., Chan, H.P., Petrick, N., Helvie, M.A., Adler, D.D., and Goodsitt, M.M. (1996), "Classification of malignant and benign breast masses: development of a high-sensitivity classifier using a genetic algorithm.," *Radiology*, vol. 201, pp. 256-257.

[91] Vyborny, C.J. and Giger, M.L. (1994), "Computer vision and artificial intelligence in mammography," *AJR*, vol. 162, pp. 699-708.

[92] Kegelmeyer Jr., W.P. (1992), "Computer detection of stellate lesions in mammograms," *Proceedings of the SPIE*, vol. 1660, pp. 446-454.

[93] Karssemeijer, N. and te Brake, G. (1996), " Detection of stellate distortions in mammograms," *IEEE Transactions on Medical Imaging*, vol. 15, pp. 611-619.

[94] Kobatake, H. and Yoshinaga, Y. (1996), " Detection of spicules on mammogram based on skeleton analysis," *IEEE Transactions on Medical Imaging*, vol. 15, pp. 235-245.

[95] Kobatake, H., Murakami, M., Takeo, H., and Nawano, S. (1999), "Computerized detection of malignant tumors on digital mammograms," *IEEE Transactions on Medical Imaging*, vol. 18, pp. 369-378.

[96] Ng, S.L. and Bischof, W.F. (1992), "Automated detection and classification of breast tumors," *Computers and Biomedical Research*, vol. 25, pp. 218-237.

[97] Laine, A.F., Schuler, S., Fan, J., and Huda, W. (1994), "Mammographic feature enhancement by multiscale analysis," *IEEE Trans Med Imaging*, vol. 13, pp. 725-740.

[98] Laine, A.F., Huda, W., Steinbach, B.G., and Honeyman, J.C. (1995), "Mammographic image processing using wavelet processing techniques," *European Radiology*, vol. 5, pp. 518-523.

[99] Kallergi, H.D., Clarke, L.P., Jain, V.K., and Clarke, R.A. (1995), "Markov random field for tumor detection in digital mammograms," *IEEE Transactions on Medical Imaging*, vol. 14, pp. 565-576.

[100] Guliato, D., Randayyan, R.M., Carnielli, W.A., Zuffo, J.A., and Desautels, J.E.L. (1998), "Segmentation of breast tumors in mammograms by fuzzy region growing," presented at *Proceedings of the 20th Annual International Conference of the IEEE Engineering in Medicine and Biology Society*, Hong Kong.

[101] Zheng, B., Chang, Y.H., and Gur, D. (1995), "Computerized detection of masses in digitized mammograms using single-image segmentation and a multilayer topographic feature analysis," *Academic Radiology*, vol. 2, pp. 959-966.

[102] Lai, S.M., Li, X., and Bischof, W.F. (1989), "On techniques for detecting circumscribed masses in mammograms," *IEEE Trans Med Imaging*, vol. 8, pp. 377-386.

[103] Yin, F.F., Giger, M.L., Doi, K., Metz, C.E., Vyborny, C.J., and Schmidt, R.A. (1991), "Computerized detection of masses in

digital mammograms: analysis of bilateral subtraction images," *Med Phys*, vol. 18, pp. 955-963.

[104] Yin, F.F., Giger, M.L., Vyborny, C.J., Doi, K., and Schmidt, R.A. (1993), "Comparison of bilateral subtraction and single-image processing techniques in the computerized detection of mammographic masses," *Investigative Radiology*, vol. 28, pp. 473-481.

[105] Brzakovic, D., Vujovic, N., Neskovic, M., Brzakovic, P., and Fogarty, K. (1994), "Mammogram analysis by comparison with previous screenings," in Gale, A.G., Astley, S.M., Dance, D.R., and Cairns, A.Y. (Eds.), *Digital Mammography*, Amsterdam: Elsevier, pp. 131-140.

[106] Good, W.F., Zheng, B., Chang, Y.H., Wang, Z.H., Maitz, G.S., and Gur, D. (1999), "Mutil-image CAD employing features derived from ipsilateral mammographic views," presented at *Proceedings of SPIE Medical Imaging*, San Diego.

[107] Petrick, N., Chan, H.P., Sahiner, B., and Wei, D. (1996), "An adaptive density-weighted contrast enhancement filter for mammographic breast mass detection," *IEEE Transactions on Medical Imaging*, vol. 15, pp. 59-67.

[108] Petrick, N., Chan, H.-P., Wei, D., Sahiner, B., Helvie, M.A., and Adler, D.D. (1996), "Automated detection of breast masses on mammograms using adaptive contrast enhancement and tissue classification," *Med Phys*, vol. 23, pp. 1685-1696.

[109] Petrick, N., Chan, H.P., Sahiner, B., and Helvie, M.A. (1999), "Combined adaptive enhancement and region-growing segmentation of breast masses on digitized mammograms," *Medical Physics*, vol. 26, pp. 1642-1654.

[110] Kupinski, M.A. and Giger, M.L. (1998), "Automated seeded lesion segmentation on digital mammograms," *IEEE Transactions on Medical Imaging*, vol. 17, pp. 510-517.

[111] te Brake, G.M. and Karssemeijer, N. (1999), "Single and multiscale detection of masses in digital mammograms," *IEEE Transactions on Medical Imaging*, vol. 18, pp. 628-639.

[112] Sanjay-Gopal, S., Chan, H.-P., Wilson, T., Helvie, M., Petrick, N., and Sahiner, B. (1999), "A regional registration technique for automated interval change analysis of breast lesions on mammograms," *Medical Physics*, vol. 26, pp. 2669-2679.

[113] Peli, T. and Lim, J.S. (1982), "Adaptive filtering for image enhancement," *Optical Engineering*, vol. 21, pp. 108-112.

[114] Lunscher, W.H.H.J. and Beddoes, M.P. (1986), "Optimal edge detection: parameter selection and noise effects," *IEEE Transactions on Pattern Analysis and Machine Intelligence*, vol. 8, pp. 154-176.

[115] Marr, D. and Hildreth, E. (1980), "Theory of edge detection," *Proceeding of the Royal Society of London, Series B, Biological Science*, vol. 207, pp. 187-217.

[116] Russ, J.C. (1992), *The Image Processing Handbook*. Boca Rato, FL: CRC Press.

[117] Hara, Y., Atkins, R.G., Yueh, S.H., Shin, R.T., and Kong, J.A. (1994), "Applications of neural networks to radar image classification," *IEEE Transactions on Geoscience and Remote Sensing*, vol. 32, pp. 100-109.

[118] Sahiner, B., Chan, H.P., Petrick, N., Wei, D., Helvie, M.A., Adler, D.D., and Goodsitt, M.M. (1995), "Classification of mass and normal breast tissue: an artificial neural network with morphological features," *Proc. of World Congress on Neural Networks*, vol. II, pp. 876-879.

[119] Kilday, J., Palmieri, F., and Fox, M.D. (1993), "Classifying mammographic lesions using computerized image analysis," *IEEE Trans Med Imaging*, vol. 12, pp. 664-669.

[120] Wei, D., Chan, H.P., Helvie, M.A., Sahiner, B., Petrick, N., Adler, D.D., and Goodsitt, M.M. (1995), "Classification of mass

and normal breast tissue on digital mammograpms: multiresolution texture analysis," *Medical Physics*, vol. 22, pp. 1501-1513.

[121] Wei, D., Chan, H.P., Petrick, N., Sahiner, B., Helvie, M.A., Adler, D.D., and Goodsitt, M.M. (1997), "False-positive reduction for detection of masses on digital mammograms: global and local multiresolution texture analysis," *Medical Physics*, vol. 24, pp. 903-914.

[122] Wei, D., Chan, H.P., Helvie, M.A., Sahiner, B., Petrick, N., Adler, D.D., and Goodsitt, M.M. (1995), "Multiresolution texture analysis for classification of mass and normal breast tissue on digital mammograms," *Proc. SPIE*, vol. 2434, pp. 606-611.

[123] Chakraborty, D.P. (1989), "Maximum likelihood analysis of free-response receiver operating characteristic (FROC) data," *Med Phys*, vol. 16, pp. 561-568.

[124] Hermann, G., Janus, C., Schwartz, I.S., Krivisky, B., Bier, S., and Rabinowitz, J.G. (1987), "Nonpalpable breast lesions: Accuracy of prebiopsy mammographic diagnosis," *Radiology*, vol. 165, pp. 323-326.

[125] Hall, F.M., Storella, J.M., Silverstond, D.Z., and Wyshak, G. (1988), "Nonpalpable breast lesions: recommendations for biopsy based on suspicion of carcinoma at mammography," *Radiology*, vol. 167, pp. 353.

[126] Jacobson, H.G. and Edeiken, J. (1990), "Biopsy of occult breast lesions: analysis of 1261 abnormalities," *JAMA*, vol. 263, pp. 2341-2343.

[127] Pohlman, S., Powell, K.A., Obuchowshi, N.A., Chilote, W.A., and Grundfest-Broniatowski, S. (1996), "Quantitative classification of breast tumors in digitized mammograms," *Med. Phys.*, vol. 23, pp. 1337-1345.

[128] Rangayyan, R.M., El-Faramawy, N., Desautels, J.E.L., and Alim, O.A. (1996), "Discrimination between benign and malignant breast tumors using a region-based measure of edge profile

acutance," in Doi, K., Giger, M.L., Nishikawa, R.M., and Schmidt, R.A., (Eds.), *Digital Mammography '96*, Amsterdam: Elsevier, pp. 213-218.

[129] Huo, Z., Giger, M.L., Vyborny, C.J., Wolverton, D.E., Schmidt, R.A., and Doi, K. (1998), "Automated computerized classification of malignant and benign masses on digitized mammograms," *Acad. Radiol.*, vol. 5, pp. 155-168.

[130] Sahiner, B., Chan, H.P., Petrick, N., Helvie, M.A., and Goodsitt, M.M. (1998), "Computerized characterization of masses on mammograms: the rubber band straightening transform and texture analysis," *Med. Phys.*, vol. 25, pp. 516-526.

[131] Sahiner, B., Chenevert, T.L., Chan, H.-P., Petrick, N., Helvie, M.A., and Sanjay-Gopal, S. (1997), "Computer-aided characterization of malignant and benign lesions on breast MR images using texture features," *Radiology*, vol. 205(P), pp. 520.

[132] Sinha, S., Lucas-Quesada, F.A., N.D., D., Sayre, J., Farria, D., Gorczyca, D.P., and Bassett, L.W. (1997), "Multifeature analysis of Gd-enhnaced MR images of breast lesions," *Journal of Magnetic Resonance Imaging*, vol. 7, pp. 1016-1026.

[133] Gilhuijs, K.G.A. and Giger, M.L. (1998), "Computerized analysis of breast lesions in three dimensions using dynamic magnetic-resonance imaging," *Medical Physics*, vol. 25, pp. 1647-1654.

[134] Garra, B.S., Krasner, B.H., Horri, S.C., Ascher, S., Mun, S.K., and Zeman, R.K. (1993), "Improving the distinction between benign and malignant breast lesions: the value of sonographic texture analysis," *Ultrasonic Imaging*, vol. 15, pp. 267-285.

[135] Giger, M.L., Al-Hallaq, H., Huo, Z., Moran, C., Wolverton, D.E., Chan, C.W., and Zhong, W. (1999), "Computerized analysis of lesions in U.S. images of the breast," *Academic Radiology*, vol. 6, pp. 665-674.

[136] Sahiner, B., LeCarpentier, G.L., Chan, H.-P., Roubidoux, M.A., Petrick, N., Goodsitt, M.M., Gopal, S.S., and Carson, P.L. (1998),

"Computerized characterization of breast masses using three-dimensional ultrasound images," *Proc. SPIE Conf. Medical Imaging*, vol. 3338, pp. 301-312.

[137] Sahiner, B., Chan, H.-P., LeCarpentier, G.L., Petrick, N., Roubidoux, M.A., and Carson, P.L. (1999), "Computerized characterization of solid breast masses using three-dimensional ultrasound images," *Radiology*, vol. 213(P), pp. 229.

[138] D'Orsi, C.J. and Kopans, D.B. (1993), "Mammographic feature analysis," *Seminars in Roentgenology*, vol. 28, pp. 204-230.

[139] Sahiner, B., Chan, H.-P., Helvie, M.A., Wilson, T.E., Gopal, S.S., and Petrick, N. (1998), "Computerized classification of mammographic masses using morphological features," *Radiology*, vol. 209(P), pp. 353.

[140] Kass, M., Witkin, A., and Terzopoulos, D. (1987), "Snakes: active contour models,," *Int. J. Comput. Vision*, vol. 1, pp. 321-331.

[141] Williams, D.J. and Shah, M. (1992), "A fast algorithm for active contours and curvature estimation," *CVGIP: Image Understanding*, vol. 55, pp. 14-26.

[142] Sahiner, B., Chan, H.P., Petrick, N., Helvie, M.A., M, G.M., and Adler, D.D. (1996), "Classification of masses on mammograms using a rubber-band straightening transform and feature analysis.," *Proc. SPIE Conf. Medical Imaging*, vol. 2710, pp. 44-50.

[143] Sahiner, B., Chan, H.P., Petrick, N., M, G.M., and Helvie, M.A. (1997), "Characterization of masses on mammograms: significance of the use of the rubber-band straightening transform," *Proc. SPIE Conf. Medical Imaging*, vol. 3034, pp. 491-500.

[144] Galloway, M.M. (1975), "Texture classification using gray level run lengths," *Computer graphics and image processing*, vol. 4, pp. 172-179.

[145] Raudys, S. and Pikelis, V. (1980), "On dimensionality, sample size, classification error, and complexity of classification

algorithm in pattern recognition," *IEEE Trans Pattern Analysis and Machine Intelligence*, vol. PAMI-2, pp. 242-252.

[146] Fukunaga, K. and Hayes, R.R. (1989), "Effects of sample size on classifier design," *IEEE Trans Pattern Analysis and Machine Intelligence*, vol. 11, pp. 873-885.

[147] Wagner, R.F., Brown, D.G., Guedon, J.-P., Myers, K.J., and Wear, K.A. (1993), "Multivariate Gaussian pattern classification: Effect of finite sample size and the addition of correlated or noisy features on summary measures of goodness," in Barrett, H.H. and Gmitro, A.F. (Eds.), *Information Processing in Medical Imaging*, *Lecture Notes in Computer Science*, vol. 687, Berlin: Springer-Verlag.

[148] Wagner, R.F., Brown, D.G., Guedon, J.-P., Myers, K.J., and Wear, K.A. (1994), "On combining a few diagnostic tests or features," *Proc. SPIE*, vol. 2167, pp. 503-512.

[149] Brown, D.G., Schneider, A.C., Anderson, M.P., and Wagner, R.F. (1994), "Effect of finite sample size and correlated/noisy input features on neural network pattern classification," *Proc. SPIE*, vol. 2167, pp. 180-190.

[150] Chan, H.P., Sahner, B., Wagner, R.F., and Petrick, N. (1998), "Effects of sample size on classifier design for computer-aided diagnosis," *Proc. SPIE*, vol. 3338, pp. 845-858.

[151] Sahiner, B., Chan, H.P., Petrick, N., Wagner, R.F., and Hadjiiski, L.M. (1999), "Stepwise linear discriminant analysis in computer-aided diagnosis: the effect of finite sample size," *Proc. SPIE*, vol. 3661, pp. 499-510.

[152] Sahiner, B., Chan, H.P., Petrick, N., Wagner, R.F., and Hadjiiski, L. (2000), "Feature selection and classifier performance in computer-aided diagnosis: the effect of finite sample size," *Med Phys*, vol. 27, (to appear).

[153] Johnson, R.A. and Wichern, D.W. (1982), *Applied Multivariate Statistical Analysis*, Englewood Cliffs, NJ: Prentice-Hall.

Chapter 7

Which Decision Support Technologies Are Appropriate for the Cytodiagnosis of Breast Cancer?

S.S. Cross, J. Downs, P. Drezet, Z. Ma, and **R.F. Harrison**

The cytodiagnosis of breast lesions is one of the definitive diagnostic modalities used in the diagnosis of breast cancer. In this chapter we examine four different decision support technologies – logistic regression, data-derived decision trees, multilayer perceptrons and adaptive resonance theory mapping neural networks, to see whether any of these can be used effectively as decision support systems in this area of laboratory medicine.

1   Introduction

Data derived decision support systems can be produced by an enormous variety of methods varying from a simple regression equation to a multilayered artificial neural network running on a comparatively powerful computer [1]. The most appropriate system for a specific problem domain will depend primarily on the effectiveness of the system as a statistical classifier but factors related to its implementation will determine whether it gains acceptance as a usable system [2]. These factors include the equipment required for implementation, the ease of use, amount of time required for use and the degree of explanation that the system gives for its decisions. In some situations a system which is a reasonable statistical classifier that requires little equipment and is quick to use will have a greater overall utility than a superior statistical classifier which requires a full specification personal computer and takes several minutes to use.

In clinical medicine there is a huge pressure on staff time, working conditions are often cramped and security for equipment is poor. Any decision support system which requires entry of information which has already been entered into another system, e.g., by writing in the patient's notes, or which requires longer than about 5 minutes to use is unlikely to be used at all in a busy clinical environment [3]. These factors also militate against computer-based decision support systems that require full specification personal computers since desktop systems occupy too much space and laptop systems are frequently stolen. Simpler decision support systems are much more likely to be widely used. Such systems might include a regression equation entered into a programmable calculator or palmheld computer and carried in staff pockets, or a printout of a decision tree pinned to the wall of the clinic.

This chapter looks at one area of clinical laboratory medicine, the cytodiagnosis of breast cancer, and uses a large dataset to generate a number of decision support systems that could be used in this area. It examines the performance of each method as a statistical classifier and then discusses practicalities of its implementation in the working environment.

2   The Problem Domain

Breast cancer is the most common cancer (excluding skin cancer) which affects women in North America, Europe and the Antipodes [4]. The prognosis for breast cancer is primarily dependent on how far the tumour has spread before treatment is instituted and this is a relatively direct function of time. If the diagnosis of breast cancer can be made earlier then the prognosis is improved since more cases will have disease localised to the breast, without spread to lymph nodes in the axilla or more distant sites. A number of countries, including the U.K. and the U.S.A., have instigated screening programmes for breast cancer which use radiographs of the breast (mammograms) as the screening modality. Mammographic abnormalities which raise the suspicion of malignancy include microcalcification and parenchymal deformity but these are not entirely specific and a confirmatory method of diagnosis is required before definitive therapy can be instituted [5]. The most common confirmatory method in the UK has been fine needle aspiration of the breast lesion (FNAB) and cytological examination [6].

In this method cells from the breast lesions are sucked into a syringe through a fine bore needle (similar to that used for taking blood samples) and are then transferred to a transport solution and sent to a pathology laboratory. In the laboratory the fluid is spun down in a cytocentrifuge to produce a deposit of cells on a glass slide [7]. This slide is stained, usually using the Papanicolaou or Giemsa methods, and is then viewed down the microscope by a trained cytopathologist.

The process by which cytopathologists make their diagnoses is largely unknown but appears to be mainly one of pattern recognition with occasional use of heuristic logic [8]. Cytopathologists are trained by an apprenticeship process in which they view slides down a double-headed microscope with an expert and are told the expert's opinion of the diagnosis. The expert may also point out specific features in the specimen and attribute a qualitative value to them in the diagnosis of either benignancy or malignancy. There are also textbooks and journals that codify this information [6]. The full training of a newly-qualified medical doctor to an independently practising cytopathologist takes a minimum of 5 years. There have been many studies of the accuracy of FNAB cytodiagnosis which has been shown to be high in specialist centres [9] but much lower in non-specialist centres when the technique is first introduced [10], [11]. There is thus considerable scope for decision aids which could accelerate the training process or assist in diagnosis in non-specialist centres.

The role of cytology in the diagnosis of breast lesions is complementary with the clinical opinion of the examining surgeon and the mammographic appearances, the so-called 'triple approach' [5], [12]. When a woman attends a clinic with a self-discovered breast lump, or with a mammographic abnormality from a screening programme, she will be examined by a surgeon who will note the features of the lesion (palpable/impalpable, fixed/mobile, tender/non-tender, etc.) and make an assessment as to the likelihood of the lesion being benign or malignant. This is often formalised as a score between 1 and 5 with 1 being normal, 2 abnormal but benign, 3 suspicious probably benign, 4 suspicious, probably malignant, and 5 definitely malignant. If the woman has not already had a mammogram then this will be performed and a radiologist will make an assessment of the likelihood of a benign or malignant diagnosis and will usually express this by the same numerical score. The cytopathologist will view the

FNAB and make a diagnosis, again expressed by the score and a text statement of the findings [13].

The information from these three sources will be reviewed in a multi-disciplinary team meeting with the surgeon, radiologist and cyto-pathologist present, and a final integrated assessment of the likelihood of a benign or malignant process will be made. A malignant diagnosis of breast cancer is highly likely to lead to surgical treatment, such as removal of the whole breast (mastectomy) or part of it (wide local excision), so the whole diagnostic process must have a very high specificity with as few false positives as possible. There is really no acceptable rate of false positives since deforming surgery on a woman without breast cancer must be avoided at all costs. However if the specificity is set very high then the sensitivity may be lower and women with breast cancer may not have their disease detected. For this reason there is often conscious, or unconscious, agreement between the surgeon, radiologist and cytopathologist that their tests, and scores, will have different ranges of sensitivity and specificity. Since mammography is used as a screening test it needs to have a relatively high sensitivity and clinical examination is often made with a high sensitivity in mind. This means that the cytodiagnosis of breast cancer must be carried out with a high specificity to reduce the number of false positives in the integrated diagnostic process. Again there is no real acceptable rate of false positive diagnosis but rates should certainly be less than 1% and preferably less than 0.1%. This requirement for high specificity is relatively unusual in the medical domain since it is usually sensitivity that is at a premium, e.g., in the microbiological diagnosis of bacterial meningitis, because usually medical treatments are fairly non-damaging, e.g., a course of antibiotic drugs, in comparison with the untreated disease.

3   Previous Work in This Area

There are a number of studies in the published literature which have sought to devise decision support systems in the cytodiagnosis of FNAB. Heathfield *et al.* [14] describe a rule-based expert system with rules derived from cytopathological textbooks and discussions with pathologists but they do not give any results for the performance of the system on a test set of data. A Bayesian belief network has been developed by Hamilton *et al.* [15]-[19]. The conditional probability matrices relating to each observed feature to the diagnosis were defined by a cytopathologist. The network was tested using self-selected 'difficult' cases and it is difficult to assess the results because four diagnostic categories were used (benign, malignant, atypical probably benign and suspicious of malignancy). However 6% of the true benign cases and 9% of the true malignant cases were assigned to an equivocal category.

Wolberg and Mangasarian [9], [20]-[22] have used machine learning techniques on a large data set with 420 training cases and 215 test cases. They used nine cytological features as input data, each given scalar values by a human observer in the range 1-10. The techniques they used were a user-modified computer-generated decision tree, the multi-surface method of pattern separation and a connectionist system with a back-propagation learning algorithm. On the test data set the decision tree method gave a specificity of 97% with a sensitivity of 93%, the connectionist network a specificity of 99% and a sensitivity of 97%, the multi-surface separation method produced 100% specificity and sensitivity. However, some cases (such as cancer judged to have been missed by the aspirating needle) were excluded before analysis.

4   The Dataset Used in Our Studies

4.1   Study Population

The study population consisted of 692 consecutive adequate specimens of fine needle aspirates of breast lumps (FNAB) that were received at the Department of Pathology, Royal Hallamshire Hospital, Sheffield during 1992 -1993. The final outcome of benign disease or malignancy was confirmed by open biopsy where this result was available. In benign aspirates with no subsequent open biopsy a benign outcome was assessed by clinical details on the request form, mammographic findings (where available) and by absence of further malignant specimens. A malignant outcome was confirmed by histology of open biopsy or clinical details where the primary treatment modality was chemotherapy or hormonal therapy.

4.2 The Defined Observations That Were Used as Input Variables

Our studies reported in this chapter have used defined human observations of FNAB cytology specimens rather than objective measurements made using image analysis techniques. The reasons for this are two fold. Firstly, despite many recent advances in technology, image analysis is still an unwieldy technique for biological specimens with many problems associated with image segmentation. We have used image analysis on low power images of FNABs in a semi-automated image analysis technique with overall accuracy's of around 80% [23] but such a system would then require automated search and selection for areas of interest to be examined at much higher magnification and the development of that part of an automated process has many unsolved difficulties. Secondly we wished to develop a decision support system that could be used in any cytopathology laboratory with a minimum of additional equipment. A system based on automated image analysis would require sophisticated and expensive equipment, such as digital cameras and motorised microscope stages, whereas one based on defined human observations could be implemented with a substrate as simple as a printed decision tree.

There are, however, problems associated with the use of human observations. Many of the features in this study, such as the presence or absence of intracytoplasmic lumina, are simple binary features and the reproducibility of these features only depends on the recognition of feature when present and a suitable level of diligence whilst searching for such features. Other features, such as cellular dyshesion, are continuous biological spectra that extend from groups of completely cohesive cells to specimens that only contain disassociated single cells. For these features a binary coding, such as used in this study, is an arbitrary cut-off boundary within a spectrum and there will be issues of reproducibility of the application of such a cut-off between different observers and the same observer at different times [24]. We choose to use simple binary coding to investigate the simplest possible system that might work in a busy clinical environment and because this allowed easier analysis of the processes by which the various methodologies produced their decisions.

The defined observations that we used are taken from those cited in the literature as being discriminatory in the cytodiagnosis of FNAB [13]. The defined observations used are listed in Table 1.

In addition to these defined observed features, the patient's age in years was used as an input feature, normalised to the interval 0,1.

Table 1. The defined human observations used as input variables.

Observed Feature	Definition
Cellular dyshesion	True if the majority of epithelial cells are dyshesive, false if the majority of epithelial cells are in cohesive groups
Intracytoplasmic lumina	True if intracytoplasmic lumina are present in some epithelial cells, false if absent
'Three-dimensionality' of epithelial cells clusters	True if some clusters of epithelial cells are not flat (more than two nuclei thick) and this is not due to artefactual folding, false if all clusters of epithelial cells are flat
Bipolar 'naked' nuclei	True if bipolar 'naked' nuclei are present, false if absent
Foamy macrophages	True if foamy macrophages are present, false if absent
Nucleoli	True if more than three easily-visible nucleoli are present in some epithelial cells, false if three or fewer easily-visible nucleoli in all epithelial cells
Nuclear pleomorphism	True if some epithelial cells have nuclear diameters twice that of other epithelial cell nuclei, false if no epithelial cell nuclei have diameters twice that of other epithelial cell nuclei
Nuclear size	True if some epithelial cell nuclei have diameters twice that of red blood cell diameters, false if all epithelial cell nuclei have diameters less than twice that of red blood cell diameters
Necrotic epithelial cells	True if necrotic epithelial cells are present, false if absent
Apocrine change	True if the majority of epithelial cell nuclei show apocrine change, false if apocrine change is not present in the majority of epithelial cells

4.3   Partitioning of the Data

The data set was randomly partitioned into a 231 case training set, a 231 case verification/optimisation set and a 230 case test set. This partitioning remained the same for all the methodologies. In methods where a verification set was not require, such as logistic regression and the C4.5 decision tree, the training and verification sets were combined to produce a 432 case training set.

5   Human Performance

The performance of any decision support system has to be compared with existing human performance. In such comparisons there should be equality between the two sets being compared. Thus a live trial of a decision support system in a working clinical environment should be compared with unassisted decisions in the same environment [2]. There are many factors that have to be considered in such comparisons including the checklist effect and the Hawthorne effect [3]. In these studies we have used the decision support systems on a dataset of observations made outside the working cytopathology laboratory by a fully-trained experienced cytopathologist. It would thus appear that the most appropriate comparison would be made with the diagnostic opinion of this experienced observer after he had made the defined observations. This would eliminate any checklist and Hawthorne effect. Comparison with the initial laboratory diagnosis of these specimens would not be appropriate since the diagnoses were made by a heterogeneous population of specialist and non-specialist, trainee and consultant, medical staff.

The expert human cytopathologist who made the defined observations did so without knowledge of outcome or patient age (which is often useful in making the diagnosis e.g., a cellular cytological specimen in a very old woman has a strong probability of being malignant even if no other cellular morphological features associated with malignancy are present). After making the defined observations the human observer gave a categorical benign or malignant diagnosis without the use of a suspicious category. The appropriate metrics for the comparison are the sensitivity, specificity and predictive values of the tests; all with calculated 95% confidence intervals. These diagnoses gave the performance illustrated in Table 2.

It can be seen that the human observer produces no false positives in the whole data set thus fulfilling the most important requirement for any system in FNAB cytodiagnosis. The long period of training and experience gained through looking at thousands of these specimens has enabled the observer to set an internal threshold for a malignant diagnosis that is high enough to eliminate false positive results. The sensitivity for this observer is reasonable but does reduce the predictive value of a negative result to 92%. This could be acceptable to referring surgeons but they would have to realise that a negative cytology result does not eliminate the possibility that the woman does have breast cancer. Some of the false negatives may have been caused by the absence of the patient's age in the information presented to the human observer. In elderly women, who are not taking hormone replacement therapy, an increased number of cells in a specimen, without much qualitative abnormality of those cells, can be the sole cytological indicator of malignancy.

Table 2. Human performance on the whole 692 item data set.

Parameter	Value with 95% confidence intervals
Sensitivity	82% (77-87)
Specificity	100%
Predictive value of a positive result	100%
Predictive value of a negative result	92% (89-94)

5.1   Logistic Regression

Logistic regression is one of the standard techniques of multivariable statistical analysis [25]. It is readily available in many statistical software packages and once a logistic equation has been derived from a training set, it can be applied to test set cases in a simple implementation on a programmable calculator or simple palmtop computer and so could be implemented quickly in any cytology laboratory. The process by which logistic regression makes its predictions is relatively transparent since the odds ratios are easily interpretable. Logistic regression is thus the standard statistical technique against which other decision support systems should be compared and which is frequently cited as the current available level of performance when seeking licensing of a decision support system for the medical market.

In this study a logistic equation was derived from the 432 combined training set entering all variables together in a main effects only model and this was applied to the test set. The logistic regression was implemented using the Statistical Package for Social Sciences (SPSS, http://www.spss.com/UK) running on a standard computer. The odds ratios from the logistic equation are given in Table 3. The receiver operating characteristic (ROC) curve (Figure 1) was calculated for the test set using standard methods [26].

Table 3. Odds ratios (with 95% confidence intervals) from logistic regression for the training set of 432 cases.

Observed Feature	Odds Ratio
Age	1.2 (1.1-1.3)
Cellular dyshesion	2490 (0-1.3×1027)
Intracytoplasmic lumina	105.3 (20.1-551.5)
'Three-dimensionality' of epithelial cells clusters	6.5 (1.1-37.8)
Bipolar 'naked' nuclei	4.8 (0.8-27.6)
Foamy macrophages	1.0 (0.3-3.2)
Nucleoli	26.8 (5.0-144.3)
Nuclear pleomorphism	31.0 (1.8-550.7)
Nuclear size	5.4 (0.4-81.5)
Necrotic epithelial cells	8.3 (0.4-176.8)
Apocrine change	0.1 (0.0-0.8)

It can be seen that logistic regression is a good overall classifier in this domain with an area under the ROC of 0.98. However although the overall accuracy is good the rate of false positives is unacceptably high when the threshold is 0.5 giving a specificity of 95% and a predictive value of a positive result of 87%. If the threshold is raised so that the specificity equals one then the sensitivity falls to 81% which gives results which are almost identical to those of the human observer. This suggests that it is the identification of the features themselves which provides the diagnosis rather than a complex integration of those features unless both the human observer and logistic regression are making that complex integration.

At a threshold of 0.5, this logistic equation gave the results in Table 4.

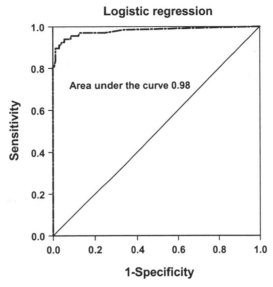

Figure 1. ROC curve for logistic regression.

Table 4. Performance of logistic regression at a threshold of 0.5.

Parameter	Value with 95% confidence intervals
Sensitivity	94% (89-99)
Specificity	95% (90-97)
Predictive value of a positive result	87% (80-95)
Predictive value of a negative result	97% (95-99)

The odds ratios show that 5 features are predictive of malignancy – increasing age, presence of intracytoplasmic lumina, presence of three dimensional cell clusters, multiple nucleoli and nuclear pleomorphism. One feature, apocrine metapalsia, is predictive of a benign diagnosis. The other 5 features all have odds ratios with 95% confidence intervals that are not totally above or below one and thus are not statistically significantly predictive of either a malignant or benign diagnosis at a 5% level of significance.

6   Data Derived Decision Tree

In the introduction the implementation of decision support systems and its effect on user compliance was discussed. One of the simplest implementations would be a decision tree that could be reproduced on a single sheet of paper and be displayed in the working cytopathology laboratory. Such a system is cheap and easily distributed.

Such decision-trees may be derived from 'rules' given by human experts or by inductive processes using input data with a known outcome [27]. The decision tree in this study was derived using the C4.5 program [28] which is an evolution of the more well-known ID3 algorithm [29]. This algorithm is an implementation of the top-down induction method where the tree is determined iteratively by adding those nodes and branches that maximise the information gain (minimise the entropy) at each step [27]. The tree that was derived from the 432 combined training set is shown in Figure 2.

Users would start at the central uppermost node ('Nuclear size') and proceed through the dichotomous branchings using their own observations to reach a terminal leaf ('benign' or 'malignant'). The 231 case test set was then applied to the tree and the predictions recorded in Table 5.

Table 5. Performance of statistically derived decision tree.

Parameter	Value with 95% confidence intervals
Sensitivity	95% (90-99)
Specificity	93% (88-97)
Predictive value of a positive result	87% (79-95)
Predictive value of a negative result	98% (95-99)

These are very similar results to those of logistic regression with a threshold of 0.5. The 7% false positive rate that would again be unacceptable in the clinical laboratory. Since this technique only produces dichotomous results no ROC curves can be constructed and no threshold can be adjusted to reduce the false positive rate.

We have tested this technique using different observers on a further 50 case test set and have shown that the performance of trainee pathologists is better without the 'aid' of the decision tree, with much higher specificity's for little reduction in sensitivity [30]. This suggests that either the decision tree technology itself is not appropriate to this domain or that the reliability of observing the features is low and so the decision tree is specific to the original observer. Examination of the agreement between the observers on individual features showed good levels of agreement on most of the features so it suggests that the technology is not appropriate to the domain, as implemented in this study. The derivation of the tree to minimise total error and the dichotomous nature of the results, without an adjustable threshold, probably account for the high false positive rate and in other domains, where specificity is not the key parameter, this technique could produce highly acceptable results.

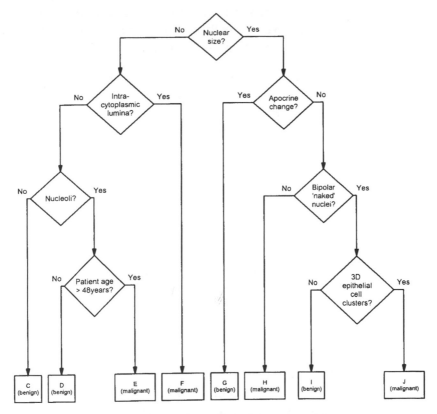

Figure 2. The decision tree derived from the training set.

7   Multilayer Perceptron Neural Networks

Multilayer perceptron (MLP) neural networks were one of the earliest types of supervised learning artificial neural networks and have now become the standard architecture with which more recent types are compared [31]. Although there are some inherent problems with the architecture, such as exponential scaling of the network connections in relation to the number of inputs, they are relatively easy to use in any modern personal computer. There are many software packages that run MLPs and most now have graphical user interfaces with a similar appearance to conventional spreadsheet programs, such as Microsoft Excel. Indeed there are MLP add-ons available for many spreadsheet packages. Whilst the training of an MLP may take some time it is relatively easy to implement a trained network in a compiled language, such as C, so that it is gives virtually instantaneous prediction on new cases and can be installed in palmtop computers.

The MLP in our studies was trained using the 231 case training set (Statistica Neural Networks, http://www.statsoft.com). The architecture of the network was 11 input neurones, one hidden layer of 6 neurones and 1 output neurone (Figure 3).

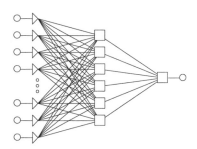

Figure 3. The architecture of the MLP.

The network was trained using a back propagation of errors method with a learning rate of 0.6 and a momentum of 0.3 [32]-[34]. There are no mathematically proven methods of deriving the optimal architecture for a MLP and there are two main variables – the number of hidden layers and the number of neurones in each hidden layer. However one of the problems of using MLPs is overfitting of the network to the training set data with subsequently poor generalisation to the test set [31]. One cause of such overfitting is a network with many more connections within it than cases in the training set. In the network architecture which we used there are $(11 \times 6) + 6 = 72$ connections which is less than a third the number of training exemplars so that cause of overfitting should be minimised. Another cause of overfitting is overtraining the MLP by using too many training epochs. There is now a trend towards the early stopping of training of MLPs to avoid this problem. By using a optimisation/verification set the effect of increasing training can be observed. In our studies we used a 231 case set for optimisation/ verification where the error for that set was displayed on the training graph alongside that of the test set but the outcome for the optimisation set was not given to the network. We used increasing numbers of training epochs and observed both errors, when the error on the optimisation set started to rise we stopped training and selected the network just before the rise. This should ensure that the trained network has adequate generalisation properties.

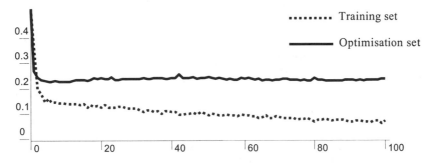

Figure 4. Training graph for the 11:6:1 architecture MLP.

At more than 100 epochs the overall error for the verification set started to rise indicating overtraining. At lower numbers of epochs the effects were variable and particular networks could be selected which gave excellent performance on training, verification and test sets. One such network was produced after 14 training epochs that had no false positives in any of the three data partitions. The results of this network on the test set at a threshold of 0.5 are given in Table 6.

This is very similar to the unaided human performance (Table 2). This is a valid result because it does use randomised training, verification and test sets and so, with the data available it is assessed to be the best MLP network. However this was one network selected out of 50, so there is reduction in the degrees of freedom due to this, and with a still further independent test set its performance might degrade. A more realistic performance is given by a network after 50 training epochs with the performance shown in Table 7.

Table 6. Performance of 11:6:1 MLP on the test set after 14 training epochs.

Parameter	Value with 95% confidence intervals
Sensitivity	85% (76-93)
Specificity	100%
Predictive value of a positive result	100%
Predictive value of a negative result	93% (90-97)

Table 7. Performance of 11:6:1 MLP on the test set after 50 training epochs.

Parameter	Value with 95% confidence intervals
Sensitivity	88% (80-95)
Specificity	98% (96-99)
Predictive value of a positive result	95% (90-99)
Predictive value of a negative result	95% (91-98)

It can be seen that this shows a reduction in specificity with modest gains in sensitivity. However the false positive rate of 2% is now too high for use in the clinical situation where this rate should be considerably less than 1% [13]. The early version of software used in this study did not facilitate the production of ROC curves so the performance of the classifiers at all thresholds cannot be quantitatively assessed. Again it appears that the human performance cannot be bettered and this may be due to the extraction of features by preprocessing in the human brain which does not give enough raw unprocessed data for the MLP to be utilised to its best advantage.

8   Adaptive Resonance Theory Mapping (ARTMAP) Neural Networks

Adaptive resonance theory mapping (ARTMAP) neural networks were developed by Grossberg and Carpenter in the late 1980s and have been evolving since then with many innovations including rule extraction [35]-[38].

8.1   Potential Advantages of ARTMAP

There are problems with MLP technology in four areas – exponential growth of network connections with increase in number of input features, number of adjustable parameters, entrapping in local minima during training and 'black box' workings [31]. The problem of exponential scaling in MLPs has been discussed above and a major advantage of ARTMAP is a linear scaling with increase in the number of input features. There are numerous parameters that can be adjusted during the training of an MLP including the number of hidden layers, the number of neurones in each hidden layer, the transfer function of the neurones, the method of training, the learning rate, momentum and number of training epochs. All of these can have significant effects on the performance of the final trained network and there are no proven algorithms for optimising them. Testing all the settings of all possible parameters in an MLP is extremely time-consuming but can be carried out automatically by a computer running for a long period of time, perhaps using genetic algorithm methods for selecting the best combination of parameters. However overtraining, e.g., by selection of a particular architecture etc., is possible given that there may be thousands of networks to test but only one verification and test set. Simplified fuzzy ARTMAPs contain only one adjustable parameter, the vigilance factor, making optimisation of the network simple.

Decision support systems in the medical environment are viewed with extreme suspicion if the reasoning by which they arrive at their decision is not transparent. Doctors and other medical staff do not feel confident in giving a potentially harmful treatment to a patient if the decision to do so comes from a black box device with no explanation for the reasoning behind that decision. This lack of confidence may not be entirely rational since most human decisions are made 'intuitively' in microseconds and only then verbalised but it does lead to a low uptake of black box decision support systems. When using an MLP data is put into the input neurones and a number, taken to be a probability, is output but there is no indication as to how that prediction was derived. A few investigators have begun to report rule extraction from MLPs but the technology is not mature. Rule extraction from ARTMAPs is a relatively simple process which can 'take the lid off the black box' [37] and could thus increase the uptake of ARTMAP-based decision support systems in a working clinical environment.

8.2   ARTMAP Architecture and Methodology

ARTMAP was developed from the competitive learning paradigm with the intention of overcoming the stability-plasticity dilemma [35], [39],

[40]. This was achieved by utilising feedback between layers of input and category nodes in addition the standard feed forward connections. So, in ARTMAP an input pattern is not automatically assigned to the category that it initially maximally activated by that input. Instead, if the feedback process rejects the initial categorisation, a search process is initiated which terminates when a category node with an acceptable match to the input is found. If no such node exists, a new category node is formed to classify the input. This can be seen as unsupervised clustering of the input data before the outcome label is linked with the clusters and allows novel clusterings to be formed outside the constraints of such labelling. Fuzzy ARTMAP consists of three modules – ART_a, ART_b and the map field (Figure 5).

During training, input patterns are presented to ART_a together with their associated teaching stimuli at ART_b. Associations between patterns at ART_a and ART_b are then formed at the map field. During testing, supervisory inputs at ART_b are omitted, and instead the inputs at ART_a are used to recall a previously learned association with an ART_b pattern via the map field. The only adjustable parameter in simplified fuzzy ARTMAP is the ART_a vigilance parameter, ρ_a. This determines how close a match is required between an ART_a input pattern and a category cluster prototype before accepting the input as a member of the cluster. This parameter indirectly controls the size of the category clusters that will form, since the higher it is set, the closer acceptable matches must be, and the smaller the coverage of the state space each cluster will have. Generally, higher vigilance provides better classification performance, although this must be balanced against the potential proliferation of category clusters, providing poor data compression and leading the network to become little more than a 'look-up table.'

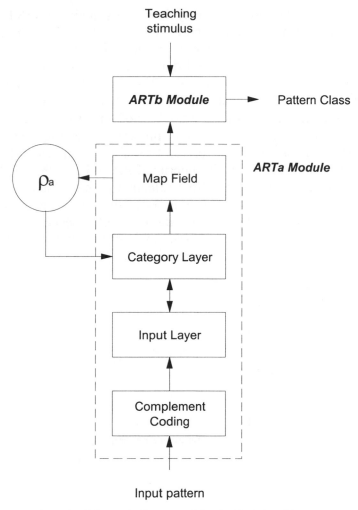

Figure 5. Schematic diagram of the ARTMAP architecture.

The formation of category clusters in ARTMAP is affected by the order of presentation of input data items [36]. Thus, the same data presented in a different order to separate networks can lead to the formation of quite different clusters within the two networks. This order dependence can be compensated by use of a voting strategy where a number of ARTMAPs are trained on different orderings of the training data and the majority decision of all the networks is taken as the prediction.

An ARTMAP often contains many low-utility nodes in ART_a after training and many of these may represent 'noise' or rare but unimportant cases. This problem is particularly acute when a high ARTa vigilance parameter is used during training. To overcome this the nodes in ARTa can be pruned. This pruning is guided by the calculation of a confidence factor (CF) for each node which is based on the node's usage and accuracy. Full details of this process are given in Carpenter and Tan [37]. The pruning process can provide significant reduction in the size of a network and usually has the side effect of improved performance over the unpruned network. In this study we have modified the process to allow selective pruning for nodes with high sensitivity or specificity. This is useful in the domain of FNAB cytodiagnosis since it allows the creation of highly specific networks. Using this specialised pruning and the voting strategy we have produced a novel cascaded configuration of ARTMAPs (Figure 6).

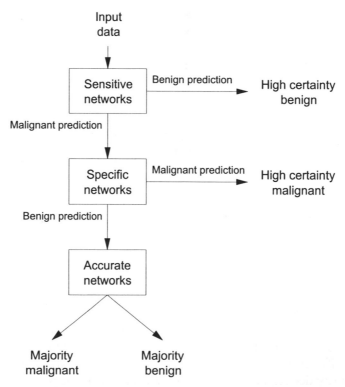

Figure 6. The cascaded voting configuration of ARTMAPs.

The first two layers are intended to identify those cases which have a very high certainty of being classified correctly, with the sensitive network being used to 'trap' the negative cases and the specific network capturing the positive cases. The reasoning being that a network which displays very high sensitivity will rarely make false negative predictions and so any negative predictions are very likely to be correct. Conversely, a highly specific network will make very few false positive predictions, and so its positive predictions have a high certainty of being correct.

8.3   Results from the Cascaded System

Table 8. Performance of the ARTMAP cascade on the test set.

	High certainty decisions	Majority decisions	Overall performance
Sensitivity	96% (92-99)	78% (64-92)	90% (84-96)
Specificity	100%	86% (74-97)	96% (93-99)
Predictive value +	100%	83% (70-97)	94% (89-99)
Predictive value −	98% (96-99)	81% (68-94)	94% (90-98)

It can be seen that the high certainty decisions produce a performance that fits the needs of the domain with 100% specificity and a very high sensitivity. This performance is better than the observing cytopathologist, with a 13% increase in sensitivity (both with 100% specificity). However the high certainty decisions only covered 71% of the test set, the remaining 29% went through to the majority decision part of the cascade where the specificity is unacceptably low. This system could be used in a laboratory environment taking action only on high certainty decisions and labeling all the majority decisions as 'suspicious.' However this would be a high rate of suspicious reports which usually runs at about 10-15% of all specimens reported by unassisted humans.

8.4   Symbolic Rule Extraction

The act of rule extraction from ARTMAP is relatively straightfoward compared with that required for feedfoward networks since there are no hidden units with implicit meaning. In essence each cluster in ARTa represents a symbolic rule whose antecedent is the category prototype weights and whose consequent is the associated ARTb category (denoted via the map field) [37]. The rules derived from ARTMAP must be contrasted with the production rules used in conventional decision support aids such as expert systems. Expert system rules are 'hard' – an input must match to each and every feature in a rule's antecedent before the consequent can be asserted. In ARTMAP the rules are 'soft,' they are derived from prototypical category clusters which are in competition with each other to match to the input data. Exact matching between inputs and categories is not necessary, a reasonably close fit suffices.

Table 9. The 12 extracted rules for a benign diagnosis.

Rule 1 - 5 occurrences	Rule 2 - 5 occurrences	Rule 3 - 5 occurrences

IF
  NOSYMPTOMS
THEN
  BENIGN
	IF
	  NAKED
	THEN
	  BENIGN
		IF
		  FOAMY
		  NUCLEOLI
		THEN
		  BENIGN

Rule 4 - 4 occurrences	**Rule 5 - 4 occurrences**	**Rule 6 - 4 occurrences**

IF
  APOCRINE
THEN
  BENIGN
	IF
	  PLEOMORPH
	THEN
	  BENIGN
		IF
		  3D
		  FOAMY
		THEN
		  BENIGN

Rule 7 - 3 occurrences	**Rule 8 - 3 occurrences**	**Rule 9 - 2 occurrences**

IF
  FOAMY
  APOCRINE
THEN
  BENIGN
	IF
	  PLEOMORPH
	  SIZE
	  APOCRINE
	THEN
	  BENIGN
		IF
		  FOAMY
		THEN
		  BENIGN

Rule 10 - 2 occurrences	**Rule 11 - 2 occurrences**	**Rule 12 - 2 occurrences**

IF
  NAKED
  FOAMY
THEN
  BENIGN
	IF
	  FOAMY
	  PLEOMORPH
	  SIZE
	  APOCRINE
	THEN
	  BENIGN
		IF
		  3D
		  NAKED
		  NECROTIC
		THEN
		  BENIGN

Table 10. The 12 most frequent extracted rules for a malignant diagnosis.

Rule 1 - 5 occurrences	Rule 2 - 5 occurrences	Rule 3 - 5 occurrences

IF
  3D
  NUCLEOLI
  PLEOMORPH
  SIZE
THEN
  MALIGNANT
	IF
	  DYSHESION
	  ICL
	  NUCLEOLI
	  PLEOMORPH
	  SIZE
	  NECROTIC
	THEN
	  MALIGNANT
		IF
		  3D
		  NUCLEOLI
		  PLEOMORPH
		  SIZE
		  NECROTIC
		THEN
		  MALIGNANT

Rule 4 - 4 occurrences	Rule 5 - 4 occurrences	Rule 6 - 4 occurrences

IF
  ICL
  3D
  NUCLEOLI
  PLEOMORPH
  SIZE
THEN
MALIGNANT
	IF
	  DYSHESION
	  NUCLEOLI
	  PLEOMORPH
	  SIZE
	THEN
	  MALIGNANT
		IF
		  NUCLEOLI
		  PLEOMORPH
		  SIZE
		THEN
		  MALIGNANT

Rule 7 - 4 occurrences	Rule 8 - 4 occurrences	Rule 9 - 4 occurrences

IF
  PLEOMORPH
  SIZE
THEN
  MALIGNANT
	IF
	  ICL
	  3D
	  FOAMY
	  NUCLEOLI
	  PLEOMORPH
	  SIZE
	  NECROTIC
	THEN
	  MALIGNANT
		IF
		  ICL
		  FOAMY
		  PLEOMORPH
		  SIZE
		THEN
		  MALIGNANT

Rule 10 - 4 occurrences	Rule 11 - 4 occurrences	Rule 12 - 4 occurrences

IF
  ICL
  NUCLEOLI
  PLEOMORPH
  SIZE
THEN
  MALIGNANT
	IF
	  DYS
	  3D
	  NUCLEOLI
	  PLEOMORPH
	  SIZE
	  NECROTIC
	THEN
	  MALIGNANT
		IF
		  3D
		  NAKED
		  NUCLEOLI
		  PLEOMORPH
		  SIZE
		THEN
		  MALIGNANT

Additionally, the rules are self-discovered through exposure to domain exemplars, rather than having been externally provided by a human expert. With these principles in mind, the most frequent rules for benign and malignant diagnoses from the uniformly pruned ARTMAPs in this study were as shown in Tables 9 and 10.

Age was not included in these rule-extracted networks since unless it is aggregated into age bands it produces separate rules for each year of age. These rules can be compared with the canonical knowledge published in the literature, such as the Cytology Working Group of the National Health Service Breast Screening Programme [13]. The extracted rules and the information in the literature are very similar with nuclear pleomorphism, multiple nucleoli and increased nuclear size cited as important predictors of malignancy in the literature and present in those rules with a malignant outcome. To test the rule extraction process we have included irrelevant information, such as the parity of the laboratory accession number, in the input features and such information has never appeared in the extracted rules.

There are some interesting explanations of decisions encoded in these rules. We have shown that nuclear pleomorphism and increased nuclear size are predictors of malignancy but the two features are present in rules 8 and 11 predicting a benign diagnosis. However also included in these two rules is the apocrine metaplasia feature. In the process of apocrine metaplasia in breast epithelial cells the whole cell, including the nucleus, does increase in size so that feature is likely to be associated with the presence of the apocrine feature. The definition of pleomorphism is that the nuclei of some epithelial cells are more than twice the diameter of other epithelial cells. This could occur with the feature apocrine when the majority of epithelial cells showed apocrine metaplasia but there were still some non-metaplastic epithelial cells present and these would be less than twice the diameter of the metaplastic cells. Thus an apparently anomalous decision is explained by the extracted rules.

The foamy macrophage feature occurs in many of the benign (3, 6, 7, 9, 10, & 11) and malignant (8, 9, & 11) rules in combination with other features. In the literature this feature is said to be associated with a malignant diagnosis but in our studies it is either non-discriminant or only discriminant when considered with other specific combinations of features. In this instance the rule extraction feature of ARTMAP may be revealing new information that has not been noted by human experts.

9   Which Technique Produces the Most Suitable Decision Support System?

In our studies we have used 4 different decision support technologies and have compared these with the performance of a human expert. We have noted that specificity is the key parameter in the domain of FNAB cytodiagnosis and should be as close to 100% as possible. The human observer attained a specificity of 100% with a sensitivity of 82% and this was only matched, on the *whole* test set, by a selected MLP which had been trained for 14 epochs. ARTMAP, in a cascaded decision system, gave a higher sensitivity with 100% specificity but only for a defined (by the system) subset of the test set. The MLP would be easy to implement on a desktop or palmtop computer and entry of the observed features could be facilitated by a graphical interface. However the MLP only equaled the human performance and it was the human who coded the observed features used as input data for the MLP. Further studies need to be carried out to examine whether this performance holds up when observations from other, perhaps less experienced, individuals are used as input data. The observed features are a simple binary encoding of very complex visual images and the human brain has evolved over millions of years to process visual images in a very efficient way. It is thus possible that almost all the processing required to solve the diagnostic problem has been carried out by the human observer during the encoding of the features, leaving little work for the decision support system. This may explain why none of the systems bettered the human performance. In order to exploit the potential advantages of techniques such as artificial neural networks, it may be necessary to use a much less processed form of data such as raw digitised images. However that process is made difficult by the large number of input features that would be present in such an image (16384 for a crude 128×128 pixel image) and problems with the exponential scaling of some neural network architectures.

The cascaded ARTMAP system performs well on a subset of the test set but the performance of the other systems is also likely to be very good on such a restricted set. The advantages of such a cascaded system are that the degree of confidence in the prediction is expressed (by the unanimity or otherwise of the voting) and the system can be modified to produce highly specific or highly sensitive results. The rule extraction facility from the trained ARTMAPs produced confirmation of many of the features described in cytopathology textbooks and new information about the role of foamy macrophages in diagnosis (probably non-discriminant).

A cautionary note about technological advances should be included at the end of a discussion about the merits of different technologies. These studies have taken a few years to carry out with verification of outcome data for the study population being the most time-consuming task. During this time a new technology for sampling breast tissue has been developed which samples a small diameter core of breast tissue. This technique does not appear to produce any greater discomfort or residual damage to the breast than fine needle aspiration. It yields a core of tissue which can be processed into paraffin wax and from which conventional histological sections (rather than cytological preparations) can be made. These histological sections are generally much easier to interpret than cytological preparations since the architecture of the tissue is preserved and so invasion and other features can be observed directly rather than be inferred from the features of individual cells in a cytological preparation. This core biopsy technique has increased in popularity enormously over the past 2 years in the UK and other European countries and has replaced much of the FNAB cytology. It would thus appear that the search for decision support technologies for FNAB cytodiagnosis has been supplanted by a simple advance in mechanical technology.

Acknowledgements

This work has been supported by the Special Trustees of the Former United Sheffield Hospitals (grant GR87727) and the Engineering and Physical Sciences Council of Great Britain (grants GR/J29916 and GR/J43233).

References

[1] Heathfield, H.A. and Wyatt, J. (1993), "Philosophies for the design and development of clinical decision-support systems," *Meth. Inform. Med.*, vol. 32, pp. 1-8.

[2] Friedman, C.P., Wyatt, J.C., Friedman, C.P., and Wyatt, J.C. (Eds.) (1997), *Evaluation Methods in Medical Informatics*, New York: Springer-Verlag.

[3] Wyatt, J. and Spiegelhalter, D. (1991), "Field trials of medical decision-aids: potential problems and solutions," *Proceedings of the 15th Symposium on Computer Applications in Medical Care*, pp. 3-7.

[4] Underwood, J.C.E. and Underwood, J.C.E. (Eds.) (1992), *General and Systematic Pathology*, 1st ed., Edinburgh: Churchill Livingstone, chapter 10 "Tumours: benign and malignant," pp. 223-246.

[5] Elston, C.W. and Ellis, I.O. (1990), "Pathology and breast screening," *Histopathology*, vol. 16, pp. 109-118.

[6] Trott, P.A. (1991), "Aspiration cytodiagnosis of the breast," *Diagn. Oncol.*, vol. 1, pp. 79-87.

[7] Howat, A.J., Armstrong, G.R., Briggs, W.A., Nicholson, C.M., and Stewart, D.J. (1993), "Fine needle aspiration of palpable breast lumps: a 1-year audit using the Cytospin method," *Cytopathology*, vol. 3, pp. 17-22.

[8] Underwood, J.C.E. (1987), *Introduction to Biopsy Interpretation and Surgical Pathology*, 2nd ed., London: Springer-Verlag.

[9] Wolberg, W.H. and Mangasarian, O.L. (1990), "Computer-aided diagnosis of breast aspirates via expert systems," *Anal. Quant. Cytol. Histol.*, vol. 12, pp. 314-320.

[10] Hitchcock, A., Hunt, C.M., Locker, A., Koslowski, J., Strudwick, S., Elston, C.W., Blamey, R.W., and Ellis, I.O. (1991), "A one

year audit of fine needle aspiration cytology for the pre- operative diagnosis of breast disease," *Cytopathology*, vol. 2, pp. 167-176.

[11] Hunt, C.M., Wilson, S., Pinder, S.E., Elston, C.W., and Ellis, I.O. (1996), "UK national audit of breast fine needle aspiration cytology in 1990-91: diagnostic criteria," *Cytopathology*, vol. 7, pp. 326-332.

[12] Pinder, S.E., Elston, C.W., and Ellis, I.O. (1996), "The role of pre-operative diagnosis in breast cancer," *Histopathol.*, vol. 28, pp. 563-566.

[13] Wells, C.A., Ellis, I.O., Zakhour, H.D., and Wilson, A.R. (1994), "Guidelines for cytology procedures and reporting on fine needle aspirates of the breast," *Cytopathology*, vol. 5, pp. 316-334.

[14] Heathfield, H.A., Kirkham, N., Ellis, I.O., and Winstanley, G. (1990), "Computer assisted diagnosis of fine needle aspirate of the breast," *J. Clin. Pathol.*, vol. 43, pp. 168-170.

[15] Hamilton, P.W., Anderson, N., Bartels, P.H., and Thompson, D. (1994), "Expert system support using Bayesian belief networks in the diagnosis of fine needle aspiration biopsy specimens of the breast," *J. Clin. Pathol.*, vol. 47, pp. 329-336.

[16] Hamilton, P.W., Bartels, P.H., Montironi, R., Anderson, N., and Thompson, D. (1995), "Improved diagnostic decision-making in pathology: do inference networks hold the key?" *J. Pathol.*, vol. 175, pp. 1-5.

[17] Hamilton, P.W., Montironi, R., Abmayr, W., Bibbo, M., Anderson, N., Thompson, D., and Bartels, P.H. (1995), "Clinical applications of Bayesian belief networks in pathology," [Review], *Pathologica*, vol. 87, pp. 237-245.

[18] Montironi, R., Whimster, W.F., Collan, Y., Hamilton, P.W., Thompson, D., and Bartels, P.H. (1996), "How to develop and use a Bayesian belief network," *J. Clin. Pathol.*, vol. 49, pp. 194-201.

[19] Whimster, W.F., Hamilton, P.W., Anderson, N.A., Humphreys, S., Boyle, M., Sundaresan, M., Rainey, A., Giles, A., Hopster, D., and

Bartels, P.H. (1996), "Reproducibility of Bayesian belief network assessment of breast fine needle aspirates," *Anal. Quant. Cytol. Histol.*, vol. 18, pp. 267-274.

[20] Wolberg, W.H. and Mangasarian, O.L. (1993), "Computer-designed expert systems for breast cytology diagnosis," *Anal. Quant. Cytol. Histol.*, vol. 15, pp. 67-74.

[21] Wolberg, W.H., Street, W.N., and Mangasarian, O.L. (1995), "Image analysis and machine learning applied to breast cancer diagnosis and prognosis," *Anal. Quant. Cytol. Histol.*, vol. 17, pp. 77-87.

[22] Wolberg, W.H., Street, W.N., and Mangasarian, O.L. (1994), "Machine learning techniques to diagnose breast cancer from image-processed nuclear features of fine needle aspirates," *Cancer Letters*, vol. 77, pp. 163-171.

[23] Cross, S.S., Bury, J.P., Stephenson, T.J., and Harrison, R.F. (1997), "Image analysis of low magnification images of fine needle aspirates of the breast produces useful discrimination between benign and malignant cases," *Cytopathology*, vol. 8, pp. 265-273.

[24] Cross, S.S. (1998), "Grading and scoring in histopathology," *Histopathol.*, vol. 33, pp. 99-106.

[25] Feinstein, A.R. Feinstein, A.R. (Eds.) (1996), *Multivariable analysis*, 1st ed., New Haven: Yale University Press, chapter 13 "Multiple logistic regression," pp. 297-330.

[26] Hanley, J.A. and McNeil, B.J. (1982), "The meaning and use of the area under a receiver operating characteristic (ROC) curve," *Radiology*, vol. 143, pp. 29-36.

[27] Jackson, P. Jackson, P. (Eds.) (1990), *Introduction to Expert Systems*, 2nd ed., Wokingham: Addison-Wesley Publishing Company, chapter 26 "Rule induction by machine learning," pp. 430-455.

[28] Quinlan, J.R. (1993), *C4.5: Programs for Machine Learning*, 1st ed., San Mateo: Morgan Kauffman.

[29] Quinlan, J.R. (1986), "Induction of decision trees," *Machine Learning*, vol. 1, pp. 81-106.

[30] Cross, S.S, Dube, A.K., Johnson, J.S., McCulloch, T.A., Quincey, C., Harrison, R.F., and Ma, Z. (1998), "Evaluation of a statistically derived decision tree for the cytodiagnosis of fine needle aspirates of the breast (FNAB)," *Cytopathology*, vol. 9, pp. 178-187.

[31] Cross, S.S., Harrison, R.F., and Kennedy, R.L. (1995), "Introduction to neural networks," *Lancet*, vol. 346, pp. 1075-1079.

[32] Fausett, L. (1994), *Fundamentals of Neural Networks: Architectures, Algorithms and Applications*, Englewood Cliffs, New Jersey: Prentice-Hall International Inc.

[33] Bishop, C.M. and Bishop, C.M. (Eds.) (1995), *Neural networks for pattern recognition*, 1st ed., Oxford: Clarendon Press, chapter 4 "The multi-layer perceptron," pp. 116-163.

[34] Ripley, B.D. (1996), *Pattern Recognition and Neural Networks*, 1st ed., Cambridge: Cambridge University Press.

[35] Carpenter, G.A., Grossberg, S., and Reynolds, J.H. (1991), "ARTMAP: supervised real-time learning and classification of non-stationary data by a self-organizing neural network," *Neural Networks*, vol. 4, pp. 565-588.

[36] Carpenter, G.A., Grossberg, S., Markuzon, S., Reynolds, J.H., and Rosen, D.B. (1992), "Fuzzy ARTMAP: a neural network architecture for incremental supervised learning of analog multidimensional maps," *IEEE Transactions on Neural Networks*, vol. 3, pp. 698-712.

[37] Carpenter, G.A. and Tan, A.-H. (1993), "Rule extraction, fuzzy ARTMAP, and medical databases," *Proc. World Congress on Neural Networks*, vol. I, pp. 501-506.

[38] Carpenter, G.A. and Markuson, N. (1998), "ARTMAP-IC and medical diagnosis: instance counting and inconsistent cases," *Neural Networks*, vol. 11, pp. 323-336.

[39] Carpenter, G.A. and Grossberg, S. (1987), "A massively parallel architecture for a self-organizing neural pattern recognition machine," *Computer Vision, Graphics and Image Processing*, vol. 37, pp. 54-115.

[40] Carpenter, G.A. and Grossberg, S. (1987), "Discovering order in chaos: stable self-organization of neural recognition codes," *Ann. N.Y. Acad. Sci.*, vol. 504, pp. 33-51.

Chapter 8

Xcyt: a System for Remote Cytological Diagnosis and Prognosis of Breast Cancer

W.N. Street

This chapter describes the current state of the ongoing Xcyt research program. Xcyt is a software system that provides expert diagnosis and prognosis of breast cancer based on fine needle aspirates. The system combines techniques of digital image analysis, inductive machine learning, mathematical programming, and statistics, including novel prediction methods developed specifically to make best use of the cytological data available. The result is a program that diagnoses breast masses with an accuracy of over 97%, and predicts recurrence of malignant samples without requiring lymph node extraction. The software is available for execution over the Internet, providing previously unavailable predictive accuracy to remote medical facilities.

1   Introduction

This chapter summarizes the current state of the Xcyt project, an ongoing interdisciplinary research effort begun at the University of Wisconsin-Madison in the early 1990s. The project addresses two important problems in breast cancer treatment: diagnosis (determination of benign from malignant cases) and prognosis (prediction of the long-term course of the disease). The resulting software system provides accurate and interpretable results to both doctor and patient to aid in the various decision-making steps in the diagnosis and treatment of the disease.

The diagnosis problem can be viewed along two axes. Foremost of these is accuracy; the ultimate measure of any predictive system is whether it is accurate enough to be used with confidence in a clinical setting. We also consider invasiveness; the determination of whether or not a breast mass is malignant should ideally be minimally invasive. In this light we can view the spectrum of diagnostic techniques to range from mammography, which is non-invasive but provides imperfect diagnostic information, to pathologic examination of excised masses, which is maximally invasive but resolves the diagnosis question completely. In our work we take a middle ground, seeking accurate predictions from fine needle aspiration (FNA). This minimally invasive procedure involves the insertion of a small-gauge needle into a localized breast mass and the extraction of a small amount of cellular material. The cellular morphometry of this sample, together with the computerized analysis described below, provides diagnoses as accurate as any non-surgical procedure. The minimally invasive nature of the procedure allows it to be performed on an outpatient basis, and its accuracy on visually indeterminate cases helps avoid unnecessary surgeries.

Once a breast mass has been diagnosed as malignant, the next issue to be addressed is that of prognosis. Different cancers behave differently, with some metastasizing much more aggressively than others. Based on a prediction of this aggressiveness, the patient may opt for different post-operative treatment regimens, including adjunctive chemotherapy or even bone marrow transplant. Traditionally, breast cancer staging is performed primarily using two pieces of information[1]: the size of the excised tumor, and the presence of cancerous cells in lymph nodes removed from the patient's armpit. However, the removal of these axillary nodes is not without attendant morbidity. A patient undergoing this procedure suffers from an increased risk of infection, and a certain number contract lymphedema, a painful swelling of the arm. We therefore wish to perform accurate prognostic prediction without using the most widely-used predictive factor, lymph node status. The techniques described here are an attempt to extract the maximum possible prognostic information from a precise morphometric analysis of the individual tumor cells, along with the size of the tumor itself.

---

[1] Many other predictors have been proposed for breast cancer prognosis; see Section 4 for a brief summary.

Underlying our approach to both of these problems is a two-stage methodology that has become widely accepted and successful in many different medical domains. The first stage is computerized image analysis, in our case, the morphometric analysis of cell nuclei to quantify predictive features such as size, shape and texture. The second stage involves the use of these features in inductive machine learning techniques, which use cases with a known (or partially known) outcome to build a mapping from the input features to the decision variable of interest. The entire process can be viewed as a data mining task, in which we search and summarize the information in a digital image to determine either diagnosis (benign or malignant) or prognosis (predicted time of recurrence).

Of course, a medical decision-making system is valuable only if it is actually being used in a clinical setting. In order to gain widespread use and acceptance of the Xcyt system, we are making it available for remote execution via the WorldWide Web. In this way, we can provide highly accurate predictive systems even in the most isolated medical facility.

The remainder of the chapter is organized as follows. Section 2 describes the details of our image analysis system, which extracts descriptive features from the prepared sample. In Section 3, we show the inductive learning technique that was used to solve the diagnostic problem. Two different methods for prognosis are shown in Section 4. Section 5 summarizes the technical issues involved with making Xcyt remotely executable. Finally, Section 6 summarizes the chapter.

2   Imaging

Previous research has demonstrated that the morphometry of cell nuclei in breast cancer samples are predictive for both diagnosis [41] and prognosis [7]. However, visual grading of nuclei is imprecise and subject to wide variation between observers. Therefore, the first task we address is the quantification of various characteristics of the nuclei captured in a digital image. We describe a three-stage approach to this analysis. First, the nuclei are located using a template-matching algorithm. Second, the exact boundaries of the nuclei are found, allowing for very precise calculation of the nuclear features. Finally, the features themselves are computed, giving the raw material for the predictive methods.

2.1 Sample Preparation

Cytological samples were collected from a consecutive series of patients with palpable breast masses at the University of Wisconsin Hospitals and Clinics beginning in 1984. A small amount of fluid is removed from each mass using a small-gauge needle. This sample, known as a fine needle aspirate (FNA), is placed on a glass slide and stained to highlight the nuclei of the constituent cells. A region of the slide is then selected visually by the attending physician and digitized using a video camera mounted on a microscope. The region is selected based on the presence of easily differentiable cell nuclei. Because of the relatively low level of magnification used (63×), the image may contain anywhere from approximately 5 to 200 nuclei. One such image is shown in Figure 1. Subsequent images are shown in gray scale, as our analysis does not require color information.

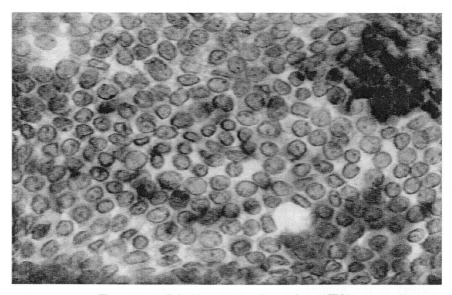

Figure 1. A digital image taken from a breast FNA.

2.2 Automatic Detection of Nuclei

Most image analysis systems rely on the user to define the region of interest. Indeed, the first version of the Xcyt software took this approach, refining user-defined boundaries in the manner described in the next section. To maximize operator independence and minimize user tedium, we have since developed an automatic method for detection and initial outlining of the nuclei. This method is based on the generalized Hough transform.

The generalized Hough transform (GHT) is a robust and powerful template-matching algorithm to detect an arbitrary, but known, shape in a digital image. Cell nuclei in our images are generally elliptical, but their size and exact shape vary widely. Therefore, our system performs the GHT with many different sizes and shapes of templates. After these GHTs are completed, the templates that best match regions of the image are chosen as matches for the corresponding nuclei.

The idea underlying both the original [18] and generalized Hough transforms [3] is the translation from image space (x and y coordinates) to a parameter space, representing the parameters of the desired shape. For instance, if we want to find lines in an image, we could choose a two-dimensional parameter space of slope m and intercept b. The parameter space is represented as an accumulator array, in which image pixels that may correspond to points on the shape "vote" for the parameters of the shape to which they belong.

Specifically, in the generalized Hough transform, a template representing the desired shape, along with a single reference point (for instance, the center), is constructed. The shape of the template is the same as the shape to be detected, but reflected through the reference point. Using this template, every edge pixel in the image votes for the possible x and y values that may correspond to the template reference point, if the edge pixel belongs to the desired shape. At the conclusion of the algorithm, high values in the accumulator will correspond to the best matches for the reference point of the desired shape.

In preparation for the template-matching step the image undergoes several preprocessing steps. First, a median filter [19] is applied to reduce image noise and smooth edges. We then perform edge detection to find pixels in the image that display a sharp gray-scale discontinuity. The Sobel edge detection method [4] is used to find both the magnitude and the direction of the edge gradients. Finally, the edges are thinned to improve processing speed. These steps are represented in Figure 2.

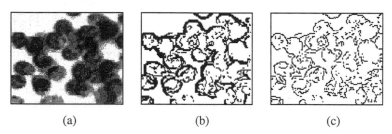

(a)   (b)   (c)

Figure 2. Image preprocessing steps: (a) median filtering; (b) Sobel edge detection; (c) edge thinning.

A straightforward implementation of the generalized Hough transform to find ellipses would require a five-dimensional parameter space: image coordinates x and y, ellipse axis sizes a and b, and ellipse rotation angle θ. In order to conserve space and avoid the difficulty of searching for peak points in a sparse five-dimensional accumulator, we adopted the following iterative approach [28]. An elliptical template is constructed using values of a, b and θ. A single GHT is performed using this template, using a two-dimensional local accumulator $A1$ of the same size as the original image. The process is then repeated for each possible value of a, b and θ. After each GHT, the values in the local accumulator are compared to a single global accumulator $A2$. The values in $A2$ are the maximum values for each pixel found in any of the local accumulators. This is reasonable since we are only interested in the determining the best-matching template for any given pixel. The iterative GHT thus reduces the use of memory from $\Theta(|x|\ |y|\ |a|\ |b|\ |c|)$ to $\Theta(|x|\ |y|)$, where $|i|$ represents the cardinality of the parameter i. This process is shown in Figure 3.

Following the completion of the iterative GHT, we wish to find the peak points in the global accumulator, which correspond to a close match of the edge pixels in the image with a particular template. However, it is often the case that a nucleus that does not closely match any of the templates will result in a plateau of relatively high accumulator values. This effect is mitigated by peak-sharpening, a filtering step applied to the global accumulator that increases the value of a point near the center of a plateau. Finally, the peak points are found, beginning with the highest and continuing until a user-defined stopping point is reached.

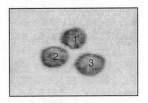

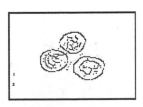

(a) Original image. Nucleus 1 is approximately 11×14 pixels; nucleus 2, 12×15; nucleus 3, 12×17.

(b) Edge image.

(c) Accumulator with 11×14 elliptical template.

(d) Accumulator with 12×15 elliptical template.

(e) Accumulator with 12×17 elliptical template.

Figure 3. Example of GHT with three different templates. Higher values in the accumulators are shown as darker pixels.

The above algorithm achieves both high positive predictive value (percentage of chosen templates that closely match the corresponding nuclei) and sensitivity (percentage of nuclei in the image that are actually found) as judged by a human operator. Experiments on two very different images resulted in both sensitivity and positive predictive value measures of over 80%. Figure 4 shows one of the images overlaid with the matching templates. The positive predictive value is naturally higher in the early stages of the matching process; hence, for images such as the one shown in Figure 4, the user would discontinue the search long before it dropped as low as 80%. For instance, at the point where the system has matched 55 templates in this image, only one of the resulting outlines is incorrect, a positive predictive value of over 98%. In most cases, outlining about 20 or 30 nuclei is sufficient to reliably compute the values of the morphometric features (described in Section 2.5).

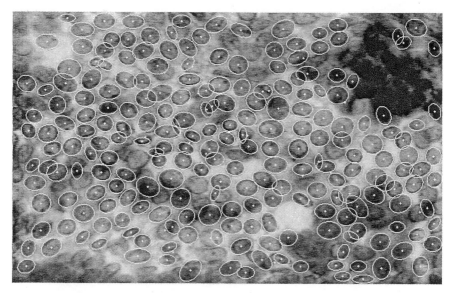

Figure 4. Result of generalized Hough transform on sample image.

2.3   Representation of Nuclear Boundaries

The desired quantification of nuclear shape requires a very precise representation of boundaries. These are generated with the aid of a deformable spline technique known as a snake [21]. The snake seeks to minimize an energy function defined over the arclength of the curve. The energy function is defined in such a way that the minimum value should occur when the curve accurately corresponds to the boundary of a nucleus. This energy function is defined as follows:

$$E = \int_s (\alpha E_{cont}(s) + \beta E_{curv}(s) + \gamma E_{image}(s)) \ ds \qquad (1)$$

Here E represents the total energy integrated along the arclength s of the spline. The energy is a weighted sum of three components E_{cont}, E_{curv} and E_{image} with respective weights α, β and γ. The continuity energy E_{cont} penalizes discontinuities in the curve. The curvature energy E_{curv} penalizes areas of the curve with abnormally high or low curvature, so that the curve tends to form a circle in the absence of other information. The spline is tied to the underlying image using the image energy term E_{image}. Here we again use a Sobel edge detector to measure the edge magnitude and direction at each point along the curve. Points with a strong gray-scale discontinuity in the appropriate direction are given low energy; others are given a high energy. The constants are empirically set so that this term dominates. Hence, the snake will settle along a boundary when edge information is available. The β weight is set high enough that, in areas of occlusion or poor focus, the snake forms an arc, in a manner similar to how a person might outline the same object. This results in a small degree of "rounding" of the resulting contour. Our experiments indicate that this reduces operator dependence and makes only a small change in the value of the computed features.

The snakes are initialized using the elliptic approximations found by the Hough transform described in the previous section. They may also be initialized manually by the operator using the mouse pointer. To simplify the necessary processing, the energy function is computed at a number of discrete points along the curve. A greedy optimization method [40] is used to move the snake points to a local minimum of the energy space.

2.4   Algorithmic Improvements

The two-stage approach of using the Hough transform for object detection and the snakes for boundary definition results in precise outlines of the well-defined nuclei in the cytological images. However, the Hough transform is very computationally expensive, requiring several minutes to search for nuclei in the observed size range. We have recently designed two heuristic approaches to reducing this computational load [23].

First, the user is given the option of performing the GHT on a scaled version of the image. This results in a rather imprecise location of the nuclei but runs about an order of magnitude faster. The GHT can then be performed on a small region of the full-sized image to precisely locate the suspected nucleus and determine the correct matching template. Our experiments indicate that this results in an acceptably small degradation of accuracy.

Second, we allow the GHT to be "seeded" with an initial boundary initialized by the user. The GHT then searches only for nuclei of about the same size as that drawn by the user. This results in a reduced search space and, again, a significant speed-up with minimal accuracy reduction. Results on two dissimilar images are shown in Figure 5. Snakes that fail to successfully conform to a nuclear boundary can be manually deleted by the user and initialized using the mouse pointer. The use of these semi-automatic object recognition techniques minimizes the dependence on a careful operator, resulting in more reliable and repeatable results.

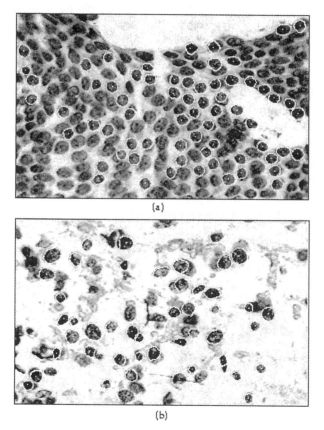

Figure 5. Results of the nuclear location algorithm on two sample images.

2.5 Nuclear Morphometric Features

The following nuclear features are computed for each identified nucleus [38].

- Radius: average length of a radial line segment, from center of mass to a snake point
- Perimeter: distance around the boundary, calculated by measuring the distance between adjacent snake points
- Area: number of pixels in the interior of the nucleus, plus one-half of the pixels on the perimeter
- Compactness: perimeter^2 / area
- Smoothness: average difference in length of adjacent radial lines
- Concavity: size of any indentations in nuclear border
- Concave points: number of points on the boundary that lie on an indentation
- Symmetry: relative difference in length between line segments perpendicular to and on either side of the major axis
- Fractal dimension: the fractal dimension of the boundary based on the "coastline approximation" [25]
- Texture: variance of gray-scale level of internal pixels

The system computes the mean value, extreme or largest value, and standard error of each of these ten features, resulting in a total of 30 predictive features for each sample. These features are used as the input in the predictive methods described in the next section.

3   Diagnosis

We frame the diagnosis problem as that of determining whether a previously detected breast lump is benign or malignant. There are three popular methods for diagnosing breast cancer: mammography, FNA with visual interpretation, and surgical biopsy. The reported sensitivity (i.e., the ability to correctly diagnose cancer when the disease is present) of mammography varies from 68% to 79% [14], of FNA with visual interpretation from 65% to 98% [15], and of surgical biopsy close to 100%. Therefore, mammography lacks sensitivity, FNA sensitivity varies widely, and surgical biopsy, although accurate, is invasive, time consuming, and costly. The goal of the diagnostic aspect of our research is to develop a relatively objective system that diagnoses FNAs with an accuracy that approaches the best achieved visually.

3.1   MSM-T: Machine Learning via Linear Programming

The image analysis system described previously represents the information present in a digital image as a 30-dimensional vector of feature values. This analysis was performed on a set of 569 images for which the true diagnosis was known, either by surgical biopsy (for malignant cases) or by subsequent periodic medical exams (for benign cases). The resulting 569 feature vectors, along with the known outcomes, represent a training set with which a classifier can be constructed to diagnose future examples. These examples were used to train a linear programming-based diagnostic system by a variant of the multisurface method (MSM) [26], [27] called MSM-Tree (MSM-T) [5], which we briefly describe now.

Let m malignant n-dimensional vectors be stored in the $m \times n$ matrix A, and k benign n-dimensional points be stored in the $k \times n$ matrix B. The points in A and B are strictly separable by a plane in the n-dimensional real space $\Re^n$ represented by

$$x^T w = \theta, \tag{2}$$

if and only if

$$Aw \geq e\theta + e, \quad Bw \leq e\theta - e. \tag{3}$$

Here, $w \in \Re^n$ is the normal to the separating plane, $|\theta|/(w^T w)^{1/2}$ is the distance of the plane to the origin in $\Re^n$, and e is a vector of ones of appropriate dimension. In general the two sets will not be strictly linearly separable and the inequalities (3) will not be satisfied. Hence, we attempt to satisfy them approximately by minimizing the average sum of their violations by solving the linear program:

$$
\begin{aligned}
\underset{w,\gamma,y,z}{\text{minimize}} \quad & \frac{e^T y}{m} + \frac{e^T z}{k} \\
\text{subject to} \quad & Aw + y \;\geq\; e\theta + e \\
& Bw - z \;\leq\; e\theta - e \\
& y, z \;\geq\; 0.
\end{aligned}
\tag{4}
$$

The linear program will generate a strict separating plane (2) that satisfies (3) if such a plane exists, in which case $y = 0$, $z = 0$. Otherwise, it will minimize the average sum of the violations y and z of the inequalities (3). This intuitively plausible linear program has significant theoretical and computational consequences [6], such as naturally eliminating the null point $w = 0$ from being a solution. Once the plane $x^T w = \theta$ has been obtained, the same procedure can be applied recursively to one or both of the newly created halfspaces $x^T w > \theta$ and $x^T w < \theta$, if warranted by the presence of an unacceptable mixture of benign and malignant points in the halfspace. Figure 6 shows an example of the types of planes generated by MSM-T. MSM-T has been shown [5] to learn concepts as well or better than more well-known decision tree learning methods such as C4.5 [30] and CART [10].

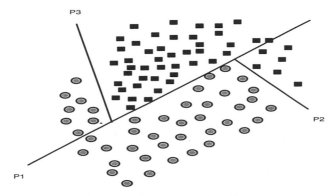

Figure 6. MSM-T separating planes.

The goal of any inductive learning procedure is to produce a classifier that generalizes well to unseen cases. This generalization can often be improved by imposing a simplicity bias on the classification method in order to avoid memorizing details of the particular training set. In our case, better generalization was achieved by reducing the number of input features considered. We performed a global search through the dimensions of the feature space, generating classifiers with a small number of planes and evaluating promising classifiers using cross-validation [35] to estimate their true accuracy. The best results were obtained with one plane and three features: extreme area, extreme smoothness, and mean texture. The predicted accuracy, estimated with cross-validation, was 97.5%. The estimated sensitivity and positive predictive value were both 96.7%, and the estimated specificity was

98.0%. This level of accuracy is as good as the best results achieved at specialized cancer institutions.

Xcyt also uses the Parzen window density estimation technique [29] to estimate the probability of malignancy for new patients. All the points used to generate the separating plane $x^T w = \theta$ in the 3-dimensional space were projected on the normal w to the separating plane. Using the Parzen window kernel technique, we then "count" the number of benign and malignant points at each position along the normal, thus associating a number of malignant and benign points with each point along this normal. Figure 7 depicts densities obtained in this fashion using the 357 benign points and 212 malignant points projected onto the normal. The probability of malignancy for a new case can then be computed with a simple Bayesian computation, taking the height of the malignant density divided by the sum of the two densities at that point and adjusting for the prior probability of malignancy.

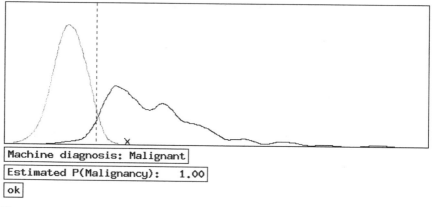

Figure 7. Densities of the benign and malignant points relative to the separating plane.

3.2   Predictive Results and Clinical Usage

The Xcyt diagnostic system has been in clinical use at the University of Wisconsin since 1993. In that period, the classifier has achieved 97.6% accuracy on the 330 consecutive new cases that it has diagnosed (223 benign, 107 malignant). The true sensitivity and positive predictive value are 96.3%, and the true specificity is 98.2%. Note the remarkably close match to the estimated predictive accuracies in the previous section.

Analysis and diagnosis of the FNA for a new patient can be performed in a few minutes by the attending physician using Xcyt. Once the FNA slide from a new patient has been analyzed, the patient is shown a density diagram as in Figure 7 along with the value of $x^T w$ for the sample. The patient can then easily appraise the diagnosis in relation to hundreds of other cases, in much the same way that an experienced physician takes advantage of years of experience. Thus the patient has a better basis on which to base a treatment decision. For instance, a value of $x^T w$ falling in the region of Figure 7 where the densities overlap would correspond to a "suspicious" diagnosis. In particular, when the probability of malignancy is between 0.3 and 0.7, it is considered to be indeterminate and a biopsy is recommended. This is a rare case, as only 10 of the 330 new cases have fallen into this suspicious region. Different patients may have very different reactions to the same readings. Masses from patients who opt for surgical biopsy have their diagnosis histologically confirmed. Patients who choose not to have the biopsy done are followed for a year at three-month intervals to check for changes in the mass.

We have successfully tested Xcyt on slides and images from researchers at other institutions who used the same preparation method. In one such study [39], a series of 56 indeterminate samples from Vanderbilt University Hospital (approximately, the most difficult 7% of their cases) were diagnosed with 75% accuracy, 73.7% sensitivity and 75.7% specificity. A slight difference in the method of slide preparation caused several of the specimens to render false negative results.

4   Prognosis

A significantly more difficult prediction problem in breast cancer treatment is the determination of long-term prognosis. Several researchers, beginning with Black *et al.* [7], have shown evidence that cellular features observed at the time of diagnosis can be used to predict whether or not the disease will metastasize elsewhere in the body following surgery. However, with the widespread use of the TNM (tumor size, lymph node, metastasis) staging system [16], nuclear grade is now rarely used as a prognostic indicator. Instead, decisions regarding post-operative treatment regimens are typically based primarily on the spread of the disease to axillary lymph nodes. Node-positive patients usually undergo post-operative chemotherapy and/or radiation therapy to slow or prevent the spread of the cancer. Surgical removal of these nodes, however, leaves the patient at increased risk for infection, as well as a risk of arm lymphedema [2], a painful swelling of the arm. Estimates of the incidence rate for lymphedema among breast cancer patients range from 10% to over 50%. Moreover, node dissection does not contribute to curing the disease [1]. Therefore, the focus of our research has been the clinical staging of breast cancer without using lymph node information.

Our attempt to get the maximum prognostic information from precisely measured nuclear "grade" (possibly together with tumor size) should be viewed in the broader context of breast prognostic factors, and area that has received much attention in recent years. In particular, many researchers have proposed the use of factors such as hormone receptor status (estrogen and progesterone) and biological factors (for instance, p53 expression) for prognostic staging. While we do not discount these approaches, we feel there is value in a system that derives prognostic predictions from the most readily available factors without the need for additional tests, and we note that many of new prognostic factors do not fare well in follow-up studies [17]. It has also been suggested that sentinel node extraction provides the value of the lymph node metastasis information while minimizing the risk of infection and lymphedema. While we applaud this attention to patient morbidity, minimizing a risk is still not the same as eliminating it. Finally, the long-standing assumption on which we base our effort is that axillary lymph dissection does not affect survival or disease-free survival rates in patients without significant tumor mass in the axilla. This assumption has recently been called into question [8]. However, pending confirmation of the hypothesis that lymph dissection leads to higher survival rates, the goal of this line of research remains the same.

The prediction of breast cancer recurrence is an example of survival data analysis. We would like to predict a time of distant recurrence or death based on predictive features available at the time of diagnosis or surgery. The problem is complicated by the fact that, for many patients, the endpoint is unavailable. For instance, the patient may change doctors, or die from some unrelated cause. The available data are therefore right censored, in that we know only a lower bound (last known disease-free time following surgery) for many of the cases, rather than an actual endpoint.

Our earlier work [37] framed the prediction of recurrence as an explicit optimization problem, known as the Recurrence Surface Approximation. While the predictive model was limited in its expressiveness, the RSA demonstrated that nuclear morphometric features could predict recurrence as well as lymph node status. Two more recent approaches are reviewed here. The first is a simple discrimination of samples into prognostic groups based on one nuclear feature and one traditional feature, tumor size. The second uses an artificial neural network approach to achieve a more fine-grained prognosis. Experiments with both of these methods indicate that they are superior to the traditional lymph node differentiation.

In these studies a subset of the diagnostic data set was used, consisting of those cancerous patients for whom follow-up data was available. We removed from this set the patients with ductal carcinoma in situ (for whom prognosis is very good) and those with distant metastasis at time of surgery (for whom prognosis is very poor), thus focusing on the more difficult cases.

4.1   Median-Based Separation

We first describe a recent attempt [43] to use simple statistical analyses to separate the cases into three prognostic groups: good, intermediate, and poor. The first step was to use a traditional approach to survival data analysis, Cox proportional-hazards regression [13], to rank the available predictive features based on their individual ability to predict time of recurrence. The features under consideration were the thirty nuclear features from the diagnosis study along with tumor size and lymph node status. The size of the tumor was found to correlate most strongly with outcome, with largest nuclear perimeter ranking second and lymph node status 7th. This analysis was repeated using breast cancer specific survival as the endpoint, with similar results.

Life table analysis [22] was then performed for each pair of the three prognostic features, tumor size, largest perimeter, and lymph node positivity. Patients were assigned to groups based on the median split for tumor size (2.4 cm), for largest perimeter (38.6 micra) and for lymph node status. This created four groups for tumor size and largest perimeter: small size, small perimeter (SS/SP); small size, large perimeter (SS/LP); large size, small perimeter (LS/SP); and large size, large perimeter (SS/LP). This is illustrated in Figure 8 where individual values for patients recurring or not recurring relative to the median-value cut points for tumor size and largest perimeter are shown. Similarly, the patients above and below the median split values for tumor size and largest perimeter were paired according to node positive (Node +) or node negative (Node −) to give four groups each. Prognostic groups were formed by considering those cases for which both features were above the median as the "poor" group, and those cases for which both features were below the median as the "good" group. Those cases for which one feature was above the median and the other below were combined to form the "intermediate" group.

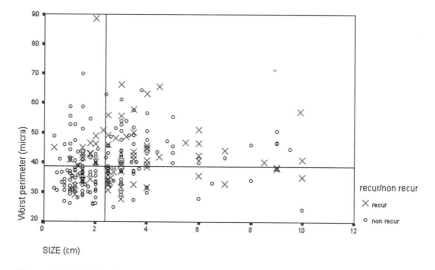

Figure 8. Distribution of recurrent and non-recurrent cases relative to median cutoffs for largest perimeter and tumor size.

Tables 1 and 2 show five-year and ten-year disease-free survival probabilities and breast cancer-specific survival probabilities, respectively, for each of the three pairs of prognostic predictors. In both cases, the pairing of tumor size and largest perimeter formed the strongest prognostic groups. This is confirmed in Table 3, which shows the p-values associated with the separation between the groups. Hence we have shown that the combination of tumor size and nuclear perimeter does a better job of separating patients into good and poor prognostic groups than either the traditional pairing of lymph node status and tumor size or the combination of nodal status with perimeter.

Table 1. Distant disease-free survival ± Standard error (%). Node: Axillary lymph node positivity. Size: Tumor size LP: Largest nuclear perimeter.

	5 Year			10 Year		
	Good	Intermed.	Poor	Good	Intermed.	Poor
Node&Size	85.1 ± 4.6	77.3 ± 4.8	55.1 ± 5.8	77.4 ± 6.7	71.5 ± 6.0	42.9 ± 6.6
Node&LP	87.4 ± 4.5	74.2 ± 4.6	55.0 ± 6.2	79.8 ± 6.6	64.7 ± 6.0	45.0 ± 7.3
Size&LP	94.8 ± 2.9	68.2 ± 5.0	55.9 ± 6.2	87.6 ± 5.6	58.1 ± 6.3	46.3 ± 7.2

Table 2. Breast cancer-specific survival ± Standard error (%).

	5 Year			10 Year		
	Good	Intermed.	Poor	Good	Intermed.	Poor
Node&Size	89.9 ± 3.9	90.3 ± 3.5	62.5 ± 5.7	85.8 ± 5.5	78.3 ± 6.4	54.7 ± 6.5
Node&LP	98.2 ± 1.8	81.6 ± 4.1	63.5 ± 6.1	90.1 ± 5.7	76.6 ± 5.2	50.1 ± 7.6
Size&LP	96.5 ± 2.4	88.4 ± 4.0	60.6 ± 6.1	92.8 ± 4.3	73.4 ± 6.2	51.3 ± 7.2

Table 3. Wilcoxon (Gehan) p values for significance between groups.

	Distant Disease-free Survival			Breast Cancer-specific Survival		
	Good vs. Poor	Good vs. Inter.	Inter. vs. Poor	Good vs. Poor	Good vs. Inter.	Inter. vs Poor
Node/Size	<0.0001	0.1877	0.0002	0.0002	0.9124	0.0001
Node/LP	<0.0001	0.0393	0.0021	<0.0001	0.0093	0.0006
Size/LP	<0.0001	0.0001	0.0114	<0.0001	0.0151	<0.0001

4.2   A Neural Network Approach

A number of researchers have used machine learning techniques such as decision trees [42], unsupervised learning [9], [34] and artificial neural networks [11], [31], [32] to predict breast cancer recurrence. Our most recent approach [36] uses a standard neural network trained with backpropagation [33] to produce precise and accurate predictions of recurrence time. The primary motivation for our approach is the observation that prediction using censored data can be viewed as a collection of classification problems. Class 1 consists of those patients known to have recurred in the first year following surgery, Class 2 corresponds to those recurring in the second year, and so on. By combining these problems into a single model, we can expect to get the most predictive power from the available data.

Our neural network contains one output node for each of the above classes, up to ten years (the length of the study). The training signal for the individual cases is a scaled probability of recurrence for each time step, as shown graphically in Figure 9. For recurrent cases, the network was trained with values of +1 for all outputs up to the observed recurrence time, and −1 thereafter. For instance, a recurrence at 32 months would have a training vector $T = \{1, 1, -1, -1, -1, -1, -1, -1, -1, -1\}$. The value of the probability formulation is seen in the censored cases. They were similarly trained with values of +1 up to the observed disease-free survival time. The probabilities of disease-free survival (DFS) for later times were computed using a variation of the standard Kaplan-Meier maximum likelihood approximation to the true population survival rate [20]. Thus the network can be viewed as learning a projected survival curve, a plot of time vs. probability of disease-free survival, for any combination of input values.

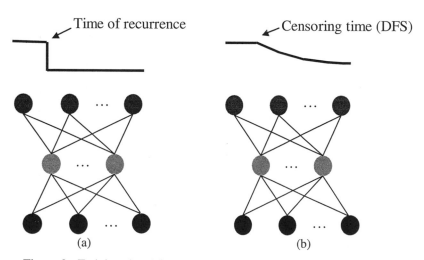

Figure 9. Training signal for neural network model: (a) recurrent case, (b) censored case.

This architecture facilitates three different uses of the resulting predictive model:
1. The output units can be divided into groups to separate good from poor prognoses. For a particular application, any prediction of

recurrence at a time greater than five years might be considered favorable, and indicate less aggressive treatment.

2. An individualized disease-free survival curve can be easily generated for a particular patient by plotting the probabilities predicted by the various output units.

3. The expected time of recurrence can be obtained merely by noting the first output unit that predicts a probability of disease-free survival of less than 0.5. This provides a convenient method of rank-ordering the cases according to the expected outcome.

Cross-validated predictive results are shown in Figures 10-12. Figure 10 shows the Kaplan-Meier disease-free survival estimates for the "poor" prognostic group (those patients predicted to recur at some point during the first five years) vs. the "good" group (all others). The difference in the two groups is statistically significant (p < 0.001). A very low risk subset can be obtained by choosing only those cases with

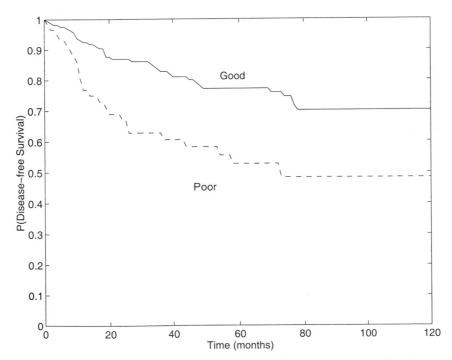

Figure 10. Actual outcomes of those cases predicted to recur in the first five years (Poor, 58 cases) compared to those predicted to recur at some time greater than five years (Good, 169 cases).

the lowest probability of recurrence in year 10. For example, of the most favorable 19 cases, only 3 have a known recurrence. More importantly, this predictive performance was again gained without use of the lymph node status feature, and the addition of this feature to the model (by adding the number of positive lymph nodes as an input feature and retraining) did not improve the results. Moreover, we again stress that these results were obtained using cross-validation, so that each case was tested against models that was trained without using the case in question.

Even more dramatic results were obtained using the SEER data set, obtained from the National Cancer Institute [12]. In this larger study of 34,545 cases, the good prognostic group had an estimated 10-year survival of 82%, while the poor prognostic group had an estimated 10-year survival of 37%.

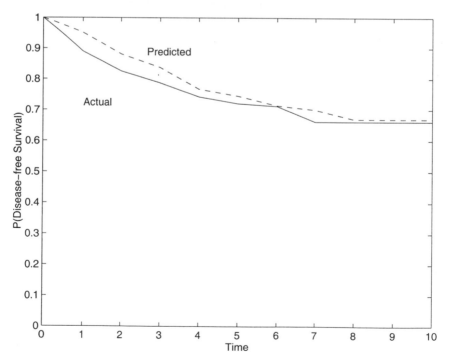

Figure 11. Kaplan-Meier estimate of true disease-free survival curve compared to predicted DFS curve.

Figure 11 plots the actual Kaplan-Meier curve for our cases along with the predicted recurrence times. There is no statistical difference between these curves (p = 0.2818). From the results in Figures 10 and 11, we conclude that the network is learning a reasonable model of recurrence based on the nuclear morphometric features. Note that direct computation of predicted-vs.-true outcome is problematic when using censored data, since, as previously noted, we often to not know the "answer."

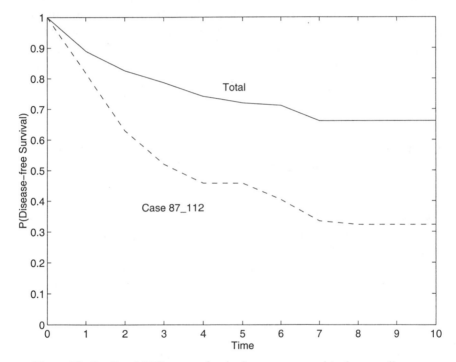

Figure 12. Predicted DFS curve of a single case compared to the overall group DFS curve.

Figure 12 shows how the predictive method is used in practice. The expected survival curve of a single patient is generated by plotting the probabilities computed by the neural network. This is compared to the overall survival curve for our study, giving an easily-interpretable visual representation of the individual prognosis. The expected time of recurrence can be computed by noting where the DFS curve crosses a probability of 50%, in this case, between three and four years. In fact, this patient did experience disease recurrence in the 44th month following surgery.

5   Remote Execution

One of the ways that the Internet is revolutionizing the way medicine is practiced is by making specialized decision-making tools available regardless of location. With only a personal computer and a modem, an urban medical center in Los Angeles or a small-town hospital in rural Iowa can now access expertise previously available only at specialized centers. Our contribution to this revolution is the implementation of Xcyt as a Java applet, suitable for execution via the World Wide Web. A trial version of the software is available at http://dollar.biz.uiowa. edu/xcyt.

Using the software available at this site, the same levels of diagnostic and prognostic accuracy we achieve can be obtained at any medical facility with the ability to prepare the FNA sample and scan a digital image.

We foresee several important benefits to patients resulting from the increased use of the Xcyt system. The diagnostic system has proven reliable for even otherwise-indeterminate cases, resulting in a reduction in unnecessary surgeries. Plus, the diagnosis can be performed in a few minutes on an outpatient basis, rather than over the course of several days, as might be the case if a tissue sample was needed at a remote lab. The prognostic system offers more detailed information for the doctor and the patient in choosing a post-operative treatment regimen, and does so without the morbidity attached to the removal of axillary lymph nodes. Finally, the entire process can be performed at very low cost, a primary concern for both health care providers and patients.

The Xcyt implementation allows users to test the software in images stored on our server, or to analyze their own images. This is achieved via file transfer accomplished with a Common Gateway Interface (CGI) [24]. Once the analysis is performed, the resulting feature values and outcomes can be saved on both the client side and the server side. In this way, we can continue to gather more samples with which to improve our predictive models. In time, this may lead to a substantial expansion of the types of information we make available to the learning methods; for instance, different sample preparation methods, patient populations, predictive features, etc. can be accommodated in future releases.

Researchers interested in collaborating in this effort are invited to contact the author. We wish to stress that the Xcyt system should be viewed as merely an objective expert advisor; a qualified physician should make all medical decisions. Further, while the analysis of nuclear features is a widely-applicable approach to disease diagnosis and prognosis, the predictive models should only be trusted when applied to breast FNA samples prepared in exactly the same way as the samples used in our training cases. See [42] for details on sample preparation.

6   Conclusions

The Xcyt software system provides remote predictive analysis for breast cancer diagnosis and prognosis. Its digital image analysis capabilities allow precise quantification of nuclear characteristics. The diagnostic system achieves the highest accuracy available with any method short of surgical biopsy. The prognostic system gives accurate, individualized predictions of breast cancer recurrence without knowledge of lymph node metastasis. The analysis process is fast, reliable, and inexpensive. The method described here is applicable to many different diseases and prediction problems. We believe that this type of system will become increasingly popular, improving the routine clinical practice of physicians all over the world by making expert diagnosis and prognosis immediately available.

Acknowledgments

The author is indebted to all of those who have contributed to the success of the Xcyt project: my mentors Olvi L. Mangasarian and William H. Wolberg, and my students Hyuk-Joon Oh, Sree R. K. R. Mallina, and Kyoung-Mi Lee. Funding for various parts of this work has been provided by the National Institutes of Health, the National Science Foundation, the Air Force Office of Scientific Research, the University of Wisconsin-Madison, and Oklahoma State University.

References

[1] Abe, O., Abe, R., Asaishi, K., Enomoto, K., Hattori, T., and Iino, Y. (1995), "Effects of radiotherapy and surgery in early breast cancer: an overview of the randomized trials," *New England Journal of Medicine*, vol. 333, pp. 1444-1455.

[2] Aitken, R.J., Gaze, M.N., Rodger, A., Chetty, U., and Forrest, A.P.M. (1989), "Arm morbidity within a trial of mastectomy and either nodal sample with selective radiotherapy or axillary clearance," *British Journal of Surgery,* vol. 76, pp. 568-571.

[3] Ballard, D.H. (1981), "Generalizing the Hough transform to detect arbitrary shapes," *Pattern Recognition*, vol. 13(2), pp. 111-122.

[4] Ballard, D.H. and Brown, C. (1982), *Computer Vision*, Prentice-Hall, Englewood Cliffs, NJ, 1982.

[5] Bennett, K.P. (1992), "Decision tree construction via linear programming," *Proceedings of the 4th Midwest Artificial Intelligence and Cognitive Science Society Conference*, pp. 97-101.

[6] Bennett, K.P. and Mangasarian, O.L. (1992), "Robust linear programming discrimination of two linearly inseparable sets," *Optimization Methods and Software*, vol. 1, pp. 23-34.

[7] Black, M.M., Opler, S.R., and Speer, F.D. (1955), "Survival in breast cancer cases in relation to the structure of the primary tumor and regional lymph nodes," *Surgery, Gynecology and Obstetrics*, vol. 100, pp. 543-551.

[8] Bland, K.I., Scott-Conner, C.E., Menck, H., and Winchester, D.P. (1999), "Axillary dissection in breast-conserving surgery for stage I and stage II breast cancer: a National Cancer Data Base study of patterns of omission and implications for survival," *Journal of the American College of Surgeons*, vol. 188(6), pp. 586-595.

[9] Bradley, P.S., Mangasarian, O.L., and Street, W.N. (1997), "Clustering via concave minimization," *Advances in Neural Information Processing Systems*, vol. 9, pp. 368-374.

[10] Breiman, L., Friedman, J., Olshen, R., and Stone, C. (1984), *Classification and Regression Trees*, Wadsworth, Pacific Grove, CA.

[11] Burke, H.B. (1994), "Artificial neural networks for cancer research: outcome prediction," *Seminars in Surgical Oncology*, vol. 10, pp. 73-79.

[12] Carter, C.L., Allen, C., and Henson, D.E. (1989), "Relation of tumor size, lymph node status, and survival in 24,740 breast cancer cases," *Cancer*, vol. 63, pp. 181-187.

[13] Cox, D.R. (1972), "Regression Models and Life-Tables," *Journal of the Royal Statistical Society B*, vol. 34, pp. 187-202.

[14] Fletcher, S.W., Black, W., Harris, R., Rimer, B.K., and Shapiro, S. (1992), "Report of the international workshop on screening for breast cancer," *Journal of the National Cancer Institute*, vol. 85, pp. 1644-1656.

[15] Giard, R.W. and Hermans, J. (1992), "The value of aspiration cytologic examination of the breast. a statistical review of the medical literature," *Cancer*, vol. 69, pp. 2104-2110.

[16] Hermanek, P. and Sobin, L.H. (Eds.) (1987), *TNM Classification of Malignant Tumors*, 4th edition, Springer-Verlag, Berlin.

[17] Hilsenbeck, S.G., Clark, G.M., and McGuire, W.L. (1992), "Why do so many prognostic factors fail to pan out?" *Breast Cancer Research and Treatment*, vol. 22, pp. 197-206.

[18] Hough, P.C. (1962) "Method and means for recognizing complex patterns," U.S. Patent 3,069,654, Dec. 18.

[19] Huang, T.S., Yang, G.T., and Yang, G.Y. (1979), "A fast two-dimensional median filtering algorithm," *IEEE Transactions on Acoustics, Speech, and Signal Processing*, vol. 27, pp. 13-18.

[20] Kaplan, E.L. and Meier, P. (1958), "Nonparametric estimation from incomplete observations," *Journal of the American Statistical Association*, vol. 53, pp. 457-481.

[21] Kass, M., Witkin, A., and Tersopoulos, D. (1988), "Snakes: active contour models," *International Journal of Computer Vision*, vol. 1(4), pp. 321-331.

[22] Lee, E.T. (1992), *Statistical Methods for Survival Data Analysis*, Wiley and Sons, New York.

[23] Lee, K.-M. and Street, W.N. (1999), "A fast and robust approach for automated segmentation of breast cancer nuclei," In *Proceedings of the Second IASTED International Conference on Computer Graphics and Imaging*, in press.

[24] Mallina, S.R.K.R. (1998), *Remote Cancer Diagnosis*, Masters Thesis, Computer Science Dept., Oklahoma State University.

[25] Mandelbrot, B.B. (1977), *The Fractal Geometry of Nature*, W.H. Freeman and Company, New York.

[26] Mangasarian, O.L. (1968), "Multisurface method of pattern separation," *IEEE Transactions on Information Theory*, vol. IT-14, pp. 801-807.

[27] Mangasarian, O.L. (1993), "Mathematical programming in neural networks," *ORSA Journal on Computing*, vol. 5, pp. 349-360.

[28] Oh, H. and Street, W.N. (1998), "A memory-efficient generalized Hough transform for segmenting cytological images." Under review.

[29] Parzen, E. (1962), "On estimation of a probability density and mode," *Annals of Mathematical Statistics*, vol. 33, pp. 1065-1076.

[30] Quinlan, J.R. (1993), *C4.5: Programs for Machine Learning*, Morgan Kaufmann, San Mateo, CA.

[31] Ravdin, P.M. and Clark, G.M. (1992), "A practical application of neural network analysis for predicting outcome of individual breast

cancer patients," *Breast Cancer Research and Treatment*, vol. 22, pp. 285-293.

[32] Ripley, R.M. (1998), *Neural Networks for Breast Cancer Prognosis*, Ph.D. Thesis, Department of Engineering Science, University of Oxford.

[33] Rumelhart, D.E., Hinton, G.E., and Williams, R.J. (1986), "Learning internal representation by error backpropagation," in Rumelhart, D.E. and McClelland, J.L. (Eds.), *Parallel Distributed Processing,* vol. 1, chapter 8, MIT Press, Cambridge, MA.

[34] Schenone, A., Andreucci, L., Sanguinetti, V., and Morasso, P. (1993), "Neural networks for prognosis in breast cancer," *Physica Medica*, vol. 9 (supplement 1), pp. 175-178.

[35] Stone, M. (1974), "Cross-validatory choice and assessment of statistical predictions," *Journal of the Royal Statistical Society (Series B)*, vol. 36, pp. 111-147.

[36] Street, W.N. (1998), "A neural network model for prognostic prediction," *Proceedings of the Fifteenth International Conference on Machine Learning*, pp. 540-546.

[37] Street, W.N., Mangasarian, O.L., and Wolberg, W.H. (1996), "An inductive learning approach to prognostic prediction," *Proceedings of the Twelfth International Conference on Machine Learning*, pp. 522-530.

[38] Street, W.N., Wolberg, W.H., and Mangasarian, O.L. (1993), "Nuclear feature extraction for breast tumor diagnosis," *IS&T/ SPIE International Symposium on Electronic Imaging: Science and Technology*, pp. 861-870.

[39] Teague, M.W., Wolberg W.H., Street W.N., Mangasarian, O.L., Lambremont, S., and Page, D.L. (1997), "Indeterminate fine needle aspiration of the breast: image analysis aided diagnosis," *Cancer Cytopathology*, vol. 81, pp.129-135.

[40] Williams, D.J. and Shah, M. (1990), "A fast algorithm for active contours," *Proceedings of the Third International Conference on Computer Vision*, pp. 592-595.

[41] Wolberg, W.H. and Mangasarian, O.L. (1990), "Multisurface method of pattern separation for medical diagnosis applied to breast cytology," *Proceedings of the National Academy of Science*, vol. 87, pp. 9193-9196.

[42] Wolberg, W.H., Street, W.N., and Mangasarian, O.L. (1994), "Machine learning techniques to diagnose breast cancer from image-processed nuclear features of fine needle aspirates," *Cancer Letters*, vol. 77, pp. 163-171.

[43] Wolberg, W.H., Street, W.N., and Mangasarian, O.L (1999), "Contribution of computer-based nuclear analysis for breast cancer staging," *Clinical Cancer Research*, vol. 5, pp. 3542-3548.

INDEX